Ripley's® Giant

Believe It or Not!®

Ripley's Giant Believe It or Not!

Introduction by Lowell Thomas

BONANZA BOOKS
New York

This 1985 edition is published by Bonanza Books, distributed by Crown Publishers, Inc. by arrangement with
Warner Books.

Printed and bound in the United States of America

ISBN: 0-517-494663
h g f e d c b a

Designed by Thomas Nozkowski
Cover design by Gene Light

Ripley's — Believe It or Not!

$1,000,000 BOOK
A FIRST EDITION OF DANTE'S "DIVINE COMEDY" OWNED BY ANTONIO MONTANTO, THE ITALIAN SCULPTOR, AND LOST IN A SHIPWRECK IN THE LIGURIAN SEA, CONTAINED HUNDREDS OF MARGINAL ILLUSTRATIONS –*EACH AN ORIGINAL DRAWING BY ITS INITIAL OWNER,* **MICHELANGELO**

THE GOLDEN TREE FROG
HAS A CROAK IN WINTER THAT SOUNDS LIKE A MALLET CHIPPING ROCK *BUT IN SUMMER IT SOUNDS LIKE A TINKLING BELL*

BALD MONEY
-BLANK ON BOTH SIDES- USED IN SAMARKAND (1918)

THE **PARTRIDGE BERRY**
IS A BOTANICAL SIAMESE TWIN *EACH BERRY DEVELOPS FROM 2 FLOWERS*

EMPEROR AUGUSTUS
(63 B.C.-14 A.D.) of Rome WAS THE FIRST NOTABLE TO **SHAVE HIMSELF**

A **HOME** In Palmaces, Spain, BUILT INSIDE A CAVE *THAT ORIGINALLY HAD BEEN A DOVECOTE*

MULTIPLY THE MAGIC FIGURE **142857** BY 1,2,3,4,5 AND 6 –AND YOU OBTAIN THE FOLLOWING SQUARE :

1	4	2	8	5	7	= 27
2	8	5	7	1	4	= 27
4	2	8	5	7	1	= 27
5	7	1	4	2	8	= 27
7	1	4	2	8	5	= 27
8	5	7	1	4	2	= 27
27	27	27	27	27	27	= 27

INTRODUCTION

by

Lowell Thomas

Do you remember Ripley's first book? Who could forget it, filled as it was with extraordinary, almost unbelievable information? Nothing like it had ever been published, and it went over like a prairie fire. Its instant success quickly led to another, and in October 1931 I was with Bob taking part in the publication day ceremonies for his second runaway best seller.

I remember taking exception to one of the cartoons in the book concerning a tourist guide in Chungking, China, who according to Ripley had bored a hole in the top of his head in which he stuck a lighted candle, supposedly to steer tourists down dark alleys. My believe-it-or-not friend, fearing I was a disbeliever, explained at length that he had his information on the best authority, plus documented proof! Nor did he stop there. A few days later I received a note from Ripley with an affidavit by Dr. J. J. Kaveney of the U.S. Navy, who had examined this man and submitted the following report:

"I found that the scalp had been cut through and a rough trepanning operation had been done. That is, an opening of sufficient diameter to hold the inserted candle had been made through the external or solid plate of the skull, and included the soft or cancellous bone tissue beneath. The opening stopped at the internal plate covering the membrane of the brain. The candle was held in place by melted sealing wax." This detailed authentication was added to later print-

THE MOST BIZARRE ACCIDENT IN ALL HISTORY

FRANCESCO delle BARCHE, VENETIAN INVENTOR OF A CATAPULT THAT COULD HURL A 3,000-POUND MISSILE, BECAME ENTANGLED IN THE WAR MACHINE DURING THE SIEGE OF ZARA, DALMATIA, AND WAS HIMSELF HURTLED INTO THE CENTER OF THE BELEAGUERED TOWN

HIS BODY STRUCK HIS OWN WIFE, WHO HAD ENTERED ZARA WITHOUT HER HUSBAND'S KNOWLEDGE AND BOTH WERE KILLED! (1346)

LAKSHMIBAI

(1827-1858) Ranee of Jhansi, India, LEARNED TO WRITE AT THE AGE OF 5 AND AS RELIGIOUS DEVOTION ALL THE REST OF HER LIFE, SPENT 2 HOURS EACH DAY WRITING THE 1,100 DIFFERENT NAMES OF THE HINDU DIVINITY, RAMACHANDRA

LIVING SKELETON
MUSSEL WITH A SHELL RESEMBLING A SKELETON -NATURE'S CAMOUFLAGE TO FOOL PREDATORS

THE COAT OF ARMS
OF THE TOWN OF LE VIGAN, FRANCE, CONSISTS OF INTERLACED V'S WHICH SIGNIFY "VIVE LE VIGAN" ("HURRAH FOR VIGAN")

LEAVES
OF THE SUMATRA BREADFRUIT TREE ARE NOTCHED WHEN THEY FIRST FORM - YET HAVE NO INDENTATIONS WHEN THE LEAVES MATURE

A TREE HOUSE ON A FARM near Savigliano, Italy, CONSTRUCTED BY SHAPING AND CUTTING THE LEAVES AND BRANCHES OF A HUGE MAPLE TREE

THE VOLCANO THAT BLOWS SMOKE RINGS
MOUNT ETNA, DURING ERUPTIONS, EMITS GIANT RINGS OF SMOKE

A MANX SHEARWATER IN A TEST OF ITS HOMING INSTINCT, FLEW FROM BOSTON, MASS., TO THE ISLAND OF SKOKHOLM, WALES- 3,050 MILES IN 12½ DAYS

Ripley's —®— Believe It or Not!

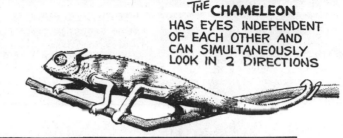

THE **CHAMELEON** HAS EYES INDEPENDENT OF EACH OTHER AND CAN SIMULTANEOUSLY LOOK IN 2 DIRECTIONS

THE **MADONNA** A PAINTING IN FIORANO CASTLE, ITALY, ESCAPED WITHOUT BEING EVEN SCORCHED WHEN INVADING SPANISH SOLDIERS SET THE CASTLE AFIRE—YET ALL *THE REST OF THE BUILDING* WAS DESTROYED

THE **CHURCH** of **CHRIST** in BASSENDEAN, AUSTRALIA, *WAS CONSTRUCTED IN A SINGLE DAY* IT WAS BUILT BY 120 VOLUNTEERS ON JAN.4,1913, AND SERVICES WERE HELD IN IT THE NEXT DAY

THE SEA HARE IN 4 MONTHS LAYS 478,000,000 EGGS

ALEJANDRO SINCHIJA an Iquito Indian of Peru BECAME A FATHER IN SEPTEMBER, 1941, AT THE AGE OF **91** *AFTER HE HAD BECOME A GREAT-GREAT-GRANDFATHER*

ings of the book. After this experience I seldom if ever questioned any of Ripley's material…and as you know, he uncovered some well-nigh unbelievable stories.

The day after Lindbergh made his historic trans-Atlantic flight in 1927, Ripley's newspaper cartoon announced that Lindbergh was the 67th person to make this nonstop journey by air from America to Europe. This, naturally, drew an avalanche of protests—more than 3000 letters and telegrams poured in from irate readers. Of course, what Lindbergh had achieved was the first across-the-Atlantic **solo** flight; Alcock and Brown had been the first, in 1919. The English dirigible **R-34** had made the flight with 31 aboard the same year, and the German **ZR** (later the **Los Angeles**) crossed in 1924 with 33 passengers. Ripley was right again…and those who had been so quick to protest became Ripley fans.

Remember his cartoon, "The Marching Chinese"? What a stir it caused! The caption read: "If all the Chinese in the world were to march four abreast past a given point they would **never** finish passing though they marched forever and ever." His research people had based their calculations on the U.S. Army marching regulations and the Chinese population of the day, but they hadn't taken into account flood, famine, war, and future family planning. However, the cartoon did bring China's huge population and rapid growth rate to our attention. Again Ripley had made his point.

He was on firm ground when, in his first radio broadcast, April 14, 1930 from NBC's WEAF, he said: "We have no National Anthem!" Listeners tuned in to the Colonial Beaconlights Program, then featuring "The Apostle of Amazement, that Titan of Truth, Robert Ripley," were shocked to learn that the tune played on formal occasions hadn't been officially made the anthem of the country, but was an old English

THE PRETZEL FUNGUS WHICH FEEDS ON NEMATODE WORMS, CAPTURES ITS PREY WHEN THE WORMS ATTEMPT *TO SLIP THROUGH THE HOLES IN ITS PRETZEL-LIKE SHAPE*

THE PELICAN EEL FOUND AT A DEPTH OF ONE MILE IN THE BERMUDA SEAS, HAS A RED TAIL THAT IS *3 TIMES AS LONG AS ITS BLACK BODY*

THE GREEK ALTAR of PERGAMUM
REBUILT 2,000 YEARS LATER IN BERLIN, GERMANY, FROM THE ORIGINAL BLOCKS OF STONE, HAS 28 STEPS THAT ARE NOT OF UNIFORM HEIGHT
THE ANCIENT GREEKS ALTERED THE HEIGHT OF THE STEPS AS A MEANS OF AVOIDING ACCIDENTS-KNOWING THAT PERSONS USING THEM WOULD BE EXTRA VIGILANT

THE REV. HENRY JOSEPH DRURY (1776-1841) AN INSTRUCTOR AT HARROW SCHOOL, HARROW-ON-THE-HILL, ENGLAND, MEMORIZED ALL THE WORKS OF VIRGIL, HORACE AND LUCAN *– A TOTAL OF 2,500 PAGES OF LATIN*

ONCE, WHILE WALKING THE 16 MILES FROM HARROW TO ETON, HE RECITED FROM MEMORY THE 8,000 VERSES OF LUCAN'S PHARSALIA

THE EYE OF HORUS, an ancient Egyptian divinity THAT WAS A SYMBOL OF PROTECTION AND HEALING, *IS THE SOURCE OF THE SIGN USED BY MODERN PHYSICIANS ON PRESCRIPTIONS --Rx*

THE MOST ARTISTIC FAMILY JOHANN HEINRICH TISCHBEIN (1682-1764) A CABINET-MAKER of Haina, Germany, WAS THE FATHER OF **7 FAMOUS PAINTERS,** THE GRANDFATHER OF **16 FAMED ARTISTS,** AND *GREAT-GRANDFATHER OF 34 ARTISTS*

THE GENERAL WHO SAVED HIS LIFE BY BUYING THE WRONG-SIZED HAT!
GENERAL HENRY HETH (1825-1888) LEADING A CONFEDERATE DIVISION IN THE BATTLE OF GETTYSBURG, WAS HIT IN THE HEAD BY A UNION BULLET *BUT HIS LIFE WAS SAVED BECAUSE HE WAS WEARING A HAT 2 SIZES TOO LARGE - WITH NEWSPAPER FOLDED INSIDE THE SWEATBAND* THE PAPER DEFLECTED THE BULLET AND THE GENERAL, UNCONSCIOUS FOR **30 HOURS,** RECOVERED AND LIVED ANOTHER **25 YEARS**

THE MODERN JONAH!

CAPTAIN EDMUND GARDNER, MASTER OF THE WHALER "WINSLOW," WAS STANDING ON THE BOW OF A WHALEBOAT OFF PERU *WHEN A GIANT WHALE HE HAD HARPOONED CLAMPED ITS TEETH DOWN ON THE WHALEBOAT'S BOW—AND ITS CAPTAIN!* THE WHALE SWALLOWED THE WOOD PLANKING, BUT THE CAPTAIN ESCAPED WITH A FRACTURED SKULL, A BROKEN COLLAR BONE AND A CRUSHED HAND—HE RECOVERED AND LIVED ANOTHER 59 YEARS (FEB. 21, 1816)

THE **BEES** THAT WEAR MOURNING WHEN A BEEKEEPER DIES IN THE SPANISH PYRENEES EACH OF HIS BEES IS SPLASHED WITH A DROP OF *BLACK INK*

THE **PARADISE WHIDAH BIRD** of AFRICA, ALWAYS LAYS ITS EGGS IN THE NEST OF A WAXWING —MAKING CERTAIN THAT THE HOST BIRD HAS THE SAME PLUMAGE AND SONG AS THE WHIDAH

A **WHITE CHAMOIS** IS CONSIDERED IN THE ALPINE REGION OF EUROPE *TO BE A PORTENT OF DEATH* SUPERSTITIOUS HUNTERS INSIST THAT ANYONE WHO KILLS A WHITE CHAMOIS WILL DIE WITHIN THE YEAR

THE **WONDER TREE OF KNYSNA FOREST** Pretoria, So. Africa A HUGE GREEN MOUND 75 FEET HIGH CONSISTING OF 13 INDIVIDUAL WILD FIG EVERGREENS *WHICH SPRANG FROM THE TRUNK OF THE ORIGINAL TREE*

drinking song, "To Anacreon In Heaven." A year later Congress acted, and "The Star Spangled Banner" was adopted as our anthem.

In his never-ending search for believe-it-or-nots, Bob collected thousands of great stories. He claimed to have traveled to 198 different countries looking for his material. Surely no one ever visited more areas, and with present boundary changes it is not likely anyone ever will. Over the years Bob and I crossed trails many times, and for every story I had to tell, Bob had one to match it. He told of visits to the Garden of Eden, of treading the Andean Inca roads Pizarro traveled in Peru, and even of buying shrunken heads from bootleggers in Panama City. He had even, he assured me, gone to Hell. In fact, he said his visit to Hell, a village in Norway, was a pleasant experience—no serpents there, not even a Devil. Ripley was indefatigable, and neither fame nor fortune blunted his curiosity.

This small-town boy from Santa Rosa, California, had come a long way. In 1908 when his father died Bob had to quit school and go to work to support the family. But for a young lad then, as now, there was opportunity for talent. Like so many westerners he found himself looking not westward but eastward to the "land of opportunity."

In New York he eventually landed a job as sports cartoonist for the **New York Globe**, with which I too was associated at one time. It was there in December 1918 that he had his Believe-It-Or-Not inspiration. At first published once a week, it soon became a regular feature and so fired the public imagination that it went on to become a national institution, was syndicated and soon was being read daily by millions in 38 countries and 14 languages.

Those of us who knew Bob Ripley in those successful

THE TREE THAT RAINS
SAMANEA SAMAN, a tropical tree,
COLLECTS MOISTURE IN ITS PODS DURING THE DAY
AND EACH EVENING DUMPS IT IN THE FORM OF
A HEAVY DOWNPOUR

THE WESTERN KINGBIRD
WHICH DINES ON BEES,
ATTRACTS THEM BY
FLASHING ON ITS HEAD A
BRILLIANT RED SPOT, WHICH
BEES MISTAKE FOR A FLOWER

THE **CISTERCIAN MONASTERY**
OF WALKENRIED, GERMANY,
WAS DEMOLISHED IN THE PEASANTS' WAR
-YET 400 YEARS LATER ITS RUINS STILL
ARE USED AS A CHURCH AND MUSEUM

THE **FROG FISH**
of Asia
CAN LIVE OUT OF
WATER FOR DAYS

THE **RUSE** THAT ENABLED A SINGLE KNIGHT TO
OVERCOME AN ENTIRE GARRISON !
DANIEL de BOUCHET, A KNIGHT OF BURGUNDY, AFTER HIS FORCES HAD
FAILED IN 8 ATTACKS AGAINST ENGLISH DEFENDERS OF THE BELGIAN
FORTRESS OF BRAINE-LE-COMTE, TRICKED THE GARRISON INTO SURRENDER-
ING WITHOUT RESISTANCE IN A 9th ATTACK BY MOUNTING A WHITE HORSE
AND DONNING ANCIENT ARMOR BEARING THE INSIGNIA IDENTIFYING HIM AS
ST. GEORGE - THE PATRON SAINT OF ENGLAND (1423)

**ELEAZAR
MORTON**
of Benton
Harbor, Mich.,
STRICKEN GRAVELY
ILL IN JAN. 1864,
COMFORTED HIS
RELATIVES BY
ASSERTING:"DON'T
WORRY, I WILL
LIVE UNTIL
INDEPENDENCE DAY."
HE DIED ON
JULY 4th, 1864

A **STONE WOLFHOUND** ON THE WALLS
OF ANTRIM CASTLE, IRELAND, IS A
MEMORIAL TO A WOLFHOUND THAT
SAVED LADY MARION CLOTWORTHY
FROM A WOLF ATTACK IN 1660 AND
ALSO ALERTED THE CASTLE TO A
SNEAK ONSLAUGHT BY AN ENEMY FORCE

Ripley's® Believe It or Not!

THE **CROSS SHELL**
(ostrea malleus)
A MOLLUSK THAT ALWAYS FORMS THE SHAPE OF A CROSS

THE **FISH THAT CARRIES A FLASHLIGHT**
GIGANTACTIS, WHICH SWIMS AT A DEPTH OF 6,000 FEET, LIGHTS IT'S WAY THROUGH THE OCEAN DEPTHS BY A BRIGHT LIGHT IT CARRIES AT THE END OF A ROD PROJECTING FROM ITS HEAD

THE **MARINE IGUANAS** of Galapagos FIGHT DUELS BY STANDING FOREHEAD TO FOREHEAD -AND PUSHING AGAINST EACH OTHER

DR. EDWARD A. HOLYOKE
(1728 - 1828)
THE FIRST MAN TO RECEIVE A MEDICAL DEGREE FROM HARVARD, PRACTICED MEDICINE IN SALEM, MASS., **FOR 80 YEARS.** HE MADE 250,000 SICK CALLS, WALKED ABOUT 7 MILES A DAY, PERFORMED SURGICAL OPERATIONS IN HIS 90'S, AND BECAME FIRST PRESIDENT OF THE SALEM SAVINGS BANK AT THE AGE OF **90**

THE JACKAL THAT BECAME A KING!
The RAJAH OF PARTABGARH in India
AS A GESTURE OF CONTEMPT FOR A DEFEATED MONARCH CROWNED A JACKAL AS RULER OF GARWARA -AND THE ANIMAL REIGNED FOR 12 YEARS!

years found him an anomaly; both a sentimentalist and a realist. A shy, awkward, buck-toothed kid, he developed into an enthusiastic and aggressive man. In his early and middle years he worked 15 hours a day (most of his drawing was done before noon), and he worked on his feature 7 days a week, 52 weeks a year, for over 20 years. Although as a young man he was often described as a hick, no one ever doubted that one day he would be one of the world's most successful cartoonists. As millions know, before he died he had achieved fame via newspapers, magazines, radio, movies, World's Fair exhibitions, and his books. I knew him as a companion and as a member of my ball team, "The Nine Old Men," who for years played against my neighbor FDR's picturesque "Roosevelt Packers."

Like all the Ripley books this one is certain to be around for many years. Indeed, for decades it will be found in second-hand book stores, at church bazaars, in school libraries, in dentists' and doctors' waiting rooms. Tattered and curled at the edges, it will catch the eye of the curious wherever it is. People will still be quoting its unbelievable contents at parties and in bars long after its pages are faded and torn, long after its cover has disappeared.

Others will create new books, and thousands more oddities will be disclosed. As Ripley himself said, "The mine is inexhaustible." That the Believe-It-Or-Not cartoon has continued on and on in over 300 newspapers for 50 years is evidence of this—for Truth is indeed stranger than Fiction.

Ripley's Believe It or Not!

A TABLET ENGRAVED WITH CHARACTERS IN THE ALPHABET OF THE TOUARIK TRIBE OF LIBYA, AFRICA, WAS FOUND IN 1839 IN AN INDIAN BURIAL GROUND AT GRAVE CREEK, NEAR THE OHIO RIVER

THE EUROPEAN STRAWBERRY TREE BEARS FRUIT AND BLOSSOMS SIMULTANEOUSLY

THE COAT OF ARMS of Camargue, France, IS A MONOGRAM FEATURING A CROSS, A HEART AND AN ANCHOR — SYMBOLIZING FAITH, CHARITY AND HOPE

A GOLDEN CALENDAR WAS PART OF THE CORONATION REGALIA OF King Charles X of France — SYMBOLIZING THAT HE ALSO WAS THE SUPREME MASTER OF TIME

THE GREAT HALL OF THE ROYAL CASTLE of Balmoral, Scotland, WAS COPIED FROM A STAGE SETTING FOR MACBETH, ADMIRED BY PRINCE ALBERT DURING A PERFORMANCE AT THE PRINCESS THEATRE IN MANCHESTER, ENGLAND

A GERMAN LAND MINE THAT DROPPED ON London, England, DURING WORLD WAR II, BUT FAILED TO EXPLODE, WAS DE-ACTIVATED AND NOW SERVES AS AN ORNAMENT IN FRONT OF THE ROYAL THAMES YACHT CLUB

THE STRANGE FLORAL TITHE TO ST. PETER

THE FOUNTAIN OF ST. PETER in the flower market of Trier, Germany, HAS BEEN DECORATED WITH ONE-TENTH OF ALL THE FLOWERS SENT TO THE MARKET DAILY FOR 800 YEARS. ST. PETER, IN RETURN, IS EXPECTED TO ASSURE A GOOD FLORAL HARVEST

THE STRANGEST DRAMATIC SCHOOL IN HISTORY

CHARLES DULLIN (1885-1949) the brilliant French actor RECEIVED HIS DRAMATIC TRAINING RECITING POETRY DAILY FOR SEVERAL YEARS IN A CAGE FULL OF LIONS

THE S.S. SKIBLADNER
of EIDSVOLL, NORWAY,
LAUNCHED AS A LAKE STEAMER IN 1856
IS STILL IN USE 114 YEARS LATER

THE RULER WHO HAD THE MOST EXTENSIVE WARDROBE IN ALL HISTORY!
MIR BAHBOOB ALI KHAN (1856-1911)
6th NIZAM OF HYDERABAD AND RICHEST PRINCE IN INDIA,
THROUGHOUT HIS LIFETIME
NEVER WORE THE SAME GARMENT TWICE
HIS CLOTHING, FASHIONED OF FINE, WHITE MUSLIN, WAS
WORN ONCE AND THEN GIVEN TO PALACE SERVANTS

THE BIGGEST BOAST
THE SEAL OF THE SOVEREIGN LAMA OF BHUTAN, INDIA, INCLUDES 16 OF HIS CLAIMED ATTRIBUTES, TYPICAL OF WHICH IS:
"I am unequalled in holiness and wisdom"

THE GHOST CRAB
IS CREAM COLORED WHEN IT IS ON DRY SAND BUT WHEN THE SAND IS WET THE CRAB BLENDS *INTO A COMBINATION OF GRAY, PURPLE AND BROWN*

THE PEACOCK WORM
WHICH LIVES IN THE MUDDY SEA BOTTOM, EXTENDS INTO THE WATER TO CAPTURE ITS FOOD FEATHERY GILLS THAT *RESEMBLE THE COLORFUL FAN OF A PEACOCK*

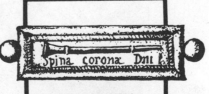

Spina corona Dni

THE HOLY THORN
A SACRED RELIC IN THE Church of Chalandry, France, IS BELIEVED TO HAVE BEEN PART OF THE CROWN OF THORNS WORN BY CHRIST AT THE CRUCIFIXION

THE TRANS-IRANIAN RAILWAY
WHICH EXTENDS 895 MILES FROM THE CASPIAN SEA TO THE PERSIAN GULF AND WAS BUILT IN 10 YEARS AT A COST OF $150,000,000 HAS **4,102** BRIDGES AND **224** TUNNELS, AND *AT ONE POINT REQUIRES 6 BRIDGES AND 4 TUNNELS TO TRAVERSE ONLY 900 FEET*

RED ROCK SALT
IS MINED IN MOROCCO AND TRANSPORTED THROUGHOUT NORTH AFRICA ON THE BACKS OF *DONKEYS*

THE RIVER THAT FLOWS IN A CIRCLE
THE TARN RIVER near Ambialet, France, *FORMS A CIRCLE 2 MILES IN DIAMETER*

HERE LIES THE BODY OF EDWARD HYDE WE LAID HIM HERE BECAUSE HE DIED ·
Epitaph IN Storrington Churchyard, England

THE STRANGEST COURTROOM IN ALL HISTORY!

GOSSAIN A CITY JUDGE OF IMPHAL, India, WHO SUFFERED FROM INVERTED VISION, PRESIDED OVER TRIALS FOR A PERIOD OF 19 YEARS *STANDING ON HIS HEAD!* (1852-1871)

PEACH SHAPED LIKE A BIRD Submitted by MRS. LORETTA HILL The Bronx, N.Y.

THE **GURNARD** A FISH THAT GRUNTS WHEN CAUGHT, HAS 3 PECTORAL PROJECTIONS WHICH IT USES LIKE FINGERS—*TO DIG FOOD FROM THE MUDDY BOTTOM OF THE SEA AND POP IT INTO ITS MOUTH*

MILITARY BANDSMEN in Saudi Arabia ARE THE ONLY INHABITANTS AMONG A POPULATION OF 6,500,000 PERMITTED TO PLAY ANY TYPE OF MUSIC

The STAR of BETHLEHEM

WHICH GUIDED THE THREE WISE MEN TO THE INFANT JESUS *APPEARS ONLY EVERY 974 YEARS!*

IT IS A BRIGHT CONJUNCTION OF JUPITER AND SATURN, IN THE CONSTELLATION OF PISCES, WAS LAST SEEN IN 1942 AND WILL NOT REAPPEAR UNTIL 2916

Ripley's® Believe It or Not!

The GENERAL who "DIED" 6 TIMES!
GENERAL BAPTISTE de MONTMORIN
(1704-1779) of the French army
WAS PRONOUNCED DEAD ON THE FIELD OF BATTLE 5 TIMES!
EACH TIME HE REVIVED JUST AS HE WAS ABOUT TO BE INTERRED.
HE SERVED IN THE FRENCH ARMY A TOTAL OF 55 YEARS AND
ACTUALLY DIED AT THE AGE OF 75

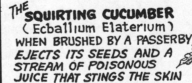

A **MONASTERY** BUILT ON A
HIGH ROCK NEAR ADUWA, ETHIOPIA,
CAN BE REACHED ONLY BY
*A ROPE LOWERED DOWN
THE SHEER CLIFF*

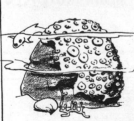

THE **SULPHUR SPONGE**
IS THE
ONLY ANIMAL
LIFE THAT CAN
DISSOLVE SEA
SHELLS INTO
THE ORIGINAL
CALCIUM FROM
WHICH THEY
WERE FORMED

THIS **TALISMAN**
IF WORN FOR
4 WEEKS,
IS BELIEVED BY
THE CHINESE
TO HAVE THE
POWER TO ASSURE
PROMOTION TO A
BETTER JOB

THE **SQUIRTING CUCUMBER**
(Ecballium Elaterium)
WHEN BRUSHED BY A PASSERBY,
*EJECTS ITS SEEDS AND A
STREAM OF POISONOUS
JUICE THAT STINGS THE SKIN*

THE CHURCH OF ST. ANNE
In Anderghem, Belgium,
HAS BEEN OPEN FOR SERVICES ONLY ONCE A YEAR
- ON THE DAY OF ST. ANNE - FOR 800 YEARS

"MICHAEL" an Irish terrier, PLAYED
IN 1,250 PERFORMANCES OF "PEG
O' MY HEART," AND HAS BEEN CALLED
A "CANINE IMMORTAL OF THE THEATRE"
- YET HE WAS OBTAINED FROM THE
LOS ANGELES POUND FOR $1 ONE
DAY BEFORE HE WAS TO HAVE
BEEN PUT TO DEATH

Ripley's Believe It or Not!

THE HUMAN CORK!

CASIMIR POLEMUS of Ploërmel, France, WAS INVOLVED IN 3 SHIPWRECKS - AND EACH TIME WAS THE SOLE SURVIVOR!

HE WAS THE SOLE SURVIVOR OF THE "JEANNE CATHERINE," WRECKED OFF BREST ON JULY 11, 1875, THE "TROIS FRÈRES," WRECKED IN THE BAY OF BISCAY ON SEPT. 4, 1880, AND "L'ODEON," WRECKED OFF NEWFOUNDLAND ON JAN. 1, 1882

SHELLS AND FEATHERS ARE ARRANGED BY THE YORUBAS OF AFRICA AS *THEIR OWN FORM OF HIEROGLYPHICS*
THIS ARRANGEMENT READS:" I love you. Hurry to me."

THE CHURCH of DENSUS in Rumania WAS CONSTRUCTED BY MAKING USE OF THE *STONE RUINS OF AN ANCIENT ROMAN TOWN WALL*

THE MUMMIFIED HAND of a NOTARY PUBLIC

CHOPPED OFF FOR FALSELY CERTIFYING A DOCUMENT HAS BEEN ON DISPLAY IN the City Hall of Münster, Germany, *AS A WARNING TO OTHER NOTARIES, FOR 400 YEARS*

THE NARTHEX PLANT WHICH GROWS ON THE SLOPES OF Mt. Panajir Dagh, in Turkey, AND WAS FIRST DESCRIBED BY HOMER, IS THE LEGENDARY PLANT IN WHICH PROMETHEUS IS SAID TO HAVE TRANSPORTED FIRE FROM HEAVEN TO EARTH. *THE STALKS CONTAIN A DRY PITH WHICH SHINES IN THE DARK FOR HOURS AFTER IT HAS BEEN REMOVED FROM THE PLANT*

THE VENUS FLOWER BASKET, A SPONGE FOUND IN BOTH THE ATLANTIC AND PACIFIC, ACTUALLY IS A GLASS CORNUCOPIA WITH AN EXQUISITE PATTERN OF SAND SPIKES--SO BEAUTIFUL THAT NATIVES OF SOUTHERN ASIA *WEAR IT AS JEWELRY*

THE DADDY LONGLEGS of the Ivory Coast DISGUISES ITSELF AS A COBWEB

THE SANCTUARY of the ASCENSION in Jerusalem MARKING THE SPOT FROM WHICH JESUS ASCENDED TO HEAVEN, IS USED FOR CHRISTIAN WORSHIP ONLY 2 DAYS IN EVERY YEAR -BEING A MOHAMMEDAN MOSQUE THE OTHER 363 DAYS

THE PEACE MEMORIAL MUSEUM in Zanzibar CONSTRUCTED IN 1925, HAS A HUGE RING PROTRUDING FROM ITS ROOF - PUT THERE BY ITS MOHAMMEDAN BUILDERS SO THAT IF AN EARTH-QUAKE OCCURRED, A GUARDIAN ANGEL COULD LIFT THE STRUCTURE INTO THE SKY

THE OLDEST THEATRE TICKET A CLAY DISK THAT ADMITTED ITS HOLDER TO A PLAY BY MENANDER -THE ANCIENT GREEK COMEDY WRITER- STAGED 2,288 YEARS AGO

THE MACQUARIE LIGHTHOUSE NEAR SYDNEY, AUSTRALIA, WAS DESIGNED BY GEORGE GREENWAY, A LONG TERM CONVICT, WHO WAS COMPENSATED BY BEING FREED ON THE DAY ITS CONSTRUCTION WAS STARTED (1818)

THE PURPLE SHORE CRAB IN PROPORTION TO ITS WEIGHT, HAS THE STRENGTH OF 40 MEN

WILLIAM BECKFORD (1760-1844) wealthy eccentric Englishman, STAYED AT HUNDREDS OF INNS DURING HIS JOURNEYS AND ALWAYS INSISTED THAT HIS SUITE BE FRESHLY WALLPAPERED BY HIS OWN DECORATORS - EVEN FOR A STAY OF ONLY A SINGLE NIGHT

THE MALE BOWFIN MUST GUARD THE EGGS LAID BY THE MOTHER BOWFIN TO PREVENT HER FROM EATING THEM

THE OLDEST KNOWN MUSICAL INSTRUMENT A BOW STRING WHICH PRODUCES A PLEASING TWANG IS STILL PLAYED BY THE SANTALS OF INDIA RECENT GENERATIONS HAVE ADDED A GOURD TO PROVIDE RESONANCE

THE MONARCH WHO COVERED HIS TRACKS WITH GOLD AND DIAMONDS! KING AROUDJ I (1474-1518) of Algeria, FLEEING A SPANISH ARMY BESIEGING THE CASTLE OF TLEMCEN, ATTEMPTED TO DELAY PURSUIT BY SCATTERING ALONG HIS TRAIL $3,000,000 WORTH OF GOLD AND PRECIOUS STONES! THE SPANIARDS COLLECTED THE FORTUNE -AND FOLLOWED ITS TRAIL TO KING AROUDJ, SLAYING HIM AT THE RIVER HUEXDA

DEMARETEIONS SILVER COINS MINTED IN SYRACUSE BY PRINCESS DEMARETE, WERE MADE FROM SILVER THE PRINCESS OBTAINED IN TRADE FOR A GIFT FROM GRATEFUL CARTHAGINIANS SPARED BY HER INTERCESSION -A 600-LB. CROWN OF SOLID GOLD (480 B.C.)

Good for $1.00 ON Demand BEACH CAMP Sign. Thos. Bernhagt Mar-6.1933 See Other Side

CLAM SHELLS
DURING THE DEPRESSION PERIOD OF THE 1930's, WERE USED IN PISMO BEACH, CALIF., AS *LEGAL TENDER*

WILLIAM WILLIS
SAILED 6,700 MILES FROM PERU TO SAMOA IN 112 DAYS ON A RAFT CONSISTING OF 7 BALSA LOGS LASHED TOGETHER *AT THE AGE OF 61* HIS ONLY COMPANIONS WERE A CAT AND A PARROT— AND THE CAT ATE THE PARROT (1954)

"EN BOUCHE CLOSE NENTRE MOUSCHE"
THE MOTTO ON JACQUES COEUR'S HOUSE IN BOURGES, FRANCE, SAYS, *"A FLY CANNOT ENTER A CLOSED MOUTH,"* MEANING - TO AVOID TROUBLE KEEP YOUR MOUTH SHUT

THE CHRISTMAS PRESENT THAT WAS NOT A GIFT AT ALL
Francois Joseph Noël (1755-1841) French envoy to the Netherlands, FOR WRITING A CONSTITUTION FOR THE BATAVIAN REPUBLIC, IN 1795 *WAS PAID 2,000,000 FLORINS ($804,000)* SINCE THE NAME NOËL IN FRENCH MEANS CHRISTMAS, THE HUGE EXPENDITURE WAS DISGUISED ON THE RECORDS AS "CHRISTMAS GIFTS"

"MR. McGREGOR"
A SCOTTISH TERRIER OWNED BY JOSEPH DUDDY, OF Pittsburgh, Pa., REGULARLY RECEIVED EACH DECEMBER 25th AS MANY AS *300 CHRISTMAS CARDS*

THE LEAF BUG
(Phyllium siccifolium) OF CEYLON HAS LEGS AND ANTENNAE THE COLOR AND SHAPE OF LEAVES, HAS INDENTATIONS ON ITS BODY LIKE THE VEIN MARKS ON A LEAF *-- AND HANGS FROM BRANCHES, SWAYING IN THE BREEZE EXACTLY LIKE A LEAF*

THE COLORADO RIVER TOAD
HAS A CROAK THAT SOUNDS LIKE A FERRYBOAT WHISTLE

THE STRANGEST PHILANTHROPY IN ALL HISTORY!
YAHYA al BARMAKI, GRAND VIZIER TO CALIPH HARUN AL RASHID OF BAGHDAD, RODE HORSEBACK THROUGH THE CITY EVERY DAY FOR 12 YEARS AND DAILY TOSSED TO 100 STRANGERS - REGARDLESS OF THEIR NEED - *PURSES FILLED WITH 100 PIECES OF SILVER* - IN THE PERIOD FROM 786 TO 798 HE DISTRIBUTED IN THIS MANNER $24,000,000 - EQUIVALENT TODAY TO $2,500,000,000 !

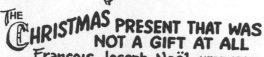

"VICKEY"
A BLACK CAT
BORN ON
"V-DAY" - DATE
OF THE FORMAL
SURRENDER OF
JAPAN IN
WORLD WAR II -
WITH A WHITE V
ON ITS CHEST

The STRANGEST JURY TRIAL IN HISTORY

RAYMOND GUI, AN OUTLAW, CAPTURED BY A
POSSE OF FARMERS NEAR MURET, FRANCE,
AFTER HE HAD KILLED 3 OF THEIR NEIGHBORS, WAS
PLACED ON TRIAL BEFORE A JURY COMPRISING
THE SHROUDED BODIES OF HIS 3 VICTIMS!
THE PROSECUTING ATTORNEY INSISTED HE WAS IN
COMMUNICATION WITH THE SPIRITS OF THE JURORS -AND
THE DEFENDANT WAS CONVICTED AND EXECUTED
(1589)

THE ALTAR CRUCIFIX

of Christ Church, in Yokohama, Japan,
WAS CARVED BY NOBUMICHI INOUYE, A
JAPANESE SCULPTOR, WHO AS A RESULT
OF HIS RESEARCH ON THE PROJECT
BECAME A CONVERT TO CHRISTIANITY

JACK CARSTENS
of Kleinzee,
Namaqualand, S. Africa,
AND A FRIEND WERE
FISHING TOGETHER
WHEN THEIR HOOKS
SIMULTANEOUSLY CAUGHT
THE SAME FISH
*THEY CUT THE FISH IN HALF
AND EACH TOOK AN EQUAL SHARE*

SALIM (1569-1627)
HEIR TO THE THRONE
of India
HAD 4 WIVES WHEN
HE WAS ONLY
8 YEARS OF AGE

Dr. James MUATT

(1656 - 1776)
of Langholm, Scotland
WAS A SURGEON
UNTIL HIS DEATH
AT THE AGE OF 120
-HAVING PRACTICED
FOR 95 YEARS !

Ripley's Believe It or Not!

A HORSE RACE WITH 2 DEAD HEATS!
THE ASTLEY STAKES RACE IN Lewes, England, IN 1880, FINISHED WITH THREE HORSES - WANDERING NOON, MAZURKA AND SCOBELL - *IN A DEAD HEAT FOR FIRST* AND THE NEXT TWO HORSES - CUMBERLAND AND THERA - *ALSO IN A DEAD HEAT*

THE **GOLD RING** WORN BY PHARAOH RAMSES II of Egypt WAS A MEMORIAL TO HIS 2 CHARIOT HORSES, NURIT AND ANAITIS, *WHICH SAVED HIS LIFE IN THE BATTLE OF KADESH*

KING LOUIS IX (1214-1270)
WAS THE ONLY FRENCH KING IN THE COUNTRY'S ENTIRE HISTORY *WHO WAS NURSED BY HIS OWN MOTHER*

THE DAY THE SKY RAINED FIRE!
THE HEAVENS OVER NORTH AMERICA WERE LIT UP ON NOVEMBER 13, 1833, *BY 200,000 SHOOTING STARS*! NONE OF THEM REACHED THE EARTH

THE **OLDEST** KNOWN NECKTIE WAS WORN BY A WOMAN
A NECKTIE NEATLY KNOTTED AT THE THROAT, IS CARVED IN STONE ON THE STATUE OF A CRETAN GIRL *CREATED 3,500 YEARS AGO*

FEMALE ARISTOCRATS on the island of Portuguese Timor, in Malaya, INDICATE THEIR SOCIAL STATUS *BY NOTCHING THEIR EARS*

THE **WOOD** THAT BURNED UNDERWATER !
A LUMBER YARD at Horsham, Australia, WAS COMPLETELY DESTROYED BY FIRE IN 1909 *ALTHOUGH THE YARD WAS DEEPLY IMMERSED BY FLOOD WATERS AND THE AREA WAS BEING SWEPT BY A TORRENTIAL RAINSTORM*
LIME STORED IN THE YARD KEPT THE LUMBER BURNING FURIOUSLY

THE **3d EARL** OF **CUMBERLAND** (1558-1605) GIVEN ONE OF HER GLOVES BY QUEEN ELIZABETH IN 1580 HAD IT STUDDED WITH DIAMONDS AND WORE IT ON HIS HAT FOR THE REMAINING 25 YEARS OF HIS LIFE

THE **STRANGEST COURT OF DOMESTIC RELATIONS IN THE WORLD**
A GUAYMI TRIBESMAN of Panama
IN A TEST OF HIS WIFE'S LOVE, TURNS HIS BACK ON A RIVAL AND LETS HIM HURL A HEAVY POLE AT HIS LEGS **30 TIMES** !
A CONTESTANT LOSES HIS WIFE TO HIS RIVAL IF HE SUFFERS A BROKEN LEG — AND HE CAN AVOID THE HEAVY STICK ONLY IF HIS *WIFE SHOUTS A WARNING AT THE PROPER MOMENT*

THE **GARDEN** of the Castle of Koburg, Germany, HAS GROWING SIDE BY SIDE ORANGE, BLACK, GREEN AND CONVENTIONAL RED ROSES

THE **OLDEST** PAIR OF PANTS IN THE WORLD
WOOL TROUSERS FOUND IN A SWAMP NEAR THORSBJERG, DENMARK, WERE 1,600 YEARS OLD
THEY HAD BELT LOOPS AND HAD BEEN MADE WITH KNITTED SOCKS ATTACHED TO THE LEGS

THE GHOST TOWN THAT COMES TO LIFE EVERY WEEK END

A COMMUNITY near Pitea, in Northern Sweden, WITH 500 HOMES AND A NUMBER OF SHOPS, BUSTLES WITH ACTIVITY EACH SATURDAY AND SUNDAY, BUT FOR 5 CENTURIES *HAS BEEN ABANDONED THE REMAINDER OF EACH WEEK*

THE HOUSES WERE BUILT BY THE LOCAL CHURCH TO ACCOMMODATE PARISHIONERS—ALL OF WHOM MUST TRAVEL SO FAR THAT THEY SPEND EACH WEEK END IN THE CHURCH TOWN

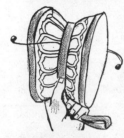

THE DRUM USED BY THE TIBETAN LAMA of Rampur, India, WAS CONSTRUCTED BY JOINING TOGETHER 2 HUMAN SKULLS

MEDICAL RINGS
ADORNED WITH THE SHELL OF THE SPINNING TOP SNAIL *WERE ONCE BELIEVED CAPABLE OF CURING THE WEARER OF COLIC, WORMS AND NOSEBLEED*

PROFESSOR JOSEPH O'CALLAGHAN
OF THE LITERATURE DEPARTMENT OF GEORGETOWN UNIVERSITY

THROUGHOUT HIS ENTIRE ADULT LIFE REFUSED TO SIT AT A DESK THAT DID NOT DISPLAY *AT LEAST ONE VOLUME OF SHAKESPEARE*

HE WAS FATALLY INJURED DURING A STORM AT SEA IN 1868 WHEN HE WAS CRUSHED BY A TABLE THAT WAS BARE OF ANY BOOKS

THE TOOTHACHE TREE
THE BARK OF THE PRICKLY ASH WAS CHEWED BY AMERICAN INDIANS *AS A REMEDY FOR TOOTHACHE*

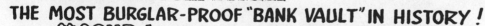

THE MOST BURGLAR-PROOF "BANK VAULT" IN HISTORY!

MASUD I, KING of GHAZNA AND RULER of INDIA, ALWAYS CARRIED THE ENTIRE STATE TREASURY —AS MUCH AS $150,000,000— *ON THE BACKS OF 3,000 PERSONALLY-TRAINED CAMELS!*

EACH CAMEL OBEYED A DIFFERENT PASSWORD KNOWN ONLY TO THE KING, WHO WOULD GIVE A CREDITOR THE PROPER PASSWORD FOR A CAMEL CARRYING EXACTLY THE SUM HE WAS TO COLLECT— *ONLY WHEN THE PROPER CODE WORD WAS UTTERED WOULD A CAMEL PERMIT ITSELF TO BE LED AWAY AND UNLOADED OF ITS PRECIOUS CARGO*

(1030—1040)

Ripley's — Believe It or Not!

A CAT TRAILING A GROUP OF ALPINISTS FROM THE HOTEL BELVEDERE, LOCATED AT AN ALTITUDE OF 10,820 FEET ON THE MATTERHORN *CLIMBED TO THE SUMMIT -AT A HEIGHT OF 14,780 FEET* (1950)

THE SIEGE THAT WAS WON BY A SINGLE ARROW!

SIR HENRY MORGAN, ATTEMPTING TO STORM THE FORTRESS OF SAN LORENZO, WHICH GUARDED THE FABULOUS RICHES OF PANAMA, *WAS REPULSED REPEATEDLY UNTIL ONE OF HIS SAILORS WAS HIT BY AN ARROW*

THE SAILOR, NAMED DIAZ, PULLED OUT THE ARROW, WRAPPED IT IN A WAD OF COTTON, AND FIRED IT FROM HIS MUSKET. THE COTTON WAS IGNITED BY THE GUN'S POWDER, AND WHEN THE ARROW LANDED ON A THATCHED ROOF IT TOUCHED OFF A BLAZE THAT EXPLODED THE SPANISH POWDER MAGAZINE *-DEMOLISHING THE FORTRESS AND KILLING 363 OF THE 400 DEFENDING SOLDIERS* (1665)

THE PITTA BIRD of Australia

IS RESPLENDENT IN FEATHERS OF 9 COLORS - BLUE, GREEN, ORANGE, BROWN, PINK, RED, WHITE, PURPLE AND BLACK

THE COWFIGHTERS WHO ARE MORE COURAGEOUS THAN BULLFIGHTERS!

COWFIGHTERS, of the Landes area of southern France, FACE THE HORNS OF WILD COWS WITH NO DEFENSE WEAPON OF ANY KIND THEY MUST ESCAPE THE COW'S SHARP HORNS BY LEAPING HIGH INTO THE AIR - AND TO AVOID A HEAD-ON CHARGE *THEIR JUMP MUST CARRY THEM OVER THE FULL LENGTH OF THE COW*

ARROWHEADS MADE BY MEDIEVAL CHINESE TO KEEP THEM FROM STRAYING HAD ENGRAVED ON THEM SUCH LINES FROM CONFUCIUS AS: "Have no depraved thoughts"

Ripley's — Believe It or Not!

THE JEWELED COSTUME THAT WEIGHED AS MUCH AS ITS WEARER
FATH ALI SHAH (1762-1834) AT HIS CORONATION AS RULER OF PERSIA IN 1797 WORE REGALIA SO HEAVILY INCRUSTED WITH DIAMONDS, RUBIES, EMERALDS AND GOLD _THAT IT WEIGHED 170 POUNDS_

THE TOWER OF THE CHURCH OF ST. ULRICH, in Rastede, Germany, WAS DEMOLISHED BY LIGHTNING 4 TIMES BETWEEN 1599 AND 1783 _EACH TIME ON APRIL 18th_

THE MOST POPULAR EMPEROR IN ROMAN HISTORY
EMPEROR CLAUDIUS II (214-270) WAS HAILED BY THE ENTIRE ROMAN SENATE, WHICH ROSE AND CHANTED: "AUGUST CLAUDIUS, YOU ARE OUR FATHER, BROTHER, FRIEND, SENATOR AND EMPEROR" THE SENATORS, SHOUTING IN UNISON, REPEATED THAT LINE **233 TIMES!**

TWIN JARS made by early Peruvians WERE SO FASHIONED THAT WHEN A LIQUID WAS POURED FROM ONE TO THE OTHER THE JARS WHISTLED MERRILY

ABUL FEIZI HINDI the Persian poet FOR TUTORING THE 3 SONS OF AKBAR, THE EMPEROR OF INDIA, WAS PAID ANNUALLY FOR 15 YEARS A SUM IN GOLD _EQUAL TO THE COMBINED WEIGHT OF HIS 3 STUDENTS_

MUREX SATATAILIS a mollusk of Senegal, TO CLOSE THE OPENING IN ITS SHELL, SECRETES A SUBSTANCE WHICH IS NOW DISTILLED TO PRODUCE _ONE OF INDIA'S MOST EXPENSIVE PERFUMES_

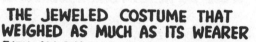

ORCHIS MASCULA AN ORCHID found in Europe and Asia, _PROVIDES BOTH FOOD AND MEDICINE_ THE DRIED TUBERS YIELD A FOOD LIKE TAPIOCA AND AN OINTMENT THAT SOOTHES WOUNDS

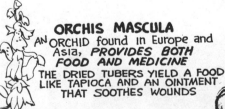

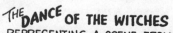

THE DANCE OF THE WITCHES REPRESENTING A SCENE FROM GOETHE'S "FAUST" CARVED FROM **A SINGLE TREE TRUNK** _IT IS NOW A CANDELABRA IN A RESTAURANT IN LEIPZIG, GERMANY_

A **LEAF** PRESSED BETWEEN THE PAGES OF A BIBLE BY A U.S. SAILOR AT SASEBO, JAPAN, IN 1945 *IS STILL GREEN NEARLY 21 YEARS LATER*
Submitted by WALT MEDICIS, Syracuse, N.Y.

THE **CEREMONIAL HEADDRESS**
of the secret Society of Sierra Leone, Africa, IS ADORNED BY HUMAN SKULLS AND THIGHBONES —IN THE BELIEF ITS WEARER WILL INHERIT FROM DECEASED MEMBERS *THEIR BRAIN POWER AND FLEETNESS OF FOOT*

THE **MAN WHO LOCATED A SOURCE OF WATER 6,000 MILES AWAY!**

FATHER ALEXIS MERMET of Saint-Prex, Switzerland, BY HOLDING A PENDULUM OVER A SET OF PLANS IN HIS STUDY *DETERMINED THE EXACT POSITION AND DEPTH OF UNDERGROUND WATER AT THE MONASTERY OF SAN CAMILO, IN POPAYAN, COLOMBIA—*

HE MARKED THE PLANS AT A POINT WHERE HE SAID WATER WOULD BE FOUND AT A DEPTH OF **27 METERS** (88 FEET, 9 INCHES) —AND THE UNDERGROUND STREAM WAS FOUND *AT THAT EXACT SPOT!*

MOREOVER HE CORRECTLY PREDICTED THAT THE WATER WOULD HAVE A FLOW RATE OF **500** LITERS PER MINUTE (1927)

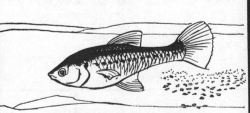

LIMIA VITTATATA
A FISH THAT BEARS LIVE YOUNG IN A SINGLE BIRTH IN THE Shedd Aquarium, Chicago, Ill. **HAD 242 BABY FISH**

"LOVERS' HOUSE" RECENTLY EXCAVATED IN POMPEII IS SO CALLED BECAUSE IT BEARS AN INSCRIPTION READING: "Lovers, like bees, live a honeyed life" ACTUALLY THE HOUSE HAD FAR FROM A HONEYED EXISTENCE, HAVING BEEN CONSTRUCTED IN THE YEAR 79 — ONLY A SHORT TIME BEFORE THE ERUPTION OF VESUVIUS DESTROYED ALL POMPEII

THE **SEA-FAN** IS ACTUALLY CORAL SHAPED LIKE A FAN

THE STRANGEST WEDDINGS IN ALL HISTORY!

RAJAH SHIVAJI of Tanjore, India,
UNHAPPY BECAUSE HE HAD NO MALE HEIR
TOOK 17 WIVES IN A SINGLE DAY!

HE MARRIED 9 GIRLS IN ONE CEREMONY AND 8 MORE THE
SAME EVENING - YET HE DIED WITHOUT A MALE HEIR,
AND THE EAST INDIA COMPANY SEIZED HIS STATE (1855)

CLAUDE CHAUVEAU-LAGARDE

(1756 - 1841)

THE LAWYER WHO RISKED HIS
OWN LIFE DEFENDING MARIE
ANTOINETTE BEFORE THE REVOLUTIONARY
TRIBUNAL, WAS ORDERED TO TURN OVER
TO THE TRIBUNAL THE FEE HE RECEIVED
**IN THE BELIEF HE HAD BEEN
PAID AN ENORMOUS SUM**

HE PROMPTLY SENT THE TRIBUNAL
HIS ONLY FEE - *A LOCK OF
THE QUEEN'S HAIR* (Oct. 1793)

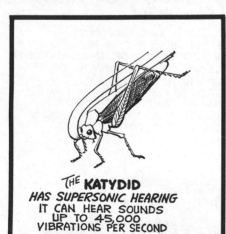

THE KATYDID

HAS SUPERSONIC HEARING
IT CAN HEAR SOUNDS
UP TO 45,000
VIBRATIONS PER SECOND

THE STRUCTURE THAT WAS COMPLETED BY CUPID

THE OLD CUSTOMS HOUSE, in Mexico City, NOW THE FEDERAL TREASURY,
WAS STARTED IN 1730, BUT WORK WAS HALTED IMMEDIATELY
BECAUSE THE BUILDERS ESTIMATED IT WOULD REQUIRE
10 YEARS TO COMPLETE THE PROJECT

A BEAUTIFUL MEXICAN GIRL, SARA DE ACUNA, PROMISED TO MARRY JUAN
GUTIERREZ IF HE WOULD FINISH THE BUILDING IN 6 MONTHS - AND
HE ACCOMPLISHED THE TASK JUST 3 DAYS SHORT OF THE DEADLINE

THE COMMON SAPSUCKER

FEEDS WITH
IMPUNITY
**ON POISON-
IVY BERRIES**

DIAMOND TURTLE

WITH
2 HEADS

Found near
Powells, Miss.,
in 1937

Ripley's — "Believe It or Not!"

THE SHIP THAT WAS SUNK BY A WHALE!
THE "WATERLOO," A FREIGHTER CARRYING GRAIN FROM LYNN, ENGLAND, TO SCHIEDAM, HOLLAND, SANK IN THE NORTH SEA ON MARCH 21, 1855 **AFTER COLLIDING WITH A WHALE!** THE CREW WAS RESCUED BY ANOTHER VESSEL

2 DOORBELLS
WERE USED BY DR. LIBORIO ANGELUCCI (1746-1811) AT HIS RESIDENCE IN ROME, ITALY— ONE FOR THOSE CALLING UPON HIM AS **GOVERNOR OF ROME,** THE OTHER FOR THOSE REQUIRING HIS SERVICES AS THE CITY'S BUSIEST **OBSTETRICIAN**

THE WORLD'S MOST-TOASTED BRIDES!
A GIRL, in the Vacococha Tribe of Peru, TO PREPARE HER FOR MARRIAGE AT THE AGE OF 12, IS PLACED IN A BASKET IN THE HUT OF HER PROSPECTIVE IN-LAWS **AND MUST REMAIN SUSPENDED OVER AN OPEN FIRE NIGHT AND DAY FOR 3 MONTHS!**

THE PALM
OF A SLAIN ENEMY'S LEFT HAND IS NAILED TO A TREE BY THE DAFLAS of India *IN THE BELIEF THAT BY PIERCING IT WITH ARROWS* **THEY WILL INHERIT THE DEAD MAN'S VALOR AND STRENGTH**

THE MOST AMAZING INSURANCE POLICY IN ALL HISTORY
EMPEROR HENRY VII (1269-1313) of Germany DURING HIS REIGN AS DUKE OF LUXEMBOURG WAS SO PROUD OF THE EFFICIENCY OF HIS POLICE *THAT HE OFFERED TO REIMBURSE PERSONALLY ANY VICTIMS OF ROBBERS WITHIN THE BOUNDARIES OF HIS DUCHY*

A WATCH
made in Germany in the 18th century **WITHOUT HANDS** THE NUMBERS INDICATING THE HOUR POP INTO VIEW AND MOVE AROUND THE DIAL

from an old print

THE MAN WHO WAS STRONGER THAN 4 HORSES!

JOHN POLTROT A FRENCHMAN WHO ASSASSINATED THE DUKE de GUISE, WAS SENTENCED TO BE QUARTERED BY 4 HORSES

- BUT THE CONDEMNED MAN WAS SO POWERFUL THE EXECUTION COULD NOT BE ACCOMPLISHED ALTHOUGH *3 TIMES FRESH HORSES WERE TIED TO HIS ARMS AND LEGS* (Feb. 1563)

THE WATERFALL YOU CAN SET YOUR WATCH BY!

THE GNADEN WATERFALL in the Tauern Mountains of Austria

REFLECTS A RAINBOW ON ITS WATERS *AT EXACTLY 3:30 P.M. EVERY DAY*

THE FLYING GURNARD

SWIMS IN WATER, WALKS ON LAND, AND FLIES THROUGH THE AIR

HOSPITAL

A SMALL **KUDU** THAT HAD CAUGHT ITS NECK IN A LOOP OF BARBED WIRE TO WHICH WAS ATTACHED A HEAVY BLOCK OF WOOD *WAS FOUND WAITING FOR HELP OUTSIDE THE HOSPITAL OF VOI, KENYA*

WHEN THE HOSPITAL'S DOORS WERE OPENED THE KUDU WALKED IN AND WAITED PATIENTLY WHILE A DOCTOR CUT THE WIRE (July, 1958)

A **SCALE** SO SENSITIVE IT CAN *WEIGH A PENCIL DOT* A DOT'S WEIGHT IS .0001 GRAM Portland, Ore.

TROPICAL ANTS, WHEN A FLOOD SWEEPS DOWN UPON THEM, ROLL THEMSELVES INTO A HUGE LIVING BALL WHICH DRIFTS UPON THE WATER - WITH THEIR YOUNG SAFE AND DRY AS ITS CORE

A **BRIDE** in Galičnik, Yugoslavia,
ONCE SHE HAS BECOME BETROTHED, MAY NOT
LOOK AT HER HUSBAND UNTIL THE WEDDING DAY
— *AND HER FIRST GLIMPSE OF HIM IS THROUGH*
THE OPENING IN HER WEDDING RING

The **BAROMETER BLOOM**
TABEBUIA NODOSA
of South America
ALWAYS SENDS FORTH
A FEW BLOSSOMS
*ON THE DAY BEFORE
A RAINSTORM*

The **ARMY** OF WAX
LIECHTENSTEIN
HAS AN ARMY CONSISTING
OF ONLY ONE SOLDIER
—*AND HE IS MADE OF WAX*
THE ARMY OF LIECHTENSTEIN
WAS REDUCED IN 1867 TO
ONE SOLDIER, ANDREAS KIEBER,
WHO SERVED UNTIL HIS
DEATH AT THE AGE OF 95
—*AND A WAX STATUE OF
KIEBER NOW GUARDS
CASTLE VADUZ*

A **HERMIT CRAB** THAT HAS
A BOARDER AND A SERVANT
THE BOARDER IS AN
ANEMONE, ATOP THE CRAB'S
SHELL, AND THE SERVANT IS
A NEREIS, A SEA WORM THAT
LIVES INSIDE THE CRAB'S
SHELL —*AND KEEPS IT CLEAN*

The **AMBER THRONE**
THE CHAIR USED
BY HASSEN ben
KENNOUN, WHO
RULED MOROCCO
FROM 954 to 973,
*WAS MADE FROM
THE WORLD'S
LARGEST
BLOCK OF
AMBER*
IT WEIGHED
110 POUNDS AND
WAS VALUED AT
$100,000

THE CITY OF 4,000,000 TEMPLES
AN AREA OF ONLY 60 SQUARE MILES surrounding Pagan, Burma,
DURING THE 255 YEARS FROM 1044 TO 1299 WAS THE SITE
OF CONSTRUCTION OF 4,000,000 TEMPLES
THE RUINS OF 5,000 TEMPLES AND PAGODAS ARE STILL VISIBLE

THE EMPEROR WHO WORKED AS A WAITER!

EMPEROR JAFFAR KHAN of Persia—
DURING THE 10 YEARS HE OCCUPIED THE THRONE,
TO DEMONSTRATE THAT HE WAS NOT ASHAMED THAT
HIS FATHER HAD BEEN A HUMBLE LABORER,
*PERSONALLY SERVED EACH COURSE WHENEVER
HIS FATHER WAS A GUEST*   (1182-1192)

THE MYXOMYCETE – A MOLD

IS BOTH AN ANIMAL AND A PLANT—
IT ABSORBS SOLID FOOD LIKE AN ANIMAL
—YET IT GROWS AND REPRODUCES LIKE A PLANT

A CUCKOO CLOCK

WAS ORDERED
REMOVED FROM
A POLLING
PLACE IN OSS,
the Netherlands,
BECAUSE ITS
CUCKOO SOUNDED
AS IF IT WERE
CALLING OUT
THE NAME OF
ONE OF THE
CANDIDATES—
KOEKOEK

THE BROKEN-HEARTED OAK

AN OAK TREE CUT DOWN ON
VALENTINE'S DAY LEFT A STUMP
*SHAPED LIKE A HEART
PIERCED BY A DAGGER*
Submitted by
Andy Preslopsky, Dallas, Pa.

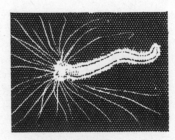

THE CORONATION CHAIR

in Westminster Abbey,
IN WHICH EVERY ENGLISH RULER
HAS BEEN CROWNED SINCE 1327,
WAS USED AS A BED FOR AN
ENTIRE NIGHT BY WILLIAM
LENNOX LORD DE ROS – *WHO
WAS 12 YEARS OF AGE AT THE TIME*

A WINDOW BOX

ON THE WALLS OF A RUINED
PALACE IN JERASH, JORDAN,
STILL CONTAINS LUSH GREEN PLANTS
*PLANTED 1,800 YEARS AGO AND TENDED
BY MORE THAN 50 GENERATIONS*

THE LUMINOUS TUBE WORM

IN THE DARKNESS
*LOOKS LIKE A
BLAZING TORCH*

Ripley's Believe It or Not!

THE **TELEGRAPH PLANT** of Asia HAS LEAVES THAT FLUTTER CONSTANTLY –EVEN WHEN THERE IS NO BREEZE

THE **TALLEST** BUILDING IN MEXICO CITY

THE LATIN-AMERICAN INSURANCE COMPANY SKYSCRAPER SURVIVED THE DEVASTATING EARTHQUAKE OF 1957 *BECAUSE ITS FOUNDATION FLOATS IN SWAMPY GROUND*

THE **KIDNAPING** THAT WAS FOILED BY A STORM!

RENEE NIVERNAS of Marseilles, France, A BABY GIRL 18 MONTHS OF AGE, WAS KIDNAPED FROM HER HOME ON AUGUST 4, 1908, AND HELD FOR RANSOM ABOARD A YACHT

A STORM SANK THE CRAFT AND ALL 8 KIDNAPERS PERISHED – YET THE LITTLE GIRL, SLEEPING IN A MAKESHIFT CRADLE OF PACKING CASES, FLOATED ASHORE AT CASSIS, FRANCE – *UNHARMED!*

3 **PIKE** WERE HOOKED SIMULTANEOUSLY ON THE AVON RIVER, ENGLAND, IN 1925 *THE FIRST FISH HOOKED HAVING BEEN SWALLOWED BY A SECOND –WHICH WAS IN TURN GULPED DOWN BY A THIRD*

A **TOMATO** GROWN BY MYRLIN WINTER *WEIGHING 3 POUNDS* Submitted by WILLIAM ROBERTS, Brooklyn, Wisc.

THE GIANT PUFFBALL
Lycoperdon Giganteum
PRODUCES 7,000,000,000,000 SPORES, EACH OF WHICH COULD GROW INTO A PUFFBALL A FOOT IN DIAMETER AND WHICH COLLECTIVELY COULD COVER AN AREA OF 280,000 SQ. MILES *–GREATER THAN THE SIZE OF TEXAS* FORTUNATELY ONLY ONE OF THE SPORES ACTUALLY BECOMES A PUFFBALL, AND THE OTHERS ALL DIE

THE CASTLE OF KARLSKRONE in Czechoslovakia, BUILT IN 1723 TO CELEBRATE THE CORONATION OF KING CHARLES VI OF BOHEMIA, WAS CONSTRUCTED IN THE SHAPE OF *THE BOHEMIAN CROWN*

Ripley's Believe It or Not!

THE MOST AMAZING NAVAL VICTORY IN ALL HISTORY!

CORT SIVARTSEN ADELAR (1622-1675) NORWEGIAN COMMANDER-IN-CHIEF OF THE VENETIAN NAVY, WITH A SINGLE SHIP MANNED BY 500 SAILORS, *ROUTED THE ENTIRE TURKISH FLEET OF 77 GALLEYS AND A FORCE OF 40,000 TURKISH SEAMEN*

THE VENETIANS SANK 18 GALLEYS, EACH OF WHICH WAS LARGER THAN THEIR OWN VESSEL -AND KILLED 5,000 TURKS (May 16, 1654)

THOMAS BABINGTON MACAULAY (1800-1859) The English historian THROUGHOUT HIS LIFETIME COULD RECITE THE 3,000 ITEMS IN THE 42-PAGE CATALOGUE OF THE ORFORD COLLECTION OF ART -WHICH HE HAD MEMORIZED AT THE AGE OF 4

THE TOWN BELL
of Uglich, Russia, BECAUSE IT WAS RUNG TO PROCLAIM AN INSURRECTION IN 1591 *WAS CONVICTED OF TREASON AND BANISHED TO SIBERIA.* AFTER 300 YEARS ITS SENTENCE WAS ANNULLED AND THE BELL NOW HANGS IN A BELFRY AT TOBOLSK

The SLIPPERS PLANT (Bulbo stylis paradoxa) of Haiti LOOKS LIKE A PAIR OF WOOLLY SLIPPERS

A HAWAIIAN STAMP OF 1851 WITH A FACE VALUE OF 2 CENTS WAS THE SOLE REASON GASTON LEROUX, A PARISIAN PHILATELIST, *MURDERED ITS OWNER, HECTOR GIROUX* (1892)

Hawaiian Postage 2 Two Cents.

A SINGLE GIANT ROLL
BAKED IN 1730 TO FEED THE SAXON ARMY ON MANEUVERS NEAR RADEWITZ, WAS 28 FEET LONG, 12 FEET WIDE, HAULED BY 8 HORSES AND *CUT WITH A KNIFE 20 FEET LONG*

THE NOBLEST GESTURE IN HISTORY

PRESIDENT MARIANO MELGAREJO of Bolivia, LEARNING OF THE OUTBREAK OF THE FRANCO-PRUSSIAN WAR, IMMEDIATELY MOBILIZED THE BOLIVIAN ARMY AT MIDNIGHT *AND STARTED A 7,000-MILE "MARCH" TO AID FRANCE*

THE ARMY MARCHED ALL NIGHT BUT THE NEXT DAY MELGAREJO ABANDONED THE EXPEDITION, WHICH WOULD HAVE NECESSITATED CROSSING DESERTS, JUNGLES AND THE ATLANTIC OCEAN (1870)

THE CRADLE THAT RULED ALL PERSIA FOR 4 YEARS

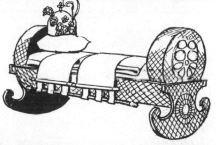

SHAH ABBAS III (1732-1736) of Persia INHERITED THE THRONE AT THE AGE OF 8 MONTHS AND BECAUSE OF HIS TENDER YEARS THE CROWN WAS PLACED ON HIS GOLDEN CRADLE

4 YEARS LATER IT WAS DISCOVERED THAT THIS ACT HAD MADE THE CRADLE EMPEROR OF PERSIA

THE CRADLE WAS MELTED DOWN AND A PRETENDER NAMED NADIR SHAH BECAME THE NEW RULER

A BROKEN TEA CUP

STILL PRESERVED IN A MUSEUM IN BERLIN, GERMANY, WAS SHATTERED BY KING FREDERICK THE GREAT OF PRUSSIA WHO PUSHED IT ASIDE ON HIS DEATH BED AS HIS LAST GESTURE

THE "SOUPER" GOURMET

EDMOND de ROSTAC, ONCE A MONTH FOR THE 22 YEARS FROM 1840 TO 1862, RESERVED THE ENTIRE MAIN DINING ROOM OF THE CAFÉ VACHETTE, IN PARIS, FRANCE, SO HE COULD LUNCH ALONE *-ALWAYS DINING ON 42 DIFFERENT KINDS OF SOUP*

from an old print

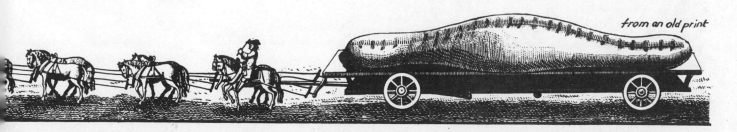

THE WARRIOR CRABS

HEIKE GANI CRABS OF THE ISLAND OF SHIKOKU, JAPAN, WHICH LOOK LIKE THE FACE OF A SAMURAI WARRIOR, ARE BELIEVED BY NATIVES TO BE THE SPIRITS OF *JAPANESE WHO DIED IN THE BATTLE OF DUN NO URA IN 1185*

MALLET EUSTACHE

GOVERNOR OF THE PROVINCE OF GUISE, FRANCE, WAS WOUNDED IN EACH OF 122 BATTLES *-BUT HE DIED IN 1349 PEACEFULLY IN HIS SLEEP*

THE GREATEST WASTREL IN ALL HISTORY

EMIR BEYSARI (1233-1293) AN EGYPTIAN OF GREAT WEALTH, DRANK WINE DAILY FROM GOLD AND SILVER CUPS *-YET IN ALL HIS LIFE HE NEVER USED THE SAME CUP TWICE* HE SPURNED THE THRONE OF EGYPT BECAUSE IT WOULD INTERFERE WITH HIS STYLE OF LIVING

PHRONIMA SEDENTARIA

A CRUSTACEAN *LIVES IN A GLASS HOUSE* IT MANUFACTURES ITS TRANSPARENT SHELTER OUT OF A GELATIN IT OBTAINS FROM SALPA, A SEA FISH

THE DEVIL'S BRIDGE

NEAR BATZ, FRANCE, A HUGE BOULDER THAT APPEARS TO BE A PROFILE OF THE DEVIL *GAZING DOWNWARD*

THE MARQUIS de NANGIS

(1682-1742) LED HIS REGIMENT OF ROYAL MARINES INTO BATTLE WITH THE RANK OF COLONEL *AT THE AGE OF 8 -* HE SERVED IN THE FRENCH ARMY 52 YEARS AND DIED A FIELD MARSHAL

A FENCE IN MIDVAAG, ONE OF DENMARK'S FAROE ISLANDS, *MADE FROM HUNDREDS OF WHALE SKULLS*

Ripley's Believe It or Not!

"BLACKIE"

A DOG OWNED BY JOHN L. QUINALTY, OF MONTGOMERY, LA., SUMMONS HIS MASTER TO ANSWER THE TELEPHONE --*ALTHOUGH IT IS ON A 6-PARTY LINE* THE DOG ALWAYS RECOGNIZES QUINALTY'S RING AND IGNORES ANY OTHER CALL

THE MOST CONSIDERATE SNORER IN HISTORY

ADOLPH SUTRO (1830-1898) MILLIONAIRE MINING ENGINEER AND MAYOR OF SAN FRANCISCO, AWARE THAT HE WAS A NOISY SLEEPER, ALWAYS RENTED 3 ADJOINING BEDROOMS IN HOTELS SO HE WOULD BE SEPARATED FROM ANY OTHER GUEST *BY A VACANT ROOM*

THE **GOAT'S BEARD** PRODUCES MANY FLOWER CLUSTERS -EACH OF WHICH CONTAINS MORE THAN 10,000 BLOSSOMS

THE AMAZING HIGH DIVERS OF CAPE DUKATO
Island of Leukas, Greece

YOUNG PRIESTS, TO QUALIFY FOR SERVICE AT THE TEMPLE OF APOLLO, WERE REQUIRED IN ANCIENT GREECE TO DON THE WINGS OF AN EAGLE AND PLUNGE FROM THE CAPE INTO THE SEA -*A DIVE OF 230 FEET!* IT WAS ASSUMED THE GODS WOULD ELIMINATE THOSE UNFIT -*BUT NO DIVER WAS EVER INJURED, ALTHOUGH THE ORDEAL WAS PERFORMED FOR CENTURIES*

THE **JAPANESE QUAIL** IS VALUED FOR ITS SONG, ITS EGGS, AS A FIGHTING COCK AND FOR ITS EATING QUALITIES -AND IN SOUTH CHINA IT *IS CARRIED IN COLD WEATHER AS A HAND WARMER*

THE **BRAZILIAN COELOXENUS BEETLE** IS SUPPORTED AS A GUEST IN ANTS' NESTS BECAUSE ITS WINGS ARE COVERED WITH LONG HAIRS *EACH OF WHICH EXUDES HONEY*

Ripley's Believe It or Not!

THE STAGE CURTAINS
FOR THEATRICAL PERFORMANCES BY THE KARENGS OF GUINEA, AFRICA, *CONSIST OF 2 HUGE BUNCHES OF HERBS SUSPENDED BY HOOKS FROM THE BRANCHES OF A TREE* THERE ARE EVEN STEPS TO PERMIT THE ACTORS TO PEEK OVER THE TOP OF THE CURTAINS TO SIZE UP THE AUDIENCE

THE MAN WHO WALKED AWAY FROM HIS OWN CREMATION!
RAJAH REMENDRA NARAYAN BOY
WHO HAD AN INCOME OF $400,000 A YEAR FROM THE STATE OF BHOWAL, INDIA, WAS PRONOUNCED DEAD IN 1909 AND HIS BODY WAS PLACED ON A FUNERAL PYRE- *WHICH WAS SET ABLAZE IN THE PRESENCE OF MANY MOURNERS* 12 YEARS LATER THE RAJAH REAPPEARED, CLAIMING THAT A MONSOON HAD SCATTERED WITNESSES, DOUSED THE FIRE AND REVIVED HIM AND THAT HE HAD BEEN A VICTIM OF AMNESIA—
THE MAN HAD FORGOTTEN HOW TO SPEAK BENGALI AND HIS WIDOW DENOUNCED HIM AS AN IMPOSTOR, *BUT IN 1935 THE BRITISH PRIVY COUNCIL REINSTATED HIS RANK AND PROPERTY*

THE **BEE ORCHID** HAS FLOWERS THAT *LOOK LIKE BEES*

TROUT WITH **2 MOUTHS** CAUGHT BY ROBERT D. TWISS, PENTICTON, B.C.

PHILIP HERRINGHAM BECAME HEADMASTER OF THE ROAN SCHOOL, ONE OF ENGLAND'S FAMOUS PUBLIC SCHOOLS, *AT THE AGE OF 16* THE TRUSTEES, IN APPOINTING PHILIP HEADMASTER IN 1749, DIRECTED HIM TO ADMINISTER THE SCHOOL AND ALSO TEACH

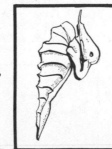

THE **PELICAN FLOWER** A BLOOM SEVERAL FEET LONG THAT *IS SHAPED LIKE A PELICAN*

A **FIELD** NEAR SAKUSHU, KOREA, IN WHICH 4 DIFFERENT TYPES OF PRODUCE - SESAME, COTTON, BEANS AND MELONS -- *ARE GROWN TOGETHER*

THE HIGHEST-PAID POET IN ALL HISTORY!
DJEHIR, ARAB POET AT THE COURT OF MOGUL EMPEROR AURANGZEB, REFUSED MONETARY COMPENSATION BUT FINALLY CONSENTED TO ACCEPT ANNUALLY *2 HANDFULS OF DIAMONDS* — FOR 10 YEARS HE VISITED THE ROYAL TREASURY ON THE BIRTHDAY OF MOHAMMED AND EXTRACTED FROM A LARGE BAG AS MANY DIAMONDS AS HE COULD HOLD IN HIS 2 HANDS

THE WATERFALL STONE
NEAR HYDEN, AUSTRALIA, A ROCK THAT GIVES THE APPEARANCE OF *A POWERFUL WATERFALL*

ANT NESTS
IN THE LOCHA FOREST OF AFRICA, ARE SO BUFFETED BY RAIN THAT THEIR OCCUPANTS BUILD A NEW ROOF EACH SEASON —*ERECTING EACH ROOF ATOP THE OLD ONE!*

THE MOST DUTIFUL SON IN ALL HISTORY
SULTAN SALADIN (1138-1193) ruler of Egypt and Syria OFFERED HIS KINGDOM TO HIS FATHER, AYYUB, *BUT AYYUB REFUSED TO ACCEPT IT* NEVERTHELESS SALADIN SEATED HIS FATHER ON THE THRONE AND BOWED LOW BEFORE HIM EVERY DAY AS LONG AS AYYUB LIVED

DEKYI CERINA

OF LHASA, TIBET, *IS THE MOTHER OF 3 LIVING BUDDHAS* ONE SON IS THE DALAI LAMA, RULER OF TIBET, AND THE OTHER 2 ARE RIMPOCHES -- ABBOTS OF GREAT MONASTERIES --*SO ALL 3 ARE CONSIDERED REINCARNATIONS OF BUDDHA*

THE NOISY SCRUB-BIRD

OF AUSTRALIA, WHICH NESTS ON THE GROUND, *IS AN EXPERT VENTRILOQUIST*— IT CAN IMITATE THE CALL OF ANY OTHER BIRD

THE SEAHORSE

OF THE AUSTRALIAN SEAS *DISGUISES ITSELF AS A SEAWEED*

THE **CASTLE OF PHARO** IN MARSEILLES, FRANCE, WAS BUILT BY THAT CITY IN 1860 AS A GIFT TO NAPOLEON III, *WHO NEVER EVEN SAW IT*— AFTER HIS DEATH MARSEILLES SUED THE EMPEROR'S WIDOW FOR OWNERSHIP OF THE STRUCTURE AND LOST THE CASE —*BUT THE WIDOW THEN DONATED THE CASTLE TO THE CITY FOR USE AS A MEDICAL SCHOOL*

SIDNEY GODOLPHIN

(1610-1643) THE ENGLISH POET WAS ELECTED TO PARLIAMENT *AT THE AGE OF 18*

VICTOR CHAUSSINAND

(1820-1887) of BESSES, FRANCE, WAS THE BROTHER OF **4 PRIESTS**, THE NEPHEW OF **3 PRIESTS**, AND THE FATHER OF **4 PRIESTS**

3-HEADED DAISY

SUBMITTED BY JACK FOWLER, BERWICK, PA.

A **PADLOCK** INVENTED BY KRISTOFER POLHEM, A SWEDISH ENGINEER, AND STILL IN USE IN THE HOUSE OF NOBLES IN STOCKHOLM *HAS PROVED BURGLAR-PROOF FOR 219 YEARS* IN 1750 POLHEM OFFERED $900 TO ANY THIEF WHO COULD FORCE IT OPEN

THE FIRST HOUSE

IN LUDINGTON, MICHIGAN, WHICH ALSO SERVED AS MASON COUNTY FIRST STORE, JAIL AND COURTHOUSE, WAS BUILT IN 1847 BY BURR CASWELL *FROM LUMBER WASHED ASHORE FROM THE WATERS OF LAKE MICHIGAN*

Ripley's Believe It or Not!

THE CRESTED PARASOL
A MUSHROOM SHAPED LIKE A PARASOL EVEN HAS A "RING" ON ITS STEM THAT CAN BE SLIPPED UP AND DOWN LIKE THE ONE THAT OPENS AND SHUTS A REAL PARASOL

THOMAS McKEAN (1734-1817)
ONE OF THE SIGNERS OF THE DECLARATION OF INDEPENDENCE, WAS CHIEF JUSTICE OF PENNSYLVANIA, GOVERNOR OF DELAWARE AND A CONGRESSMAN FROM DELAWARE *SIMULTANEOUSLY*

THE HUMMINGBIRD
HAS A CLEFT TONGUE COMPRISING 2 BLADES WHICH IT MANIPULATES LIKE A PAIR OF FORCEPS TO EXTRACT MINUTE INSECTS FROM FLOWERS

THE UNLUCKIEST SPY IN ALL HISTORY!
PETER KARPIN, A GERMAN ESPIONAGE AGENT IN WORLD WAR I, WAS SEIZED BY FRENCH INTELLIGENCE AGENTS IN 1914 AS SOON AS HE ENTERED THE COUNTRY- KEEPING HIS CAPTURE SECRET, THE FRENCH SENT FAKED REPORTS FROM KARPIN TO GERMANY, AND INTERCEPTED THE AGENT'S WAGES AND EXPENSE MONEY UNTIL KARPIN ESCAPED IN 1917 -- *WITH THOSE FUNDS THE FRENCH PURCHASED AN AUTOMOBILE WHICH IN 1919, IN OCCUPIED RUHR, ACCIDENTALLY RAN DOWN AND KILLED A MAN* -- WHO PROVED TO BE **PETER KARPIN!**

NATURE'S FLOWER CHILDREN
EACH PINK FLOWER OF THE PURPLE ORCHID LOOKS REMARKABLY LIKE A SMALL CHILD WEARING A HAT TOO LARGE FOR IT

THE CALLING HARE
WHICH BLEATS LIKE A SHEEP. *IS AN EXPERT VENTRILOQUIST-* IN FACT IT CAN MAKE ITS VOICE APPEAR TO COME SIMULTANEOUSLY FROM SEVERAL DIFFERENT POINTS

Ripley's® Believe It or Not!

THE MOST BIZARRE MILITARY PROCESSION IN HISTORY

ARCHDUKE FERDINAND SON OF EMPRESS MARIA THERESA OF AUSTRIA, SO HE COULD WEAR A NEW HAT AT HIS 21st BIRTHDAY PARTY, SENT AN EXPEDITION COMPRISING OFFICIALS IN ROYAL CARRIAGES AND SEVERAL HUNDRED MOUNTED SOLDIERS *TO ESCORT HIS HAT HOME FROM A CITY 20 MILES AWAY* (1765)

GENERAL POSTUMUS

WAS ELECTED ROMAN EMPEROR BY HIS TROOPS IN 257 FOR ALLOWING THEM TO LOOT CAPTURED CITIES IN GAUL, BUT WHEN HE REFUSED TO PERMIT LOOTING OF THE GERMAN CITY OF MAINZ 10 YEARS LATER *HE WAS SLAIN BY THOSE SAME SOLDIERS*

THE **CRAB'S EYES PLANT** (Abrus Precatorius) of the Tropics PRODUCES SEEDS THAT ARE USED IN INDIA TO *WEIGH GOLD*

A *DOE* SHOT BY WILLIAM COON. of Bear's Hell, Hardy County, W.Va., HAD ANTLERS COMPRISING **8 POINTS**

TOMATO WITH A STRAWBERRY GROWING INSIDE IT Submitted by Mary Cortez Los Angeles, Calif.

NAILS USED BY ANCIENT ROMAN SHIPBUILDERS PIERCED THE WOOD - AND THEN WRAPPED THEMSELVES AROUND IT IN AS MANY AS FOUR SPIRAL COILS

QUAHIR BILLAH

WHO TWICE WAS CALIPH OF BAGHDAD AND WAS BLINDED AND IMPRISONED AFTER HIS SECOND DETHRONEMENT IN 934, WAS FREED WHEN HIS NEPHEW ASCENDED THE THRONE - *BUT SPENT THE LAST 16 YEARS OF HIS LIFE ON THE STREETS BEGGING PASSERSBY FOR ALMS*

APUS AUSTRALIENSIS
A SHRIMP-LIKE CRUSTACEAN OF ARID CENTRAL AUSTRALIA, SURVIVES WHERE OTHER WATER ANIMALS WOULD PERISH BECAUSE ITS EGGS HATCH ONLY AFTER *THEY HAVE BEEN DRIED OUT IN THE SUN*

THE STEAMER "WALLABI"
WENT AGROUND AT GREYMOUTH, N.Z., ON NOV. 5, 1870, AND WAS REFLOATED AND RETURNED TO SERVICE
-BUT 16 YEARS LATER IT BECAME A TOTAL LOSS WHEN IT AGAIN PILED UP ON THE BEACH AT THE SAME SPOT

THE SMALLEST CHURCH IN THE U.S.
Wiscasset, Maine

A CHAPEL BUILT BY THE REV. LOUIS W. WEST

MEASURING 4½ BY 7 FEET

THE MOST PROLIFIC PLAYWRIGHT OF ALL TIME
MARIE de LAMBERT THEAULON (1787-1841) of Paris, France, WROTE 50 THREE-ACT PLAYS IN A SINGLE YEAR AND PRODUCED MOST OF THEM HIMSELF

HE ALSO WROTE 3 PLAYS IN A SINGLE DAY AND PRODUCED THEM HIMSELF ON THE SAME DAY IN 3 DIFFERENT THEATRES

EMPEROR JUSTINIAN THE GREAT
(483 - 565) ruler of the Eastern Roman Empire, ENACTED A LAW TO STOP HIS SUBJECTS FROM SWEARING *"BY THE HAIR OF THEIR HEADS"* - BECAUSE HE BELIEVED THAT PARTICULAR OATH CAUSED **EARTHQUAKES AND THUNDERSTORMS**

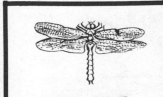

ANAX JUNIUS
a dragon fly CAN ROTATE ITS HEAD **180 DEGREES**

THE WHIRLING CLOUD of MOUNT JIRINAJ (Indonesia)
A FLAT CLOUD HOVERING OVER THE PEAK OF AN EXTINCT VOLCANO AFFECTED BY HOT AIR RISING FROM THE CRATER, *SPINS SWIFTLY AROUND AND AROUND*

A COCONUT SENT TO MRS. HELEN SZUMILAS AS A WORLD WAR II SOUVENIR FROM OKINAWA WAS OPENED AFTER 22 YEARS – AND PROVED TO BE A BOMB! FORTUNATELY THE BOOBY TRAP, WHICH HAD BEEN TAKEN TO SCHOOL BY EACH OF MRS. SZUMILA'S 4 CHILDREN, DID NOT EXPLODE WHEN IT WAS OPENED
Southbridge, Mass.

THE MASSACRE THAT WAS TOUCHED OFF BY A SINGLE WORD!

NORMAN GUARDS STATIONED OUTSIDE WESTMINSTER ABBEY AT THE CORONATION OF KING WILLIAM I OF ENGLAND, IN THE BELIEF SAXONS INSIDE THE ABBEY WERE RIOTING, SET FIRE TO THE CITY OF WESTMINSTER ON CHRISTMAS DAY, 1066, AND MASSACRED ITS POPULATION!
ACTUALLY, THE OFFICIATING BISHOP HAD MERELY ASKED THE TRADITIONAL QUESTION OF WHETHER THOSE ATTENDING THE CEREMONY ACCEPTED THEIR NEW MONARCH – AND THE CROWD HAD SHOUTED "YES!"

THE MAGIC CLOCK

AN ORNATE CLOCK CONSTRUCTED BY ROBERT-HOUDIN, A FRENCH MAGICIAN, THAT HAS ITS WORKS IN ITS STAND AND A DIAL CONSISTING OF A SOLID PIECE OF TRANSPARENT GLASS, KEEPS PERFECT TIME, ALTHOUGH THERE IS NO APPARENT CONNECTION BETWEEN THE HOUR HAND AND THE CLOCK'S MECHANISM

JACK TERRY CROSSED THE ENGLISH CHANNEL FROM DOVER TO CALAIS ON A TRICYCLE
HE MADE THE TRIP IN 8 HOURS, KEPT AFLOAT BY THE RUBBER TIRES AND STEERING WITH HIS REAR WHEEL
July 28, 1883

THE WORLD'S HIGHEST HEDGE

Cirencester Park, Gloucestershire, England
IT TOWERS 30 FEET HIGH AND ITS ANNUAL CLIPPING TAKES 10 DAYS

A BLUE HOMING PIGEON TRANSPORTED FROM SAIGON, VIETNAM, TO ARRAS, FRANCE, IN THE DARK HOLD OF A SHIP, FOUND ITS WAY BACK TO SAIGON IN 25 DAYS – A JOURNEY OF 7,200 MILES WITHOUT A SINGLE FAMILIAR LANDMARK
August, 1931

Ripley's Believe It or Not!

A **SILVER BUTTERFLY** WAS ONCE USED IN CHINA **AS CURRENCY**

THE **MUSICAL FOUNTAIN** OF **TIVOLI**
Italy

ITS TUMBLING WATER HAS BEEN PRODUCING ORGAN MUSIC FOR **400** YEARS

THE BUILDING A MEDAL BUILT

THE CASINO in Homburg von der Höhe, Germany, WAS CONSTRUCTED WITH FUNDS OBTAINED BY SELLING A DIAMOND-STUDDED DECORATION FOUND IN A BOX OF WORTHLESS PAPERS WHICH *HAD LAIN UNOPENED FOR 93 YEARS* THE MEDAL HAD BEEN AWARDED TO PRINCE LUDWIG OF HESSE-HOMBURG IN RUSSIA AND WAS SOLD FOR $16,975 WHEN IT WAS DISCOVERED IN 1838

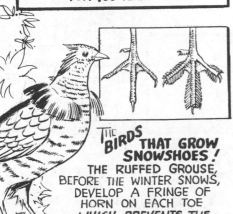

THE **BIRDS THAT GROW SNOWSHOES!**
THE RUFFED GROUSE, BEFORE THE WINTER SNOWS, DEVELOP A FRINGE OF HORN ON EACH TOE *WHICH PREVENTS THE BIRD FROM SINKING INTO SNOW*

THE FISH WITH RUNNING LIGHTS
PHOTOSTOMIAS GUERNI IS EQUIPPED WITH 2 ROWS OF PHOSPHORESCENT SPOTS *TO LIGHT ITS WAY THROUGH THE DEPTHS OF THE OCEAN*

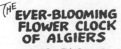

THE **EVER-BLOOMING FLOWER CLOCK OF ALGIERS**

LIVING BLOOMS COMPRISE ITS DIAL THROUGHOUT THE YEAR

THE RUSE THAT SAVED 40,000 LIVES!

FRANÇOIS de MONTMORIN (1522-1582)
governor of the French province of Auvergne, TO THWART A COMMAND BY KING CHARLES IX THAT HE EXECUTE EVERY HUGUENOT IN HIS DISTRICT, SENT THE MONARCH THIS MESSAGE: "I RESPECT YOUR MAJESTY TOO MUCH NOT TO BELIEVE THAT THE ORDER IS A FORGERY"

EVERY OTHER GOVERNOR FOLLOWED MONTMORIN'S LEAD—AND THE LIVES OF 40,000 MEN, WOMEN AND CHILDREN WERE SPARED

A **PRAYER BOOK** STILL USED IN the Royal Chapel of Granada, Spain, WAS ORIGINALLY THAT OF QUEEN ISABELLA—WHO *DIED 462 YEARS AGO*

Ripley's Believe It or Not!

THE SHRINE TO A MAN WHO CONDEMNED HIMSELF TO DEATH!

A SHRINE on the Khokkham Canal, in Thailand, HONORING THE HELMSMAN OF A ROYAL BARGE WHO RAN THE VESSEL AGROUND AT THAT POINT AND INSISTED THAT HE BE EXECUTED AS PUNISHMENT! KING PHRACHAO SÜA, WHO WAS RIDING IN THE BARGE, OFFERED TO PARDON HIS HELMSMAN -BUT THE MAN DECLINED

THE LAND OF 5 SUNS
EARLY MORNING MISTS near Sing-nying-chu, China, CREATE AS AN OPTICAL ILLUSION IN THE SKY

THE MOST BIZARRE DUELS IN HISTORY

THE CHEVALIER de FIRMIN (1681-1722) FOUGHT 13 DUELS WITH SWORDS, KILLING 3 OPPONENTS AND WOUNDING 3 OTHERS, TO ENFORCE HIS INSISTENCE THAT CHARLES COFFIN SURPASSED JEAN SANTEUL AS A MODERN LATIN POET

JUST BEFORE HE DIED FIRMIN CONFESSED HE HAD NEVER READ A SINGLE LINE WRITTEN BY EITHER MAN

THE DEEP-SEA BENTHAL OCTOPUS
HAS EYES THAT ARE ONE-THIRD THE SIZE OF ITS ENTIRE BODY

A TALISMAN
CONTAINING A FRAGMENT OF THE TRUE CROSS WAS CARRIED ALL HIS LIFE BY ROMAN EMPEROR CONSTANTINE THE GREAT -YET HE DID NOT BECOME A CHRISTIAN UNTIL A FEW HOURS BEFORE HIS DEATH

THE BUTCHER'S BROOM PLANT
(Ruscu aculeatus) GROWS NO LEAVES BUT DEVELOPS BRANCHES SHAPED LIKE LEAVES

FLOWERS GROW FROM THE CENTER OF THESE FALSE LEAVES

THE RULER WHO WALKED 50,000 MILES ON A PATHWAY OF SILVER COINS!

CALIPH HASSAN (625-669) of BAGHDAD, MADE THE 2,000-MILE ROUND TRIP FROM KUFA, IRAQ, TO MECCA A TOTAL OF 25 TIMES, AND EACH TIME ATTENDANTS STREWED THE GROUND IN FRONT OF HIS FEET WITH SILVER COINS -A THIRD OF THEM WERE ALWAYS LEFT BEHIND TO ENCOURAGE OTHER PILGRIMS TO FOLLOW IN HIS FOOTSTEPS

THE STRANGEST STEAMBOAT— THE WESTERN ENGINEER, FIRST STEAMBOAT TO ASCEND THE MISSOURI RIVER, WAS BUILT IN 1819 IN THE SHAPE OF A DRAGON TO FRIGHTEN OFF INDIANS —WITH ITS BOW A HEAD THAT SPEWED SMOKE FROM ITS MOUTH AND ITS STERN A TAIL THAT ISSUED A STREAM OF FOAMING WATER

THE WHEAT THAT PRODUCES A ONE-POUND LOAF OF BREAD REQUIRES 2 TONS OF WATER TO GROW

MUSSAENDA ERYTHROPHYLLA HAS A FLOWER SO DRAB THAT INSECTS WOULD NEVER POLLINATE IT, SO NATURE PROVIDED IT WITH ONE BRIGHT RED SEPAL

KARL WILHELM DIEFENBACH (1851-1913) famed German painter, SO WEAKENED FOR YEARS BY A LONG SIEGE OF TYPHOID THAT HIS HANDS WERE UNABLE TO HOLD A BRUSH, PUT HIS PAINT ON THE CANVAS WITH A BRICKLAYER'S TROWEL

THE STEPMOTHER WATERBUG (Belostomatid) DEPOSITS ITS EGGS ON THE BACK OF ANY PASSING BUG THE EGGS REMAIN GLUED THERE UNTIL THEY HATCH

THE CANDLESTICKS OF THE SUN A PLANT IN CENTRAL AUSTRALIA THAT GROWS A CANDLE-SHAPED FLOWER ONCE EVERY 7 YEARS

A DECK OF PLAYING CARDS CONTAINS 52 CARDS— AND "ACE, TWO, THREE, FOUR, FIVE, SIX, SEVEN, EIGHT, NINE, TEN, JACK, QUEEN, KING" ADD UP TO EXACTLY 52 LETTERS

PROFESSOR RUDOLF VIRCHOW (1821-1902) famed German physician and scientist, FOR THE LAST 60 YEARS OF HIS LIFE SLEPT ONLY 4 HOURS EACH NIGHT

THE BIRCHENOUGH BRIDGE
1,080 FEET LONG
WHICH SPANS THE SABI RIVER IN RHODESIA WAS NAMED FOR SIR SAMUEL BIRCHENOUGH, WHO FINANCED ITS CONSTRUCTION —AND THE ASHES OF SIR SAMUEL AND HIS WIFE ARE IN ONE OF THE SPAN'S PILLARS

THE WOMAN WHO WAS RESCUED FROM THE GRAVE
MINNA BRAUN, a nurse in Berlin, Germany, WAS PRONOUNCED DEAD FROM AN OVERDOSE OF SLEEPING PILLS, AND AS WAS CUSTOMARY IN SUICIDES WAS BURIED IN AN OPEN GRAVE— THE NEXT DAY THE COFFIN'S NAILED LID WAS OPENED TO PERMIT IDENTIFICATION OF THE BODY —AND THE GIRL WAS FOUND TO BE ALIVE! SHE RECOVERED AND RETURNED TO HER NURSING DUTIES
Oct. 28, 1919

MEN OF Miloti, Albania, STILL WEAR A DOUBLET OF BLACK WOOL AS MOURNING FOR THE DEATH OF ALBANIA'S NATIONAL HERO, SKANDERBEG, WHO DIED 501 YEARS AGO

THE SHIPWRECKED CREW THAT SAILED TO SAFETY ON AN ICEBERG
19 SAILORS, WHO SURVIVED WHEN THE "U.S. POLARIS" WAS CRUSHED BY ICE IN THE ARCTIC, WERE RESCUED IN GOOD HEALTH OFF THE COAST OF LABRADOR AFTER THEY HAD DRIFTED 1,200 MILES AND FOR 196 DAYS ON AN ICEBERG!
(Oct. 15, 1872 - April 30, 1873)

VENUS' FLOWER BASKET a deep-sea sponge IS A POPULAR JAPANESE WEDDING PRESENT BECAUSE IT ALWAYS SHELTERS 2 CRUSTACEANS - WHICH TO THE JAPANESE ARE SYMBOLS OF GOOD LUCK

THE PECTORAL FIN OF A WHALE IS AMAZINGLY SIMILAR TO A HUMAN ARM WITH A "SHOULDER BLADE," AN "UPPER ARM," AN "ELBOW," A "WRIST" AND 5 "FINGERS"

THE ICHNEUMON FLY HAS SO KEEN A SENSE OF SMELL THAT IT CAN LOCATE A CATERPILLAR DEEP INSIDE A TREE TRUNK

Ripley's Believe It or Not!

THE TOMB of MOHAMMED ASKIA, RULER of GAO, West Africa, WAS BUILT DURING HIS LIFETIME FROM A VERBAL DESCRIPTION OF THE PYRAMIDS OF EGYPT
BEFORE HIS DEATH THE KING VISITED EGYPT IN 1493 AND DISCOVERED HIS TOMB WAS NOTHING LIKE THE PYRAMIDS-BUT HE LIKED HIS IMPERFECT COPY BETTER THAN THE ORIGINAL

$$1 \div 9 = 0.11111---$$
$$2 \div 9 = 0.22222---$$
$$3 \div 9 = 0.33333---$$
$$4 \div 9 = 0.44444---$$
$$5 \div 9 = 0.55555---$$
etc.

THE NEST of the ACADIAN FLYCATCHER IS ALWAYS BUILT WITH A TAIL THAT HANGS NEARLY A FOOT BELOW THE NEST

BEAN POD (Entada Pursoetha) IN EASTERN PAKISTAN, GROWS TO A HEIGHT OF 4 FEET AND IS SO STURDY THAT THE ARAKANESE USE IT AS A STAIRWAY TO THEIR DWELLINGS

John William CONGER (1857-1920) of Faulkner County, Arkansas, SERVED AT VARIOUS TIMES AS PRESIDENT OF 5 DIFFERENT COLLEGES

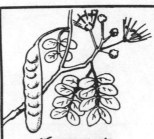

THE WOMAN'S TONGUE of Zanzibar IS A PLANT WITH PODS FULL OF SEEDS *WHICH RATTLE CONTINUOUSLY*

THE TAILLESS TENREC of Madagascar REGULARLY PRODUCES THE LARGEST LITTERS OF ANY MAMMAL -AS MANY AS 32 YOUNG AT EACH BIRTH

A FOUNDLING ABANDONED AT THE HOTEL ST. GERMAIN AT LA CHÂTRE, FRANCE, WHO WAS ADOPTED BY THE HOTEL OWNER AND NAMED NAPOLEON DE PARIS, *GREW UP TO BECOME MAYOR OF THE TOWN OF THEVET ST. JULIEN*

TULIP WITH A PETAL *GROWING OUT OF A LEAF*

Submitted by Kathy and Billy SALTZ Aurora, Ill.

A NEW RAILROAD BRIDGE
FOR MANY YEARS WAS BUILT EACH FALL OVER THE FROZEN MISSOURI RIVER AT OMAHA, NEBR., AND EVERY SPRING THE RAILS WERE REMOVED *AND THE RAGING RIVER CARRIED AWAY THE BRIDGE*

THE BIRD WITH A BUILT-IN TIMETABLE

THE REEF HERON, WHICH FEEDS ON SHELLFISH ON THE GREAT BARRIER REEF, DAILY FLIES 30 MILES FROM THE AUSTRALIAN MAINLAND, AND ALTHOUGH THE TIDE CHANGES VARY BY 45 MINUTES A DAY *THE HERON ALWAYS ARRIVES AT THE EXACT TIME THE WATER RECEDES*

THE WORLD'S MOST AMAZING LINGUIST

SADDHU TERIM AN INDIAN HERMIT WHO LIVES IN A CAVE NEAR BADRINATH, INDIA, UNDERSTANDS ONLY HINDU AND ENGLISH--*YET HE CAN ANSWER QUESTIONS IN ANY OF THE WORLD'S 1,000 LANGUAGES* HE DOES NOT UNDERSTAND WHAT HE IS SAYING, BUT IF THE QUESTIONER CONCENTRATES ON THE ANSWER THE SADDHU WILL VOICE IT IN THE SAME LANGUAGE *BY MENTAL TELEPATHY!*

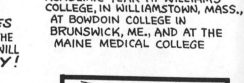

SIAMESE DAHLIAS

GROWING ON A SINGLE STEM-- *ONE RED AND THE OTHER WHITE WITH A RED BORDER* Submitted by MRS. RUTH E. MEYERS, Hanover, Md.

PROFESSOR PAUL A. CHADBOURNE
(1823-1883)

TAUGHT CHEMISTRY AND BOTANY FOR 9 YEARS AT **3 COLLEGES SIMULTANEOUSLY** HE SPENT PART OF EACH ACADEMIC YEAR AT WILLIAMS COLLEGE, IN WILLIAMSTOWN, MASS., AT BOWDOIN COLLEGE IN BRUNSWICK, ME., AND AT THE MAINE MEDICAL COLLEGE

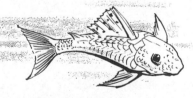

THE **ACARI FISH** of SOUTH AMERICA, WHICH GROWS TO A FOOT IN LENGTH, IS COMPLETELY ENCASED IN *A BONY SUIT OF ARMOR THAT IS TRANSPARENT*

THE OLDEST BELL IN ALL GERMANY

THE BELL IN THE TOWER OF THE MONASTERY OF HERSFELD HAS BEEN RUNG PERIODICALLY FOR **919 YEARS**

LAKE ARU TSO in Tibet IS ALTERNATELY DRINKABLE AND SALT WATER *EVERY 12 YEARS*

A MARBLE ARCH

CONSTRUCTED IN TRIPOLI, LIBYA, IN 164 BY ROMAN EMPEROR MARCUS AURELIUS, WAS ONE OF THE MOST SPLENDID MONUMENTS OF ANTIQUITY -YET A GROCER HAS CEMENTED IT UP AND CONVERTED IT INTO A SHOP *SELLING DRIED FISH, SPICES AND OTHER GROCERIES*

THE EAGLE FERN

SO NAMED BECAUSE A CROSS SECTION OF ITS ROOT ALWAYS HAS THE *OUTLINE OF AN EAGLE IN FLIGHT*

THE MAN WITH HANDS LIKE HAMPERS!
FYODOR MACHNOV (1880-1905) a Russian "giant" HAD SUCH ENORMOUS HANDS THAT HE COULD HOLD A DOZEN EGGS IN EACH -*WITHOUT CRACKING A SINGLE SHELL*

THE DEER HEAD TREE

NATURAL GROWTH ON JOHN W. SNYDER'S FARM IN TELL CITY, IND. SUBMITTED BY CAROL HAUENSTEIN, TELL CITY, IND.

THE KURTUS GULLIVERI MALE

A FISH OF NEW GUINEA HAS A HOOK ON ITS NECK TO WHICH THE FEMALE ATTACHES HER NEWLY LAID EGGS, AND THE POOR HOOKED MALE HAS TO CARRY THE EGGS AROUND UNTIL THEY HATCH

THE TRIBE THAT HAS NO SPINSTERS

GIRLS OF THE NEWAR TRIBE, IN THE KATMANDU VALLEY, NEPAL, TO MAKE CERTAIN THEY WILL NEVER BE OLD MAIDS, ARE MARRIED AT THE AGE OF 6 *TO A GOLDEN ORANGE* ANY HUSBANDS THE GIRLS ACQUIRE LATER IN LIFE ARE CONSIDERED LIVING REPRESENTATIVES OF THE FRUIT

SLOW
RATTLESNAKE CROSSING

HIGHWAY SIGN ERECTED IN 1939 IN PLEASANT GROVE, MINN.

CLAUDE CREBILLON

(1707-1777) ONE OF FRANCE'S STRICTEST OFFICIAL CENSORS, PREVIOUSLY HAD BEEN IMPRISONED AND BANISHED FOR 5 YEARS *FOR HAVING HIMSELF WRITTEN BOOKS OFFENSIVE TO PUBLIC MORALS*

THE MOST DESTRUCTIVE HAILSTORM IN ALL HISTORY!

HAILSTONES AS LARGE AS BASEBALLS SMASHED MORADABAD, INDIA, ON APRIL 30, 1888, *KILLING 230 PEOPLE*

THE OPOSSUM SHRIMP HAS ITS EYES IN ITS TAIL

THE MASONRY STEEPLE OF ST. JOHANN'S CHURCH IN DAVOS, SWITZERLAND, HAS BEEN TWISTED INTO A GRACEFUL SPIRAL *BY 500 YEARS OF INTENSE SUNSHINE*

THE **REV. SHADROCK SIMPSON** (1848-1912) WAS ELECTED PRESIDENT OF YADKIN COLLEGE IN NORTH CAROLINA *WHILE HE WAS STILL AN UNDER- GRADUATE IN TRINITY COLLEGE*

IN 1883 HE WAS APPOINTED PROFESSOR OF NATURAL SCIENCE AT WESTERN MARYLAND COLLEGE -AND ONLY THEN TOOK A COURSE IN NATURAL SCIENCE TO QUALIFY FOR THE POSITION

THE SMALLEST FLOWERING PLANT IN THE WORLD PILOSTYLES THURBERI, A PARASITE THAT GROWS ON THE STEMS OF THE DALEA SHRUB, LOOKS LIKE A TINY BLACK KERNEL - *YET EACH IS AN INDIVIDUAL PLANT*

THE MOST CAUTIOUS TRAVELER IN HISTORY!

SENATOR ALEXANDER SLUCHEVSKY A WEALTHY RESIDENT of Kharkov, in the Ukraine, TRAVELED BY TRAIN TO ST. PETERSBURG SEVERAL TIMES EACH YEAR -*BUT HE ALWAYS RODE ON A FLAT CAR, SEATED IN HIS OWN CARRIAGE, TO WHICH WERE HITCHED A TEAM OF WHITE HORSES SO HE COULD CONTINUE HIS JOURNEY IF THE TRAIN BROKE DOWN*

SOUP LADLES CARVED IN THE LOWER CONGO BY A WOODCARVER WHO, GIVEN A REPAIRED SAMPLE, FAITHFULLY REPRODUCED THE BROKEN HANDLE AND SCREW -*YET EACH LADLE WAS A SOLID PIECE OF WOOD*

Ripley's — Believe It or Not!

THE **CHAPEL of GLÖCKLEHOF** in Bad Krozingen, Germany, *EXCAVATED IN 1936* HAS BEEN LEFT EXACTLY IN THE CONDITION IN WHICH IT WAS FOUND -*AFTER HAVING BEEN BURIED FOR 1,100 YEARS*

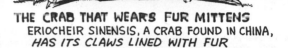

THE CRAB THAT WEARS FUR MITTENS
ERIOCHEIR SINENSIS, A CRAB FOUND IN CHINA, *HAS ITS CLAWS LINED WITH FUR*

THE MOST FRAGILE BRIDGES IN THE WORLD
NATIVES CROSSING THE ORINOCO RIVER AT RAUDAL, COLOMBIA, BUILD BRIDGES 100 FEET LONG -*USING ONLY THE STEMS OF FOREST PLANTS*
EACH INDIAN PARTY MUST BUILD A NEW BRIDGE BECAUSE THE FRAIL SPANS ARE ALWAYS SWEPT AWAY BY WIND AND RISING WATERS

THE FIELD MARSHAL'S BATON
CARRIED BY AUSTRIA'S MILITARY LEADER, PRINCE EUGENE OF SAVOY - IN RECOGNITION OF THE CONTRIBUTIONS TO VICTORY OF HIS COMMON SOLDIERS - CONSISTED OF 2 INFANTRY MUSKET BARRELS WELDED TOGETHER TO FORM A SINGLE STAFF

HOLLYHOCK
19'5½" HIGH *AND STILL GROWING*
Grown by WILLIAM RANDALL Buena Park, Calif.

MARTIN J. SPALDING
(1810-1872)
A STUDENT AT ST. MARY'S COLLEGE, in Lebanon, Kentucky, WAS APPOINTED A PROFESSOR OF MATHEMATICS *2 YEARS BEFORE HE GRADUATED -AND WHILE HE WAS ONLY 14 YEARS OF AGE!*
HE LATER BECAME ARCHBISHOP OF BALTIMORE

WORSHIPERS in the Temple of Kiyomizu, in Kyoto, Japan, MUST SAY THEIR PRAYERS WHILE STANDING BENEATH *3 SPOUTS OF PURIFYING WATER*

Ripley's Believe It or Not!

THE LIVING TORCHES
PUYA RAIMONDI - ONE OF THE EARTH'S OLDEST PLANTS - WHICH GROWS IN THE CORDILLERA MOUNTAINS OF PERU AND HAS A SHAFT OF BLOSSOMS 33 FEET HIGH, IS SO SATURATED WITH RESIN THAT SHEPHERDS LIGHT IT TO ILLUMINATE THE COUNTRYSIDE

A COMPASS USED IN THE 18th CENTURY BY MOSLEM PILGRIMS TO MECCA, HAD A REPLICA OF THE HOLY CITY DEPICTED ON IT WHICH ALWAYS POINTED THE WAY TO THE EAST

CROCE
AN INDIAN INSECT HAS REAR WINGS 3½ TIMES AS LONG AS ITS BODY

BERRIES OF THE YEW TREE AND THE BRANCHES THEMSELVES ARE HIGHLY POISONOUS TO CATTLE - YET BIRDS CAN EAT THEM WITHOUT ILL EFFECTS

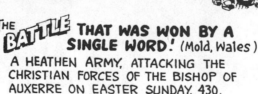

THE THEATRE ROYAL IN JOHANNESBURG, SO. AFRICA, WAS BUILT IN AUSTRALIA AND TRANSPORTED TO ITS PRESENT SITE BY SHIP, OXCART AND COACH - A DISTANCE OF 6,000 MILES

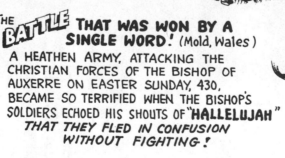

THE BATTLE THAT WAS WON BY A SINGLE WORD! (Mold, Wales)
A HEATHEN ARMY, ATTACKING THE CHRISTIAN FORCES OF THE BISHOP OF AUXERRE ON EASTER SUNDAY, 430, BECAME SO TERRIFIED WHEN THE BISHOP'S SOLDIERS ECHOED HIS SHOUTS OF "HALLELUJAH" THAT THEY FLED IN CONFUSION WITHOUT FIGHTING!

THE MANTLE OF ZEUS
STALACTITE FORMATION IN THE CAVE OF LIKTAION, CRETE - THE CAVE IS REPUTED TO HAVE BEEN THE BIRTHPLACE OF ZEUS, AND LEGEND HAS IT THAT HE HUNG UP HIS MANTLE - WHICH BECAME FOSSILIZED

THE GRAVESTONES OF THOSE WHO DIED UNMARRIED IN ANCIENT GREECE WERE ALWAYS REPLICAS OF AN HONOR DENIED THEM IN LIFE - THE VASE OUT OF WHICH WATER WAS POURED ON THE HANDS OF THE BRIDE AND GROOM AT EVERY WEDDING

RAMIE
A WEST INDIAN SHRUB THAT YIELDS A NETTLE FIBER THAT IS WOVEN INTO CLOTH, CAN BE HARVESTED 7 TIMES EACH YEAR

THE TUSK SHELL
A MARINE SNAIL OFTEN FOUND AT OCEAN DEPTHS OF 10,000 FEET, HAS A SHELL RESEMBLING THE TUSK OF AN ELEPHANT

THE STAR-SHAPED LANTERN

of the Alhambra Palace in Granada, Spain, WAS CONSIDERED SO DISTINCTIVE THAT KING YUSUF PROCLAIMED IN 1354 THAT COPYING ITS DESIGN WAS **A CRIME PUNISHABLE BY DEATH**

SIR WILLIAM STANLEY

(1548-1630) English soldier and adventurer

WAS CONSIDERED SUCH A HERO BY THE NETHERLANDS GOVERNMENT THAT IT OFFERED ENGLAND 1,000 POUNDS OF GOLD FOR THE PRIVILEGE OF BURYING HIM ON DUTCH SOIL

THE BRITISH REFUSED — YET *IT WAS REVEALED YEARS LATER THAT STANLEY HAD BETRAYED BOTH COUNTRIES*

THE UNDERSEA BALLOON

THE NAUTILUS WHICH IS RELATED TO THE OCTOPUS, OCCUPIES A SHELL DIVIDED INTO MANY COMPARTMENTS AND MOVES ITS HOME UP AND DOWN IN THE WATER *BY PUMPING GAS INTO OR OUT OF THE VARIOUS COMPARTMENTS*

THE MANCHURIAN LOTUS

IN THE KENILWORTH AQUATIC GARDENS, WASHINGTON, D.C., GREW FROM SEEDS THAT HAD LAIN DORMANT IN THE BED OF A LAKE IN MANCHURIA FOR SEVERAL THOUSAND YEARS

THE HAWK MOTH

WHICH SUCKS NECTAR FROM BLOSSOMS, LIKE A HUMMINGBIRD, FLIES SO SWIFTLY THAT IT CAN POLLINATE 200 DIFFERENT BLOOMS IN ONLY *10 MINUTES*

THE RUSE THAT DETERMINED THE CAPITAL OF MINNESOTA

JOSEPH ROLETTE, A MEMBER OF THE 1857 LEGISLATURE OF THE TERRITORY OF MINNESOTA, PREVENTED TRANSFER OF THE CAPITAL FROM ST. PAUL TO ST. PETER *BY DISAPPEARING FOR 123 HOURS WITH THE BILL THAT ORDERED THE CHANGE* ROLETTE DID NOT REAPPEAR UNTIL THE LEGISLATURE HAD ADJOURNED — AND ST. PAUL HAS REMAINED THE CAPITAL TO THIS DAY

THE ASHAR MAHAL

MOST SACRED STRUCTURE IN BIJAPUR, INDIA — BUILT TO *SAFEGUARD 2 HAIRS FROM MOHAMMED'S BEARD!* THE ADJACENT POOL SERVES ONLY TO PROVIDE MOISTURE TO KEEP THE HAIRS CURLY

THE PIGMY PINES

OF NEW ZEALAND ARE SO TINY THAT HUNDREDS OF THEM GROW IN AN AREA NO LARGER *THAN A CUSHION*

BARON CHRISTOPHE de TURSANNE
of Bigorres, France,
WHEN HIS PONY BECAME LAME IN
A HUNTING ACCIDENT, CARRIED THE **420-LB.**
ANIMAL TO A VETERINARIAN ON HIS
OWN SHOULDERS - *A DISTANCE
OF 1¼ MILES!*

The **ENGLISH GARDEN FROM WHICH
AMERICA'S TEXTILE INDUSTRY GREW**
THE TINY APOTHECARIES' GARDEN
in London
PRODUCED THE SEEDS THAT WERE
EXPORTED TO START THE FIRST
AMERICAN COTTON PLANTATION

The **SHADOW BIRDS**
ALWAYS BUILD A
3-ROOM NEST
ONE SECTION IS A
NURSERY, THE SECOND
IS A PANTRY, AND IN
THE THIRD THE MALE
PARENT STANDS GUARD
AGAINST INTRUDERS

CROSS SECTION

HOUSES
in the Casbah
of Melilla,
Morocco,
CONSTRUCTED FROM
DECAYED FLOUR

BUDDHIST

The **CASTLE**
THAT WAS SAVED BY A GHOST
ESTERNAY CASTLE in the Champagne province of France WAS ORDERED
DEMOLISHED DURING THE FRENCH REVOLUTION, BUT AUTHORITIES
RESCINDED THE DIRECTIVE WHEN THEY WERE TOLD THE CASTLE
WAS HAUNTED NIGHTLY BY THE GHOST OF ITS FORMER OWNER, FIELD
MARSHAL ABRAHAM FABERT - *BECAUSE HE WAS TOO POPULAR TO
INCONVENIENCE, ALTHOUGH HE HAD BEEN DEAD FOR MORE THAN 135 YEARS!*

JOSEPH R. BROWN
(1805-1870)
famed Minnesota pioneer
SOLD THE SITE OF WHAT
IS NOW DOWNTOWN
ST. PAUL FOR $125

HE ALSO TRADED WHAT IS
NOW A SOLID BLOCK OF
DOWNTOWN MINNEAPOLIS
FOR A BOX OF CIGARS
-AND GAVE AWAY THE SITE
OF DAVENPORT, IOWA, IN
EXCHANGE FOR A COOKSTOVE

Ripley's Believe It or Not!

"SANDY" A COLLIE HAS CHEWED 6 PACKS OF GUM EVERY DAY FOR 5 YEARS
Submitted by DOROTHY ANNE SPICE, Toronto, Ont.

TABLE KNIVES USED BY WEALTHY EGYPTIANS IN ANCIENT TIMES *WERE RECTANGLES OF SOLID GOLD -WITH 4 CUTTING EDGES*

A *WATERMILL* ON THE RIVER SOAR in Cossington, England, HAS BEEN OPERATING CONTINUOUSLY *FOR MORE THAN 700 YEARS*

MONKS
ALWAYS WEAR GARMENTS COLORED OCHRE TO COMMEMORATE THE FACT THAT BUDDHA DONNED THE CLOTHING OF A POOR HUNTER *TAINED OCHRE BY THE DUST OF THE HIGHWAYS*

A DIAMOND OWNED BY THE 6th NIZAM of Hyderabad, India, WEIGHING 182½ CARATS AND VALUED AT $5,000,000, WAS USED AS A PAPERWEIGHT
IT WAS MISLAID FOR A PERIOD OF 6 YEARS AND WAS FINALLY FOUND AFTER HIS DEATH IN 1911 — IN A SLIPPER

STRANGE HALO AROUND THE SUN
SEEN IN Springfield, Missouri, Nov. 1, 1913

THE **CHILD WHOSE COURAGE SAVED HER MOTHER'S LIFE**
Nantes, France
ZOE de BONCHAMPS, ASKED TO SING BEFORE A FRENCH REVOLUTIONARY TRIBUNAL THAT HAD SENTENCED HER MOTHER TO DEATH AS THE WIFE OF A ROYALIST GENERAL, CHANTED: "LONG LIVE THE KING -DOWN WITH THE REVOLUTION!"
THE CHILD'S EFFRONTERY SO AMUSED THE JUDGES THAT HER MOTHER WAS GIVEN HER FREEDOM —AND SURVIVED FOR ANOTHER 52 YEARS (1794)

Ripley's ® Believe It or Not!

THE MOST TERRIFYING RIVER CROSSING IN THE WORLD!

THE ROPE BRIDGE across the Sarda River, near Dharchula, India, CAN BE TRAVERSED ONLY BY LYING ON YOUR BACK, SUPPORTED BY A TRIANGULAR BLOCK OF WOOD, AND PULLING YOURSELF HAND OVER HAND BY AN OVERHEAD ROPE WHICH YOU *ALSO MUST CLING TO WITH YOUR FEET*

THE "SWAN" GREBE
SWIMS AND MAKES DEEP DIVES WITH ITS *YOUNG BALANCED ON ITS BACK*

PREHISTORIC BURIAL URN
excavated near Kematen, Austria, WITH A HUMAN FACE AND 2 SMALL AUXILIARY URNS ATTACHED TO IT – FOR THE *SOULS OF 2 UNBORN CHILDREN THE DEPARTED MIGHT HAVE HAD IF SHE HAD LIVED LONGER*

THE CELESTIAL RAILWAY
SO CALLED BECAUSE ITS TERMINALS WERE THE FLORIDA TOWNS OF JUPITER AND JUNO, HAD NO MEANS OF TURNING ITS ENGINE AROUND – SO ON THE RUN FROM JUNO TO JUPITER THE TRAIN ALWAYS *BACKED UP THE ENTIRE 7½ MILES*

THE FLAG of the Australian Commonwealth WAS DESIGNED IN 1901 BY IVOR EVANS –A SCHOOLBOY– HE WON A DESIGN COMPETITION OVER 30,000 OTHER ENTRIES

FARMS on the island of Izu, Japan, RAISE 2 CROPS EACH YEAR ON THE LAND–ALTERNATING *HARVESTS OF RICE AND WHEAT*

THE FIRST DENTAL PLATE
A DENTURE FOUND IN AN ETRUSCAN GRAVE in Italy WAS MADE OF SOLID GOLD *2,100 YEARS AGO*

A SAXON RING
THAT WAS CONSIDERED
A CHARM PROTECTION
AGAINST THE PLAGUE

**THE FIRST CALENDAR WAS
THE GREAT PYRAMID OF CHEOPS!**
THE SHADOW CAST BY THE PYRAMID ENABLED THE EGYPTIANS
TO DISCOVER THE RELATIONSHIP OF THE EARTH AND THE SUN,
THE 4 SEASONS, AND OUR MODERN METHOD OF MEASURING TIME—
THE FIRST YEAR DETERMINED BY THIS CALENDAR WAS 4236 B.C.

SCHOOLGIRLS
in Japan
OFTEN CARRY A YOUNGER
SISTER TO SCHOOL WITH THEM
ON THEIR BACKS

**THE
RIBBED LIMPET**
(Acmaea Scabra)
a shellfish,
HAS SUCH A
**POWERFUL
SUCTION** THAT TO
PRY ITS SINGLE
FOOT FROM A
ROCK REQUIRES
A FORCE OF
**70 POUNDS PER
SQUARE INCH**

THE 2 EYES OF A LOBSTER—
EACH HAS 13,000 LENSES
AND 13,000 INDIVIDUAL
NERVE RODS
IF A LOBSTER LOSES AN EYE, IT
CAN REGROW ANOTHER— WITH ITS
13,000 LENSES AND 13,000 NERVE RODS

STUDENTS at the University
of Groningen, Holland,
ANNOUNCE THE SUBJECTS IN
WHICH THEY ARE MAJORING
*BY THE COLOR
OF THEIR CAPS*

**A CHINESE
REBUS AMULET**
2 MUSICAL STONES
(Ch'ing)
ARE JOINED BY A DISC (pi)
AND THE CHINESE WORDS
ALSO MEAN, *"May you be
assured double good fortune"*

**THE STRANGE FATE OF A SOLDIER WHOSE
NAME HELD THE SECRET OF HIS DESTINY**
GENERAL COUNT ARKADI SUVOROV-RIMNIKSKY
(1784-1811) ON A JOURNEY FROM RUSSIA TO RUMANIA,
DROWNED IN THE WATERS OF THE RIMNIK RIVER
— *THE VERY RIVER WHICH HAD GIVEN
HIS FATHER THE FAMILY NAME!*

HINDUS BELIEVE SALVATION IS ASSURED IF THEY DIE ON THE NORTH BANK OF THE GANGES RIVER IN BENARES AND THEIR ASHES ARE CAST INTO THE HOLY RIVER. YET THEY ARE CONVINCED THAT ANYONE WHO DIES ON THE SOUTH BANK OF THE SAME RIVER *WILL BE REBORN A DONKEY*

THE MAN WHO ESCAPED DEATH BY A WHISKER

SIR JOHN PAKINGTON FOUGHT A PISTOL DUEL WITH JOHN PARKER IN 1852 AND BOTH MEN ESCAPED INJURY — *BUT PARKER'S BULLET CLIPPED OFF PART OF SIR JOHN'S WHISKERS*

"WHEN YOU WRITE 'WRIGHT', WRIGHT, WRITE 'WRIGHT' RIGHT! RIGHT, WRIGHT?" "RIGHT, WRIGHT!"
CONVERSATION BETWEEN PAUL WRIGHT OF San Antonio, Texas, AND ROBERT WRIGHT AT PITTSBURG STATE COLLEGE, Pittsburg, Kansas

BUTTERFLY BUTTONS *OF SOLID GOLD* WERE SEWN ON THE SHROUDS of the ancient Etruscans TO AID EACH SOUL IN ITS FLIGHT TO ETERNITY

ILE de SEIN IS THE ONLY COMMUNITY IN ALL FRANCE IN WHICH NO TAX IS LEVIED — *EXCEPT FOR A TAX ON DOGS*

THE TAIKIH A CHINESE AND KOREAN RELIGIOUS SYMBOL CONSISTING OF A CIRCLE ENCLOSING 2 COMMAS, WAS ALSO REVERED AT THE TIME COLUMBUS VOYAGED TO THE NEW WORLD BY BOTH THE MEXICANS AND THE PERUVIANS

GARRETT D. WALL (1783-1850) WAS ELECTED GOVERNOR OF NEW JERSEY IN 1829 — *BUT REFUSED TO SERVE* HE WAS THE ONLY ELECTED GOVERNOR IN AMERICAN HISTORY WHO DECLINED THE OFFICE

THE OLDEST PLOWMAN IN ALL HISTORY !
CLEMENT OLHEIM (1690-1812) a farmer near Peronne, France, *PLOWED HIS FIELDS REGULARLY AT THE AGE OF 122 !*

Ripley's Believe It or Not!

ICE CREAM FRUIT
THE CHIRIMOYA, of Ecuador, HAS A WHITE PULP THAT IS SCOOPED OUT WITH A SPOON AND COMBINES 3 DELICIOUS FLAVORS —PINEAPPLE, BANANA AND STRAWBERRY

THE BANK OF SCOTLAND-
THE ONLY BANK EMPOWERED TO GRANT ITS STOCKHOLDERS IN ANY COUNTRY BRITISH AND SCOTTISH CITIZENSHIP
IT ENJOYED THAT PRIVILEGE FROM 1695 TO 1818 -A PERIOD OF 123 YEARS

THE WEDDINGS OF THE LOVE BIRDS
KHANDERAV -Ruler of Baroda, India,
INVITED ALL THE NOTABLES IN HIS KINGDOM TO **42** MARRIAGE CEREMONIES
— THE BRIDE AND GROOM IN EACH CASE BEING
A PAIR OF PIGEONS !
KHANDERAV SPENT **$2,000,000** IN THIS EFFORT TO CURRY FAVOR WITH THE GODS

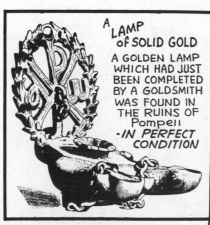

A LAMP of SOLID GOLD
A GOLDEN LAMP WHICH HAD JUST BEEN COMPLETED BY A GOLDSMITH WAS FOUND IN THE RUINS OF Pompeii -IN PERFECT CONDITION

A FIRE
in the Royal Palace of Rwanda, Africa, HAS BEEN KEPT BURNING NIGHT AND DAY FOR **200** YEARS

Ripley's — "Believe It or Not"

A GLASS CHIMNEY
LOST FROM A LANTERN
BY PAT LANAHAN WHILE
FISHING IN PLEASANT POND,
at Monticello, N.Y.,
WAS RECOVERED BY LANAHAN 5 YEARS LATER
*WHEN HE CAUGHT A BASS THAT WAS
WEARING THE UNBROKEN CHIMNEY AS
IF IT WERE A BATHING SUIT*

ROBERT FELLOWES
(1850-1924) of Southampton, England,
AWARE THAT HE WAS GOING BLIND
*READ THE BIBLE FROM
COVER TO COVER 7 TIMES*
THROUGH 40 YEARS OF BLINDNESS
HE RECEIVED SPIRITUAL COMFORT
FROM HAVING MEMORIZED
PAGES OF THE SCRIPTURES

SQUARE COINS
MINTED IN 1621
In Pforzheim,
Germany

A GOLDEN CROSS
WORN BY KING
SAMSI VUL IV of Assyria
*835 YEARS BEFORE THE
BIRTH OF CHRIST*

THE **JOCKEY** WHO CHANGED HORSES
IN THE MIDDLE OF A RACE!
MICHAEL MORRISSEY
British steeplechaser
THROWN BY ONE HORSE AT A JUMP
LANDED IN THE SADDLE OF ANOTHER
Southwell Race Track
Oct. 15, 1953

CIRCULAR BRICKS
WERE USED BY
THE ANCIENT INCAS
OF PERU IN
*THE CONSTRUCTION
OF THEIR SACRED
BUILDINGS*

GRAPE VINES
In Valais, Switzerland,
ARE GROWN IN SOIL
*PACKED INTO THE
NARROW CRACKS
IN STONE WALLS*

THE **MOST COMMEMORATED MONUMENT**
THE ANCIENT
LIGHTHOUSE
of Alexandria,
Egypt,
DESTROYED
BY AN
EARTHQUAKE
700 YEARS AGO,
*HAS BEEN
REPRODUCED
IN MINIATURE
IN THE FORM
OF THOUSANDS
OF MINARETS
IN
MOHAMMEDAN
MOSQUES
THROUGHOUT
THE WORLD*

SEI DEO·SEI·DEIVAE·SAC
SEXT IVS ET CALVINVS
DE SENATI SENTENTIA
RESTITVIT

AN **ANCIENT ALTAR**
on Palatine Hill,
Rome, Italy,
HONORS AN
"UNKNOWN DEITY"
*AN ATTEMPT BY
THE ROMANS TO
MAKE CERTAIN NO
GOD WOULD BE
ANGERED BY
HAVING BEEN
IGNORED*

MINIATURE
CANNON
used in Borneo
AS MONEY

THE WAR THAT WAS WAGED FOR A POT COVER!

EMIR ALI IBN al HAJ, RULER OF BORNU, in Africa, LED 1,000 CAVALRYMEN IN AN INVASION OF NEIGHBORING AHIR SOLELY TO RECOVER THE STRAW LID OF A GOURD STOLEN FROM A BORNU WOMAN BY AN AHIR WARRIOR!

THE EMIR RECOVERED THE POT COVER - BUT 70 OF HIS WARRIORS WERE KILLED IN THE BATTLE FOR ITS POSSESSION

THE BOUQUET BUSH
Oleander
PRODUCING BLOOMS
IN 20 DIFFERENT
COLORS

Grown by
NICHOLAS SIDERAKIS,
Whittier, Calif.

THESE HIEROGLYPHICS
IN THE TIME OF THE ANCIENT
PHARAOHS REPRESENTED
THE FIGURE 1,235,326

BARLOW
TRECOTHICK
A NATIVE OF
Boston, Mass.,
WAS ELECTED LORD
MAYOR OF LONDON,
ENGLAND, IN 1770
- THE ONLY AMERICAN
TO BECOME CHIEF
EXECUTIVE OF LONDON

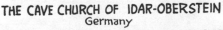

THE CAVE CHURCH OF IDAR-OBERSTEIN
Germany

BUILT IN A NATURAL CAVERN IN THE SIDE
OF A MOUNTAIN 600 YEARS AGO

MESHROB MASHDOTS
(361-441)
CREATED 2 ALPHABETS
- THOSE OF ARMENIA
AND GEORGIA -
*BOTH STILL IN USE MORE
THAN 1,500 YEARS LATER*

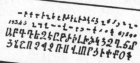

TIMOTHY MURPHY (1751-1818)
FAMED HERO OF THE AMERICAN REVOLUTION,
ESCAPED FROM AN INDIAN WAR PARTY
BY HIDING FOR AN ENTIRE NIGHT UNDER
Bouck's Falls, near Middleburg, N.Y.
-WHILE WATER THUNDERED DOWN UPON
HIM FROM A HEIGHT OF 125 FEET !

THE **MOST HEROIC** NAUTICAL RESCUE
IN ALL HISTORY !

CAPT. THOMAS A. SCOTT
BROUGHT HIS TUG ALONGSIDE A
FERRYBOAT SINKING IN NEW YORK'S
NORTH RIVER WITH HUNDREDS OF
WOMEN AND CHILDREN ABOARD AND
PLUGGED A HOLE IN THE LISTING BOAT
AT THE WATER LINE WITH
HIS OWN BODY !
CAPT. SCOTT'S ARM, WHICH PROTRUDED
THROUGH THE HOLE, WAS SEVERELY
LACERATED BY ICE CAKES -*BUT ALL
ABOARD THE VESSEL WERE SAVED*
January 30, 1870

THE TOMATO RED CANARY
BRED BY
CROSSING
A CANARY
AND A
VENEZUELAN
SISKIN

THE GREATEST CHESS
PLAYER OF ALL TIME
A ROBOT CHESS PLAYER BUILT
BY WOLFGANG von KEMPELEN
of Slovakia in 1783
PLAYED EVERY CHESS EXPERT
OF ITS TIME - YET IT
NEVER LOST A MATCH
*THE ROBOT SHOOK THE
CHESS BOARD IF ITS OPPONENT
MADE AN IMPROPER MOVE*

THE **HARDEST-WORKING POET** IN HISTORY

CHARLES-SIMON THEVENEAU (1759-1821)
FRENCH POET WHO WAS A COLLEGE PROFESSOR
AT THE AGE OF 15, COULD NOT WRITE HIS
VERSES UNTIL HE HAD JOGGED HIS THINKING
*BY ROCKING VIOLENTLY IN BED
FOR A FULL 24 HOURS*

Ripley's Believe It or Not!

THIS STATUE in the Cathedral of St. Etienne, Meaux, France, HONORS AN ANONYMOUS BENEFACTOR WHO DURING THE CATHEDRAL'S CONSTRUCTION GAVE AN APPLE TO EACH LABORER EVERY DAY **FOR 25 YEARS**

THE **SWANS** IN THE ROYAL WATERS OF VERSAILLES WERE REQUIRED BY KING LOUIS XIV TO SERVE AN APPRENTICESHIP ON Swan Island, in Paris, IN THE BELIEF THEY WOULD LEARN FROM OLDER SWANS THE ART OF MAJESTIC BEHAVIOR

THE **PROPHET** WHO WAS SO ACCURATE HE TERRIFIED HIMSELF! SHEIK ABDUL REZEGH of Khaw, Jordan, WHOSE PREDICTION THAT KING ABDULLAH of Jordan WOULD BE ASSASSINATED WAS TRAGICALLY FULFILLED IN 1951 TOOK A VOW OF ETERNAL SILENCE AND HAS NOT SPOKEN ANOTHER WORD FOR 13 YEARS!

THE **FIRST INFLATED MONEY** GOLD DISCS MINTED IN Germany 2,000 YEARS AGO AS COINS WITHOUT INSCRIPTIONS INDICATING THEIR VALUE, INCREASED IN WORTH WHEN THE MINT SPREAD A RUMOR THEY HAD BEEN FOUND AT THE END OF A RAINBOW

ONLY ONE COIN A SILVER ECU WORTH ABOUT 58 CENTS WAS EVER MINTED BY CORSICA 1736

The **KING** of the Bubis, of Spanish Guinea, Africa, SITS ON A NEW THRONE **EVERY DAY OF HIS REIGN** ANOTHER THRONE IS CONSTRUCTED FOR THE MONARCH EACH NIGHT

THE STRANGEST NAVAL BATTLE IN HISTORY! COMMODORE PERRY'S FLEET, WHICH OPENED JAPAN TO THE WESTERN WORLD IN 1854, WAS ATTACKED BY SMALL SAMPANS ARMED ONLY WITH STRAW ROPES THE JAPANESE, HAVING NO KNOWLEDGE OF THE POWER OF STEAM ENGINES, USED ROPES IN AN ATTEMPT TO HOLD BACK THE FRIGATES SUSQUEHANNA (2,213 TONS) AND POWHATAN (2,182 TON) BUT WERE FRIGHTENED OFF BY BLASTS FROM THE SHIPS' WHISTLES!

Ripley's® Believe It or Not!

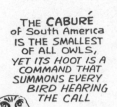

THE CABURÉ of South America IS THE SMALLEST OF ALL OWLS, YET ITS HOOT IS A COMMAND THAT SUMMONS EVERY BIRD HEARING THE CALL

A TON OF HAY
A RANCHER VITALLY NEEDED IN SNOWBOUND SILVERTON, COLO., TO FEED HIS CATTLE, WAS MAILED FROM DURANGO BY PARCEL POST
THE HAY WAS WRAPPED IN SMALL PACKAGES AND CARRIED OVER THE MOUNTAIN TRAILS ON PACK MULES FOR $14 IN POSTAGE -BUT IT COST THE POST OFFICE $100 TO HIRE THE MULES !
(1932)

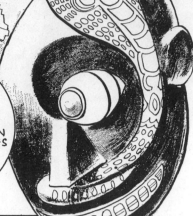

VALONIA THE LARGEST VEGETABLE CELL IN NATURE, IS 2,000 TIMES AS LARGE AS THE AVERAGE CELL !

THE CATHEDRAL OF LUCERA
in Italy
WAS CONSTRUCTED BY KING CHARLES II IN 1300 FROM THE DEBRIS OF A SARACEN MOSQUE -WHICH ITSELF HAD BEEN BUILT FROM THE STONES OF A CATHEDRAL

NATIVES OF Ceylon BELIEVED THAT DEAFNESS COULD BE CURED BY WEARING A MASK REPRESENTING THE DEMON OF DEAFNESS

THE STRANGEST DINNERS IN ALL HISTORY!
CLODIUS, SON OF ESOPUS, the famed Roman actor, WAS HOST AT AN ANNUAL BANQUET IN WHICH THE APPETIZER WAS ALWAYS A DISH CONSISTING OF 100 BIRDS -EACH OF WHICH COST $250 BECAUSE THEY HAD BEEN PREPARED FOR THE FEAST BY RECEIVING YEARS OF VOICE TRAINING FROM ROME'S OUTSTANDING ELOCUTION TEACHERS !
THE GUESTS WASHED DOWN THE APPETIZER WITH A DRINK IN WHICH THE HOST HAD DISSOLVED A PEARL VALUED AT $400,000

17 BROTHERS
THE SONS OF SIR DAVID MURRAY of Tullibardine, ALL SLEPT IN BLAIR CASTLE, Atholl, Scotland, IN ONE HUGE CIRCULAR BED

THE TRUNK OF AN ELEPHANT IS OPERATED BY 40,000 MUSCLES

THE MAN WHO WEPT CONTINUOUSLY FOR 168 HOURS!

PRINCE CHAO of China, REFUSED MILITARY AID BY HIS ALLY, PRINCE TSIN, AGAINST AN INVASION BY BARBARIANS, WEPT WITHOUT INTERRUPTION FOR **7 DAYS AND 7 NIGHTS!** PRINCE TSIN FINALLY CHANGED HIS MIND—AND THE AID HE SENT SAVED BOTH THEIR COUNTRIES

THE OFFICIAL SEAL of the Republic of Mount Athos, Greece, CONSISTS OF 4 PARTS, EACH HELD BY A DIFFERENT OFFICIAL —AND THEY MUST MEET TO VALIDATE ANY DOCUMENT

THE THORN OF CHRIST (Spina Christi) THE TYPE OF BUSH FROM WHICH CAME THE CROWN OF THORNS CHRIST WORE ON THE CROSS — STILL GROWS ONLY IN THE HOLY LAND

THE MEMORIAL TO A STRING OF POLO PONIES

THE DOORWAY TO THE MOSQUE OF FATEHPUR, IN INDIA, HAS BEEN ADORNED FOR 362 YEARS BY *HORSESHOES FROM EMPEROR AKBAR'S POLO PONIES*

GEORGE E. CHAMBERLAIN (1854-1928) of Oregon IS THE ONLY **DEMOCRAT** IN HISTORY WHO WAS ELECTED TO THE U.S. SENATE *BY A REPUBLICAN LEGISLATURE* (1909)

THE SEA BUTTERFLY ISN'T A BUTTERFLY *IT IS A WINGED SNAIL*

A COIN PRIVATELY MINTED DURING THE CIVIL WAR TO AVOID CONFLICT WITH LAWS AGAINST SUCH CURRENCY BORE THE LEGEND **"NOT ONE CENT"**

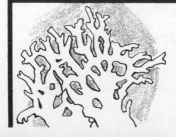

A CRADLE CARVED IN Belgium IN 1450 AND SOLD 480 YEARS LATER FOR $12,250

FIRE CORAL of the Red Sea *IS INTENSELY HOT* TOUCHING IT CAUSES PAINFUL BURNS, BLISTERS AND PERMANENT SCARS

THE CHURCH A MAN SACRIFICED A KINGDOM TO BUILD

THE CATHEDRAL OF ST. MAGNUS in Kirkwall, The Orkney Islands, WAS CONSTRUCTED IN 1137 BY KOL, WHO LET HIS SON ASSUME THE THRONE OF THE ORKNEYS *IN EXCHANGE FOR PERMISSION TO DESIGN THIS CATHEDRAL*

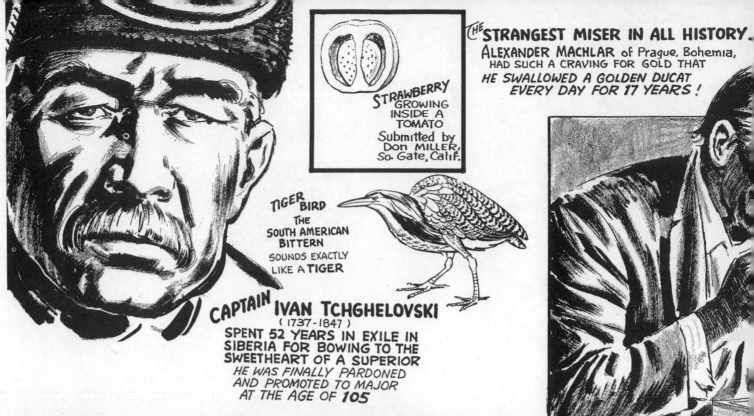

STRAWBERRY GROWING INSIDE A TOMATO
Submitted by Don MILLER, So. Gate, Calif.

THE STRANGEST MISER IN ALL HISTORY.
ALEXANDER MACHLAR of Prague, Bohemia, HAD SUCH A CRAVING FOR GOLD THAT HE SWALLOWED A GOLDEN DUCAT EVERY DAY FOR 17 YEARS!

TIGER BIRD THE SOUTH AMERICAN BITTERN SOUNDS EXACTLY LIKE A TIGER

CAPTAIN IVAN TCHGHELOVSKI (1737-1847)
SPENT 52 YEARS IN EXILE IN SIBERIA FOR BOWING TO THE SWEETHEART OF A SUPERIOR
HE WAS FINALLY PARDONED AND PROMOTED TO MAJOR AT THE AGE OF 105

The STRANGEST QUALIFICATION TEST IN HISTORY!
EMPEROR AKBAR (1542-1602) of India
FORCED EVERY CANDIDATE FOR HIGH OFFICE TO VIE WITH HIM IN A GAME OF NIGHT POLO
—USING BALLS OF FIRE!

DUKE CHARLES OF LORRAINE (1643-1690) FAMED AUSTRIAN MILITARY LEADER WAS SLAIN WITH A POISON WIG BY A BRIBED SERVANT

Ripley's — ® Believe It or Not!

5 Tulips GROWING ON ONE STEM
Submitted by JACK VALIS Yonkers, N.Y.

A **WATCH** made in Switzerland in 1825 *IN THE SHAPE OF A TULIP*

THE TEMPLE BUILT TO ATONE FOR A MURDER PROPHESIED AT THE KILLER'S BIRTH!
A MEMORIAL TO KING PHYA KONG, CONSTRUCTED AT NAKORN PATHOM, THAILAND, BY HIS SON, KING PHARN, WHO KILLED THE ELDER MONARCH IN BATTLE AND SUCCEEDED TO HIS THRONE AND ONLY THEN LEARNED THAT **HE HAD SLAIN HIS OWN FATHER!**
KING PHYA KONG HAD CAST OUT HIS SON AT BIRTH BECAUSE A SOOTHSAYER HAD WARNED HIM THE BOY WAS DESTINED TO SLAY HIM

THE NAME THAT MEANT LIFE AND DEATH TO 3 GENERATIONS!
SIETE SETIEMBRE of Barcelona, Spain, WHOSE NAME MEANS "SEVENTH SEPTEMBER"
WAS BORN ON SEPTEMBER 7, 1749 AND DIED ON SEPTEMBER 7, 1801
HIS SON, ALSO NAMED SIETE SETIEMBRE *WAS BORN ON SEPTEMBER 7, 1774 AND DIED ON SEPTEMBER 7, 1826*
HIS GRANDSON, NAMED SIETE SETIEMBRE *WAS BORN ON SEPTEMBER 7, 1814 AND DIED ON SEPTEMBER 7, 1862*

A FRENCH TRANSLATION OF A HISTORY OF ROME BY TITUS LIVIUS WAS PRINTED WITH INK MIXED WITH COFFEE GROUNDS AND SOOT BECAUSE THE ORIGINAL BOOK WAS WRITTEN IN PRISON *WITH AN INK MADE BY MIXING COFFEE GROUNDS AND SOOT*

A **CHECK** FOR **$15** WRITTEN ON THE SHELL OF AN EGG WAS CASHED BY A BANK IN VICTORIA, B.C.

SHAH MOHAMMED ruler of Iran, **REZA** SHOT AT 3 TIMES BY AN ASSASSIN FROM A DISTANCE OF ONLY 6 FEET, ESCAPED WITHOUT INJURY ALTHOUGH *ALL 3 BULLETS RIPPED THROUGH HIS HAT* (Feb. 4, 1949)

Ripley's Believe It or Not!

DEEP-SEA SHRIMP BAFFLE PURSUERS BY RELEASING CLOUDS OF LUMINOUS FLUID

THE FIGUREHEAD of the M.S. Bonnard, a Norwegian ship, CONSISTS OF 25,000 PIECES OF GLASS

GERANIUM GROWING FROM THE CENTER OF ANOTHER GERANIUM BLOOM

Submitted by MRS. M. FREDERICI Arborg, Manitoba

THE LARGEST INSECT IN THE WORLD THE MEGANEURON, A PREHISTORIC DRAGONFLY, MEASURED 29 INCHES FROM WINGTIP TO WINGTIP

THE OSTRICH TREE Monterey, Calif.

THE REV. JEROME C. BERRYMAN (1810-1906) WAS A MINISTER IN Arcadia, Mo., FOR 75 YEARS

A PALACE BUILT IN ROME, ITALY, BY PIETRO RIARIO, AND STILL USED AS A GOVERNMENT OFFICE BUILDING WAS FINANCED BY $60,000 WON IN A SINGLE CARD GAME (1471)

A MILITARY HELMET THAT COST HALF A MILLION DOLLARS CHARLES THE BOLD (1433-1477) WORE IN BATTLE AN IRON HAT STUDDED WITH PEARLS, RUBIES AND EMERALDS

BEET WITH 2 BUNCHES OF LEAVES Submitted by MRS. JOHN GRAY Prince George,

RASPBERRIES
AND
BLUEBERRIES
ARE
CHERRIES

**THE MOSQUE THAT WAS SO BEAUTIFUL
ITS ARCHITECT WAS BLINDED !**
THE MOSQUE OF MOHAMMED ALI , in Cairo, Egypt,
WHICH TOOK 28 YEARS TO COMPLETE,
PLEASED THE PASHA OF EGYPT SO
MUCH THAT HE GRANTED A GENEROUS
PENSION TO ARCHITECT YUSIF BULIM
-*THEN ORDERED HIM BLINDED SO HE
COULD NEVER DUPLICATE IT* (1857)

**Armand
BREZELLE**
of Nonancourt, France,
WHO WAS BORN AT 2:10 A.M.,
WAS FOUND TO HAVE ON THE
PUPIL OF HIS LEFT EYE A
PERFECT REPRODUCTION
OF A CLOCK DIAL
-WITH THE HOUR HAND
POINTING TO 2:10
July 11, 1849

SIX (O'CLOCK) SHOOTER
A **PISTOL** WITH A BUILT-IN WATCH-
WHEN THE TRIGGER IS PRESSED IT SHOOTS
PERFUME -*IT WAS MANUFACTURED IN
SWITZERLAND IN THE EARLY 19th CENTURY*

**THE MAN WHOSE MURDER
WAS AVENGED 5 TIMES !**
PIERS GAVESTON, A FAVORITE OF KING
EDWARD II, of England, WAS KILLED BY 5
CONSPIRATORS JEALOUS OF HIS POWER
-*AND SUBSEQUENTLY EACH OF THE
5 DIED A VIOLENT DEATH !*
THE EARL OF LANCASTER AND THE EARL OF
ARUNDEL WERE EXECUTED, THE EARL OF
HEREFORD WAS SLAIN IN BATTLE, THE EARL
OF PEMBROKE WAS ASSASSINATED, AND THE
EARL OF WARWICK DIED BY POISON

from an old print

THE SPANISH STEPS in Rome, Italy
THE FAMED STAIRWAY OF 136 STEPS
ACTUALLY IS OWNED BY FRANCE, TO WHICH ITALY PAYS
AN ANNUAL RENTAL OF ONE LIRA (1/6 OF A CENT)

THE MAN WHO WAS KILLED BY A SKELETON

PIETER PEUTEMAN - famed Dutch painter
DIED OF FRIGHT WHEN HE SAW
A SKELETON DANCING IN HIS STUDIO
*HE WAS UNAWARE THAT THE SKELETON HE USED AS A MODEL
WAS BEING SHAKEN BY AN EARTHQUAKE*
Sept. 18, 1692

THE RIVER THAT RUNS RED

THE **RIO TINTO** -Spain- CONTAINS A MINERAL
SOLUTION THAT UPON CONTACT WITH THE AIR
TURNS THE ENTIRE RIVER BLOOD RED

THE **IRON KEY**
STILL USED TO LOCK
THE STATE HOUSE OF ANDORRA,
IS **400** YEARS OLD, WEIGHS
3 POUNDS, AND MEASURES ONE
FOOT, FIVE INCHES IN LENGTH

THE **MAUSOLEUM** of **CAESAR AUGUSTUS**
in Rome, Italy,
BENEATH WHICH THE EMPEROR'S ASHES STILL REST IN AN URN,
WAS CONVERTED 1,500 YEARS AFTER HIS DEATH INTO A
CONCERT HALL, WORLD-FAMOUS FOR ITS ACOUSTICS-
*IN 1935 MUSSOLINI ORDERED THE CONCERT HALL CONVERTED
BACK TO ITS ORIGINAL STATE AS A RUIN*

THE
TOMB OF THE MAHDI
CONSTRUCTED TO HOLD THE BODY OF THE
RELIGIOUS LEADER OF OMDURMAN, SUDAN,
HAS A DOME OF SOLID SILVER-
*NO ONE HAS TRIED TO MAKE OFF WITH
THE SILVER -BUT THE BODY OF
THE MAHDI HAS DISAPPEARED*

Ripley's Believe It or Not!

A GOLDEN JAR in the Monastery of St. Maurice d'Augune, Switzerland, FASHIONED FROM THE SCEPTER OF A HUNGARIAN CHIEFTAIN SLAIN BY EMPEROR CHARLEMAGNE

THE SPONGE CRAB TO MAKE ITSELF UNAPPETIZING TO PREDATORS, CUTS A PIECE OF SPONGE THAT FITS PERFECTLY OVER ITS BACK

THE DREAM THAT CLEARED THE WAY FOR A RAILROAD!

ARTHUR STILWELL, of Kansas City, AFTER BEING TOLD BY SURVEYORS THAT LAND HE NEEDED FOR HIS RAILROAD WAS OWNED BY A RIVAL LINE, DREAMED THAT THE PROPERTY ACTUALLY WAS IN THE NAME OF HEIRS OF A MAN NAMED KERSEY COATES

THE HEIRS OF COATES WERE UNAWARE THEY OWNED THE LAND UNTIL A NEW SURVEY PROVED STILWELL'S DREAM WAS TRUE, AND ENABLED HIM TO PURCHASE THE PROPERTY

THE FIRST BRICK HOUSE IN AMERICA THE HOME OF WILLIAM PENN in Philadelphia WAS THE FIRST BUILT IN THIS COUNTRY ENTIRELY OF BRICK

THE BERRY BUTTERFLIES HYPSA MONYCHA BUTTERFLIES of Singapore IN THEIR CATERPILLAR STAGE GROUP AROUND THE TOP OF A STEM TO FOIL PREDATORY BIRDS *BY IMITATING THE APPEARANCE OF A POISONOUS BERRY*

THE MOST STRENUOUS RACE IN HISTORY

GIPSY MOTH III, A YACHT WEIGHING 13 TONS, AND 39 FEET, 7 INCHES LONG, WHICH NORMALLY REQUIRES A CREW OF 6 MEN, WON A RACE FROM PLYMOUTH, ENGLAND, TO NEW YORK WITH ONLY FRANCIS CHARLES CHICHESTER, AGED 59, ABOARD- *CHICHESTER, RACING FOUR OTHER YACHTS EACH MANNED BY A SINGLE SAILOR, COVERED 4,000 MILES IN 40½ DAYS* (June 11 to July 21, 1960)

THE PEACE POPLAR PLANTED IN JENA, GERMANY, IN 1815, TO MARK THE END OF THE NAPOLEONIC WARS, COLLAPSED SUDDENLY ON AUGUST 1, 1914 -THE DAY WORLD WAR I BEGAN IN GERMANY

Ripley's Believe It or Not!

THE OLDEST-KNOWN COMPACT

A GOLD VANITY CASE FOUND IN THE TOMB OF AN INDIAN BEAUTY HAD BEEN INTERRED WITH HER 5,000 YEARS AGO

THE BELL TOWER of the Cathedral of Chartres, France, AS THE RESULT OF A HURRICANE IN 1691 *LEANED 12 FEET FROM THE PERPENDICULAR FOR AN ENTIRE YEAR*

IT WAS STRAIGHTENED IN 1692 AND EXTENDED AN ADDITIONAL 4 FEET TO A TOTAL HEIGHT OF 346 FEET

A CHERRY TOMATO GROWING ON THE BOTTOM OF A PEAR TOMATO

Submitted by MRS. W.E. DUNSTANE, East Northport, N.Y.

THE MOST HAZARDOUS BRIDGE IN HISTORY !

A WOODEN BRIDGE over Lake Zurich, Switzerland, THAT LINKED RAPPERSWIL AND HURDEN BETWEEN 1358 AND 1850, TOSSED SO VIOLENTLY IN STORMY WEATHER THAT **1,000 PERSONS DIED ATTEMPTING TO CROSS IT.**

IN BAD WEATHER IT COULD BE TRAVERSED ONLY ON HANDS AND KNEES

IPOKRITOS

FROM WHICH THE ENGLISH "HYPOCRITE" IS DERIVED, ORIGINALLY WAS THE WORD FOR AN ACTOR OF ANCIENT GREECE

THE STRANGEST PILGRIMAGE IN THE WORLD !

THE 4-MOUNTAIN RUN STAGED IN CARINTHIA, AUSTRIA, FOR CENTURIES REQUIRES EACH PILGRIM TO WALK 24 MILES, CLIMB MOUNT MAGDALEN (3,553 FT.), MOUNT ULRICH (3,330 FT.), MOUNT LORENZI (3,160 FT.) AND MOUNT VEIT (3,855 FT.) AND ATTEND CHAPEL SERVICES ON EACH PEAK - *ALL IN A PERIOD OF 24 HOURS STARTING AT MIDNIGHT OF EACH 3d SUNDAY FOLLOWING EASTER*

THE PILGRIMAGE IS SO STRENUOUS THAT MANY DIE OF EXHAUSTION

WHIP-MA-WHOP-MA-

A STREET in York, England, SO NAMED BECAUSE CRIMINALS ONCE WERE WHIPPED THERE

THE **LITTORINA PERIWINKLE**
GRADUALLY CHANGING FROM A MARINE ANIMAL TO A LAND DWELLER, CAN LIVE OUT OF WATER FOR MORE THAN 40 DAYS *AND IS THE ONLY OCEAN CREATURE THAT CAN SURVIVE IN SWEET WATER*

FRANCOIS-AUGUSTE de **THOU**
(1607-1642)
BECAME GRAND MASTER OF THE ROYAL LIBRARY OF PARIS AND CHIEF LIBRARIAN OF ALL FRANCE **AT THE AGE OF 10**- 25 YEARS LATER HE WAS EXECUTED FOR TREASON

CIGAR BANDS
WERE INTRODUCED IN CUBA BY *FEMININE SMOKERS* SO THE STOGIES WOULDN'T STAIN THEIR DAINTY FINGERS

A CIRCULAR HOUSE
at Arzachena, Sardinia, *BUILT IN A HOLLOW BOULDER*

THE **OWL** BUTTERFLY
IS NOT HARMED BY PREDATORS BECAUSE ITS CAMOUFLAGE MAKES IT LOOK LIKE A *FIERCE BIRD OF PREY*

SIR **GEORGE ROOKE**
(1650-1709)
SENT TO SEA AS A BOY BY HIS FATHER AS A PUNISHMENT FOR PETTY THIEVERY -BECAME THE BRITISH ADMIRAL WHO CONQUERED GIBRALTAR

THE **FAMOUS VOYAGE** THAT OWED ITS SUCCESS TO CHOPPED CABBAGE!

CAPTAIN COOK (1728-1779) WHEN HE SET SAIL AROUND THE WORLD WITH 2 SHIPS IN 1776, EXPECTED TO LOSE **60%** OF HIS CREW TO SCURVY, BUT THE 4-YEAR EXPEDITION DID NOT LOSE A SINGLE MAN TO THAT SCOURGE BECAUSE **COOK PRESCRIBED A STEADY DIET OF SAUERKRAUT.** THE ONLY DEATHS WERE THE CAPTAIN HIMSELF, WHO WAS KILLED BY NATIVES, AND THE SHIP'S SURGEON, WHO SUCCUMBED TO TUBERCULOSIS

THE **GREAT WILLOW TREE**
IN THE GARDEN OF THE GOVERNOR'S
PALACE, IN WILLIAMSBURG, VA.,
WAS PLANTED AS THE ONLY MEMORIAL
TO 156 REVOLUTIONARY SOLDIERS,
WHOSE BODIES WERE FOUND BURIED
IN A MASS GRAVE AT THAT SPOT

THE SIEGE THAT WAS WON BY A SWARM OF BEES!
THE FORTRESS OF ACRE IN THE HOLY LAND,
AFTER RESISTING ATTACKS BY THE CRUSADERS FOR 2 YEARS,
FINALLY WAS CAPTURED IN 1191 BY KING RICHARD THE LIONHEARTED,
WHO ORDERED 100 BEEHIVES TOSSED OVER ITS WALLS
THE SARACEN DEFENDERS SURRENDERED AT ONCE

THE **STRANGEST CHRISTMAS TREE**
SCUBA DIVERS
IN THE ITALIAN NATIONAL UNDERSEA EXPEDITION OF 1952
CELEBRATED CHRISTMAS BY DECORATING A CORAL BUSH
WITH COLORED LIGHTS 100 FEET BELOW THE SURFACE
OF THE RED SEA

THE **CHAPEL DEDICATED
TO A SONG**
Oberndorf, Austria
IT WAS ERECTED ON THE
SITE OF A DEMOLISHED
CHURCH IN WHICH COMPOSER
FRANZ GRUBER FIRST
RENDERED HIS SONG,
"Holy Night"

A GIRL IN THE OSSAU VALLEY, FRANCE, MAY WEAR A RED DRESS ONLY IF SHE IS AN HEIRESS GIRLS WHO HAVE BROTHERS OR OLDER SISTERS WEAR BLACK DRESSES

THE **PROFESSOR WHO ALWAYS LECTURED TO HIS DONKEY!** AMMONIUS DRAMATICUS (319-396) CELEBRATED PROFESSOR OF GREEK GRAMMAR AT THE UNIVERSITY OF ALEXANDRIA, RODE TO SCHOOL EACH DAY ON A DONKEY, WHICH THEN *SAT IN THE LECTURE HALL AMONG HIS STUDENTS —LISTENING ATTENTIVELY TO ITS MASTER'S VOICE*

ASTROPHYTUM MYRIOSTIGMA A CACTUS —*LOOKS LIKE AN ORNATE BISHOP'S CAP TOPPED BY A FEATHER*

THE OYSTERCATCHER GIVEN A CHOICE OF HATCHING HER OWN EGG, THAT OF ANOTHER BIRD, OR ONE MADE OF WOOD —*ALWAYS SITS ON THE WOODEN EGG*

 "GOOD" IS WRITTEN IN CHINESE BY AN IDEOGRAPH DEPICTING A BOY MEETING A GIRL

好

CANOES IN THE NGARUAWAHIA REGATTA, IN NEW ZEALAND, *MUST RACE OVER SCORES OF HURDLES WITHOUT TIPPING*

THE **ARTIST** WHO COULD NOT SURVIVE SUCCESS CORREGGIO (1494-1534) one of the greatest painters of all time WAS PAID FOR ONE OF HIS CANVASES WITH A 50-POUND BAG OF COPPERS —*AND DIED AS THE RESULT OF THE EXERTION OF CARRYING IT HOME*

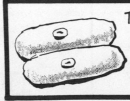

THE **AFRICAN MASON WASP** (Sceliphron) BUILDS NESTS WITH MANY CUBICLES IN WHICH IT IMPRISONS SPIDERS, *SEALING THEM IN WITH CLAY CORKS* - THE WASPS ABANDON EACH NEST AFTER A YEAR AND IT IS TAKEN OVER BY OTHER INSECTS THAT PREY ON SPIDERS

Ripley's® Believe It or Not!

THE CATASTROPHE THAT OCCURRED 6 TIMES ON THE SAME DATE!

SEVERE EARTHQUAKES DEVASTATED JAPANESE CITIES ON SEPTEMBER 1, 827
SEPTEMBER 1, 859
SEPTEMBER 1, 867
SEPTEMBER 1, 1185
SEPTEMBER 1, 1649
AND SEPTEMBER 1, 1923

ON SEPTEMBER 1, 1923, TOKYO AND YOKOHAMA WERE LEVELED BY THE GREATEST EARTHQUAKE IN JAPAN'S HISTORY -WITH A LOSS OF 143,000 LIVES!

BONE SHAPED LIKE A HUMAN SKULL
Submitted by Roy P. Maricondo, Brooklyn, N.Y.

THE STRANGEST HORSE RACE IN THE WORLD!

A GRUELLING CROSS-COUNTRY RACE, STAGED ANNUALLY IN MONGOLIA TO DETERMINE THE COUNTRY'S THREE FASTEST HORSES, ALWAYS HAS 200 HORSES RIDDEN MADLY OVER AN 18-MILE COURSE BY CHILDREN 5 TO 8 YEARS. OF AGE!

YOUNGSTERS—MANY OF WHOM HAVE TO BE TIED ON THEIR MOUNTS—ARE USED AS JOCKEYS TO GIVE A TRUE TEST OF THE HORSES' NATURAL ABILITY. YET IN CENTURIES THERE HAS NOT BEEN A SINGLE ACCIDENT

THE MOST AMAZING DIVING FEAT IN HISTORY!

ALEXANDER LAMBERT, a French deep-sea diver, SINGLEHANDEDLY SALVAGED $350,000 IN GOLD FROM THE WRECKED STEAMER "ALFONSO XII IN 162 FEET OF WATER OFF THE CANARY ISLANDS BY MAKING 3 DIVES A DAY FOR 11 SUCCESSIVE DAYS - EACH TIME MAKING HIS ASCENT IN 5 MINUTES INSTEAD OF THE NORMAL 60 MINUTES CONSIDERED MINIMUM TIME TO AVOID THE DREADED "BENDS"

HE HAD NO ILL EFFECTS UNTIL HE REMAINED DOWN 45 MINUTES ON HIS LAST DIVE AND, AFTER AGAIN ASCENDING IN 5 MINUTES, WAS PERMANENTLY PARALYZED

THE OBSIDIAN CROWN A MILITARY DECORATION AWARDED in ancient Rome TO GENERALS WHO CAPTURED A FORTRESS AFTER A HEROIC SIEGE WAS WOVEN ENTIRELY FROM GRASS TAKEN FROM THE SEIZED CITY

THE GOLDEN MUMMY
THE LAST GRAND LAMA OF MONGOLIA, AS A MUMMY WITH OPEN EYES AND A LIFELIKE SMILE, SITS OUTSIDE THE Choisy Temple, in Ulan Bator
HIS BODY COVERED FROM HEAD TO TOES WITH GOLD

JEAN-BAPTISTE TESTE
(1780-1852) WAS ELECTED TO THE GRAND ASSEMBLY, HIGHEST LEGISLATIVE BODY OF THE FRENCH REVOLUTION, *WHEN HE WAS ONLY 13 YEARS OF AGE*

The CHAPEL of ST. QUIRINUS
in Luxembourg
WAS CONSTRUCTED IN THE 13th CENTURY IN THE SOLID ROCK *OF A MOUNTAIN*

SPERM WHALE HAS AN EFFICIENT DEPTH GAUGE —*THE OUTER MEMBRANE OF ITS EYE*— HICH FLASHES A WARNING TO ITS BRAIN WHEN THE ALE HAS DESCENDED TO THE DANGER POINT

CHARLES C. WEAVER
1875-1946
WAS NAMED PRESIDENT OF RUTHERFORD COLLEGE, N.C., IN 1900
THE SAME YEAR IN WHICH HE COMPLETED HIS OWN COLLEGE EDUCATION

The TEMPLE of the COUGHS
A RUINED TEMPLE in Rome, Italy, THAT WAS BELIEVED TO HAVE THE POWER TO *CURE THE COUGH OF ANYONE WHO SPENT A SINGLE NIGHT IN THE DRAFTY STRUCTURE*

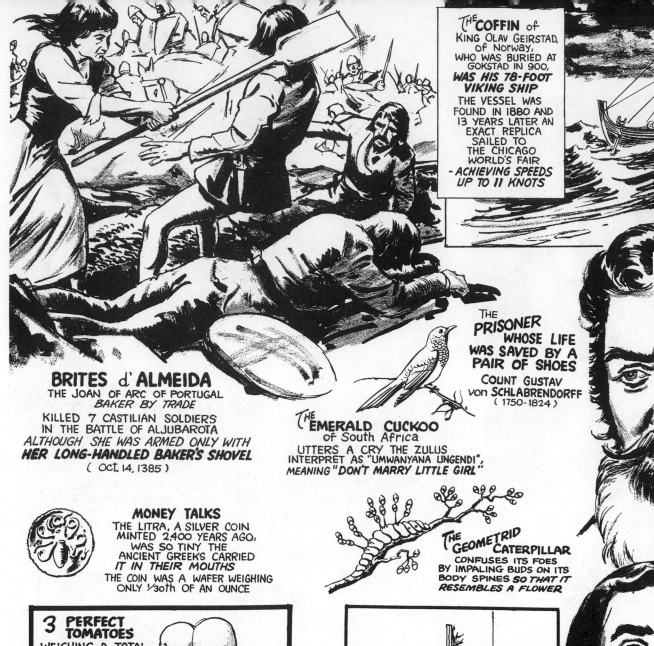

THE **COFFIN** of KING OLAV GEIRSTAD, of Norway, WHO WAS BURIED AT GOKSTAD IN 900, **WAS HIS 78-FOOT VIKING SHIP** THE VESSEL WAS FOUND IN 1880 AND 13 YEARS LATER AN EXACT REPLICA SAILED TO THE CHICAGO WORLD'S FAIR - ACHIEVING SPEEDS UP TO 11 KNOTS

BRITES d'ALMEIDA THE JOAN OF ARC OF PORTUGAL *BAKER BY TRADE* KILLED 7 CASTILIAN SOLDIERS IN THE BATTLE OF ALJUBAROTA *ALTHOUGH SHE WAS ARMED ONLY WITH* **HER LONG-HANDLED BAKER'S SHOVEL** (OCT. 14, 1385)

THE **PRISONER** WHOSE LIFE WAS SAVED BY A PAIR OF SHOES COUNT GUSTAV von SCHLABRENDORFF (1750-1824)

THE **EMERALD CUCKOO** of South Africa UTTERS A CRY THE ZULUS INTERPRET AS "UMWANYANA UNGENDI", MEANING *"DON'T MARRY LITTLE GIRL"*

MONEY TALKS THE LITRA, A SILVER COIN MINTED 2,400 YEARS AGO, WAS SO TINY THE ANCIENT GREEKS CARRIED *IT IN THEIR MOUTHS* THE COIN WAS A WAFER WEIGHING ONLY 1/30th OF AN OUNCE

THE **GEOMETRID CATERPILLAR** CONFUSES ITS FOES BY IMPALING BUDS ON ITS BODY SPINES *SO THAT IT RESEMBLES A FLOWER*

3 PERFECT TOMATOES WEIGHING A TOTAL OF 36½ OUNCES *GROWING ON ONE STEM* THE SAME BUSH SIMULTANEOUSLY PRODUCED 6 TWIN TOMATOES Submitted by Wallace M. Depew, Scranton, Pa.

A **BEET PLANT** THAT GREW TO A HEIGHT OF **7** FEET Submitted by Julian Collins, Los Angeles, Calif.

A **SPECIAL TAX** LEVIED IN Schweinfurt, Germany, in 1819, TO DEFRAY THE COST OF STREET ILLUMINATION, WAS AN ANNUAL FEE OF $3.55 -TO BE PAID BY THE OWNER OF *EVERY CAPTIVE NIGHTINGALE*

THE **BIG BORE** ERICUS AURIVILLIUS (1643-1702) Professor of Law at the University of Uppsala, Sweden, LECTURED DAILY AT THE UNIVERSITY *YET IN 18 YEARS ONLY ONE STUDENT EVER ATTENDED HIS CLASS !*

A **TYPEWRITER** INVENTED PRIOR TO 1860 -WITH A *PIANO KEYBOARD*

THE **MUMMIFIED HAND** OF A WOMAN MURDERED IN MARKT BIBART, GERMANY, IS STILL BEING HELD IN COURT AS EVIDENCE AGAINST HER UNKNOWN KILLER *412 YEARS AFTER HER DEATH* IN ANCIENT MURDER TRIALS THE HAND OF THE VICTIM WAS ALWAYS KEPT IN COURT UNTIL THE MURDERER HAD BEEN CONVICTED

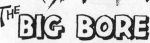

Ripley's Believe It or Not!

THE BLEEDING HEART PIGEON of Luzon, in the Philippines, HAS ON ITS WHITE BREAST A BRIGHT RED PATCH *THAT LOOKS EXACTLY LIKE A MORTAL WOUND*

SUMMONED FROM HIS CELL FOR EXECUTION IN THE FRENCH REVOLUTION, HAD HIS TRIP TO THE GUILLOTINE POSTPONED *BECAUSE HE COULD NOT FIND HIS SHOES* THE SHOES WERE LOCATED, BUT THE COUNT'S NAME SOMEHOW WAS DROPPED FROM THE LIST OF THOSE TO BE KILLED

THE LOVE TRAP Levoca, Czechoslovakia A JILTED GIRL, WHO REPORTED THE NAME OF HER FIANCE TO THE AUTHORITIES, WAS LOCKED INSIDE AN IRON CAGE IN THE MARKET PLACE OF LEVOCA, AND THE YOUNG MAN WAS CHAINED OUTSIDE IT THEY WERE KEPT IMPRISONED UNTIL THE MAN AGREED TO MARRY

A **PET POODLE** WAS TRAINED BY LORD ERSKINE, England's highest judicial officer, TO SIT FOR HOURS WITH ITS PAWS UPON AN OPEN LAW BOOK *WEARING A JURIST'S WIG*

THE **FAÇADE** of the Monastery of San Bruno, Italy, IS STILL STANDING **872** YEARS AFTER ITS CONSTRUCTION, ALTHOUGH AN EARTHQUAKE IN 1783 WRECKED THE STRUCTURE, WHIRLED ITS FACADE ENTIRELY AROUND — AND THEN *TURNED IT BACK TO ITS ORIGINAL POSITION!*

THE GREATEST GLUTTON IN ALL HISTORY!

PHAGON an official in the court of Roman Emperor Aurelianus, IN THE PRESENCE OF THE EMPEROR, CONSUMED IN A SINGLE BANQUET *AN ENTIRE BOAR, A SHEEP, A PIG, 100 LOAVES OF BREAD AND A BARREL OF WINE!*

Ripley's — "Believe It or Not!"

WILLIAM RAINEY HARPER (1856-1906) founder of the University of Chicago ENTERED Muskingum COLLEGE IN OHIO **AT THE AGE OF 10** HIS REPUTATION AS AN EDUCATOR WAS SO GREAT THAT WHEN HE CREATED THE UNIVERSITY OF CHICAGO **9 COLLEGE PRESIDENTS RESIGNED THEIR POSTS TO TEACH ON HIS FACULTY**

THE MOST DRAMATIC TAX CUT IN HISTORY! EMPEROR AURELIAN (212-275) of Rome WIPED OUT ALL THE TAX LIABILITIES OF HIS SUBJECTS IN 274 *BY BURNING ALL THE TAX RECORDS IN A HUGE BONFIRE!*

THE COMPASS PLANT (Pachypodium namaquanam) S. Africa, IS USED AS A GUIDE BY TRAVELERS BECAUSE IT ALWAYS *LEANS TOWARD THE NORTH*

COUNT von PAPPENHEIM (1594-1632) WAS ELECTED RECTOR OF THE UNIVERSITY OF ALTDORF Germany **AT THE AGE OF 14** HE LATER BECAME A FAMOUS GENERAL AND DIED OF HIS *101st BATTLE WOUND*

THE "FISH HOUSE," a private club in Philadelphia, Pa., FOUNDED AS "THE CASTLE OF THE STATE" IN 1732, *IS THE OLDEST ENGLISH-SPEAKING CLUB IN THE WORLD*

ADDING ALL THE DIVISORS OF **220**
$1+2+4+5+10+11+20+22+44+55+110$ EQUALS **284**
ADDING ALL THE DIVISORS OF **284**
$1+2+4+71+142$ EQUALS **220**
SUCH PAIRS OF FIGURES WERE CARRIED BY FRIENDS IN TIMES PAST IN THE BELIEF THAT IF EACH POSSESSED ONE OF THE FIGURES *THEY WOULD ALWAYS BE COMPATIBLE*

THE MAN WHOSE DEATH SENTENCE MADE HIM A SULTAN!

MUSTAPHA III (1717-1773) of Turkey
WAS ORDERED POISONED BY COMMAND OF SULTAN OSMAN
HIS OWN UNCLE!
WHEN MUSTAPHA FORCED THE SULTAN'S MESSENGER, THE COURT PHYSICIAN,
TO DRINK THE POTION HIMSELF, SULTAN OSMAN DIED OF FRIGHT
—AND MUSTAPHA *SUCCEEDED HIM ON THE THRONE*

THE 'PALACE' THAT WAS BUILT FOR ONE DAY

A MASONRY FACADE WITH INTRICATE
STAIRWAYS, ORNAMENTS AND GALLERIES
BUILT IN VENICE, ITALY, IN 1782, FOR A
VISIT BY PIUS VI – *AND DEMOLISHED
IMMEDIATELY AFTER HIS DEPARTURE*

A **1927 AUTOMOBILE**
owned by Whitney Miller
of Walla Walla, Wash.,
WHICH RECENTLY MADE
AN 8,000-MILE TRIP
*HAS ITS BODY ALMOST
COVERED WITH BUFFALO
NICKELS AND INDIAN-
HEAD PENNIES*

ANDREAS MULLER
(1630-1694)
GERMAN STUDENT OF
ORIENTAL CULTURE
WROTE POETRY IN
GREEK, LATIN AND HEBREW
AT THE AGE OF 16

THE **FIRST
U.S. EXPRESS
SERVICE**
founded in 1839
CONSISTED OF
DELIVERIES BY
CARPET BAG

A **FIG TREE**
on the slope of Mt. Etna,
near Catania, Italy,
*GROWING OUT OF
AN OLIVE TREE*

ROBERT GIBSON (1766-1885)
of College Mound, Missouri,
VOTED FOR **22** U.S. PRESIDENTS

GEORGE WASHINGTON	ZACHARY TAYLOR
JOHN ADAMS	MILLARD FILLMORE
THOMAS JEFFERSON	FRANKLIN PIERCE
JAMES MADISON	JAMES BUCHANAN
JAMES MONROE	ABRAHAM LINCOLN
JOHN QUINCY ADAMS	ANDREW JOHNSON
ANDREW JACKSON	ULYSSES S. GRANT
MARTIN VAN BUREN	RUTHERFORD HAYES
WILLIAM H. HARRISON	JAMES GARFIELD
JOHN TYLER	CHESTER ARTHUR
JAMES POLK	GROVER CLEVELAND

DENIS LE FEVRE (1488-1558)
BECAME A PROFESSOR OF GREEK AND LATIN AT THE University of Paris, France *AT THE AGE OF 16*

THE MOST CONCEITED DESPOT IN ALL HISTORY!

SULTAN MULEY ISMAEL (1646-1727) of Morocco, CONVINCED THAT ANYONE WOULD BE HONORED TO DIE AT HIS HANDS, ALWAYS EXPRESSED HIS THANKS TO THE SERVANT WHO HELD HIS STIRRUP *BY CUTTING OFF THE MAN'S HEAD!* THE MONARCH PERSONALLY SO KILLED 10,000 SERVANTS

2 WHITE PARROTS, BROUGHT TO INDIA BY EMPEROR TUGHLAK SHAH IN 1320, LIVED IN HIS PALACE AT FIROZABAD DURING THE ENTIRE PERIOD OF HIS DYNASTY *-A TOTAL OF 79 YEARS*

THE GRAVE In Wilmot, N.H., OF A BUCKSKIN HORSE NAMED "BROWNIE" WHICH PULLED A CHUCKWAGON IN THE CIVIL WAR *IS STILL DECORATED WITH AN AMERICAN FLAG EACH MEMORIAL DAY*

THE SEA ORANGE A MEDITERRANEAN SPONGE WRAPS ITSELF AROUND THE SHELL OF A HERMIT CRAB *-EXCHANGING SECURITY FOR TRANSPORTATION*

THE ICE FENCES OF THE HIMALAYAS FIELDS in the Himalaya Mountains, AS A RESULT OF HIGH WINDS WHIPPING THE ICE, OFTEN ARE SURROUNDED *BY SHARP PICKETS OF ICE 10 FEET HIGH*

THE GREEN TREE FROG *IS A VENTRILOQUIST* IT THROWS ITS VOICE SO PREDATORS CAN NEVER LOCATE IT BY ITS CROAKING

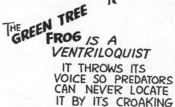

RED ROSE GROWING FROM THE CENTER OF A YELLOW ROSE Submitted by MRS. ANNE CHASE, So. San Gabriel, Calif.

Ripley's—® Believe It or Not!

THE **DÜRKHEIM CASK**
AN INN in Dürkheim, Germany,
IS BUILT IN THE SHAPE OF
A HUGE WINE BARREL
AND THE 2 LAMPPOSTS IN
FRONT RESEMBLE BOTTLES

THE **MOST REMARKABLE QUINTUPLETS IN HISTORY**
5 BROTHERS BORN TOGETHER IN LLANPUMPSAINT,
WALES, IN THE 10th CENTURY
EACH BECAME A SAINT
THE TOWN OF LLANPUMPSAINT (*MEANING THE CHURCH OF TI*
QUINTUPLET SAINTS) IS NAMED FOR THE CHURCH IN WHICH ST. GWY!
ST. CEITHO, ST. CELYMEN, ST. GWYNO AND ST. GWYNORO ARE INTERRE!

THE **MEMORIAL** TO THE
"DUNBAR"
A SAILING SHIP THAT
WENT DOWN NEAR
Sydney, Australia,
in 1857
WITH A LOSS
OF 121 MEN
**DISPLAYS THE
VESSEL'S OWN
ANCHOR**

A **RED CEDAR**
WITH ITS BRANCHES PASSING
*THROUGH THE TRUNK
OF A HICKORY TREE*
Submitted by Angelo Cots,
Shelton, Conn.

THE **BUMBLEBEE**
CONSIDERING
ITS SIZE, SHAPE
AND WINGSPAN, IS AN
AERODYNAMIC MISFIT—WHICH
SHOULD BE UNABLE TO FLY

THE **PRUNING
KNIFE
FISH**
(*Zanclus*)
of New Guinea,
HAS A
WHIP-LIKE
APPENDAGE
ON ITS
DORSAL FIN
**3 TIMES
AS LONG
AS ITS
BODY**

PIETRO ZUCCHI
(1602 - 1670)
of Parma, Italy,
WAS THE FATHER
OF 7 CHILDREN—
**A PRIEST,
3 MONKS
AND 3 NUNS**

Ripley's Believe It or Not!

THE LARGEST MOTHS IN THE WORLD

THE HERCULES, A GIANT MOTH of NEW GUINEA, MEASURES 14 INCHES FROM WING TIP TO WING TIP. IT LIVES ONLY 14 DAYS AND TAKES NO NOURISHMENT DURING ITS BRIEF LIFE SPAN

WAFER MONEY
BRACTEATES, GOLD AND SILVER COINS ISSUED IN 12th-CENTURY EUROPE WERE SO THIN THAT A DOZEN PILED ONE ATOP ANOTHER COULD BE CURLED TOGETHER BY A PINCH OF THE FINGERS FOR CONVENIENCE IN CARRYING THEM

COWS DURING THE JANUARY HARVEST FESTIVAL IN MYSORE, India, ARE PURIFIED BY DRIVING THEM THROUGH A BLAZING FIRE!

PHARAOH RAMSES II
WHO RULED EGYPT FOR 77 YEARS, WAS THE FATHER OF 119 CHILDREN - **60 BOYS AND 59 GIRLS** HE HAD A LIKENESS OF EACH OF THEM CARVED ON THE FRONT WALL OF THE TEMPLE OF ABYDOS

A **BABY RATTLE**
ONCE OWNED BY KING FAROUK, of Egypt HAS A JADE HANDLE TOPPED BY A CROWN ENCRUSTED WITH DIAMONDS -AND THE "PEBBLES" THAT RATTLE INSIDE IT ARE RUBIES

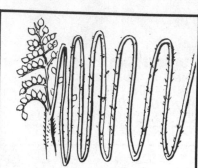

THE CLIMBING PALM
(Calamus wightii)
HAS A THREADLIKE STEM SO LONG THAT WHEN IT IS CONFINED IN A LIMITED SPACE IT GROWS IN FOLDS

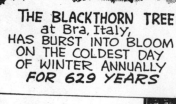

THE BLACKTHORN TREE
at Bra, Italy, HAS BURST INTO BLOOM ON THE COLDEST DAY OF WINTER ANNUALLY **FOR 629 YEARS**

BARON GUSTAF de HELMFELT
(1651-1674) of Sweden
HAD MASTERED THE 9 PRINCIPAL LANGUAGES OF EUROPE, AS WELL AS GREEK, LATIN AND HEBREW, AT THE AGE OF 10- HE BECAME A SUPREME COURT JUSTICE IN SWEDEN AT 19

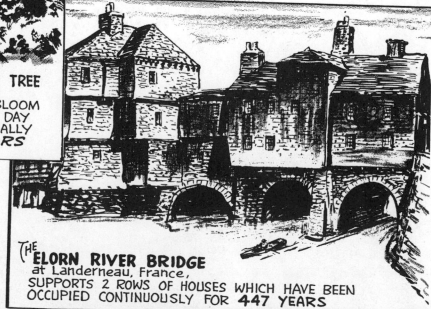

THE **ELORN RIVER BRIDGE**
at Landerneau, France, SUPPORTS 2 ROWS OF HOUSES WHICH HAVE BEEN OCCUPIED CONTINUOUSLY FOR **447 YEARS**

MONARCH WHO RULED IN CHAINS!

CALIPH DHAHER (1172-1226) of Baghdad, WHO HAD BEEN IMPRISONED BY HIS FATHER FOR 19 YEARS BEFORE HE INHERITED THE CROWN, HAD BECOME SO ACCUSTOMED TO HIS CHAINS *THAT HE DONNED THEM FROM TIME TO TIME ON THE THRONE!*

A PAWN THAT CAST A SHADOW RESEMBLING THE PROFILE OF KING LOUIS XVI OF France, WAS THE SECRET CHESS PIECE THAT IDENTIFIED ITS OWNER DURING THE FRENCH REVOLUTION *AS FAVORING THE RESTORATION OF THE BOURBON DYNASTY*

THE ROYAL CAMBRIAN ACADEMY OF ART

IN CONWAY, WALES, BUILT IN 1585, HAS **365** WINDOWS –ONE FOR EACH DAY OF THE YEAR –**52** DOORS– ONE FOR EACH WEEK IN THE YEAR–AND **52** STEPS LEADING TO ITS TOWER

THE CHILDREN WHO DANCE BAREFOOTED ON FIRE!

THE SANGHYANG, A RITUAL PERFORMED BY CHILDREN ON THE ISLAND OF BALI, REQUIRES THEM TO DANCE WITHOUT SHOES, ON **GLOWING EMBERS!** THEY ARE PUT INTO A TRANCE DURING WHICH THEY FEEL NO PAIN, AND SUSTAIN NO INJURY

THE MOST EXPENSIVE CREMATION IN ALL HISTORY! (Babylon)

HEPHESTION, THE DEAREST FRIEND OF ALEXANDER THE GREAT, WAS CREMATED IN 323 B.C. ON A PYRE ON WHICH THE MONARCH PILED *GOLD INGOTS, PRECIOUS JEWELS, IVORY, RARE SPICES AND FABRICS VALUED AT $12,000,000*

THE MAN WHO BORE A CHARMED LIFE!

FRANK TOWER AN OILER,
SWAM AWAY FROM 3 MAJOR SEA DISASTERS
- THE TITANIC, IN 1912
THE EMPRESS OF IRELAND, IN 1914
AND THE LUSITANIA IN 1915
Submitted by RICHARD E. BROWN, Bakersfield, Calif.

THE GREAT TOWER

of the Castle of Chateaubriant, France,
WHICH HAS WALLS 13 FEET THICK,
HAS NO FOUNDATION AND MERELY
RESTS ON SMOOTH ROCK - YET
IT HAS ENDURED FOR 953 YEARS

THE PARROT THAT REALLY WAS A STOOL PIGEON!

A FRENCH DETECTIVE, INVESTIGATING THE MURDER IN LYONS
OF A WIDOW NAMED ANNETTE ROQUES, WHO OFTEN GAVE MEALS TO
JOBLESS SAILORS, HAD ONLY ONE CLUE - THE DISCOVERY, NEAR
THE BODY, OF A FLUTE THAT HAD A DEFECTIVE G NOTE.
A YEAR LATER THE DETECTIVE ARRESTED A SAILOR CARRYING
A PARROT WHICH IMITATED THE SOUND OF A FLUTE WITH
A FLAT G - THE SAILOR CONFESSED TO THE MURDER AND
WAS SENTENCED TO LIFE IMPRISONMENT (1922-1923)

Ripley's Believe It or Not!

THE STRONGEST PITCHING ARM IN HISTORY!
ADOLPH von LUETZOW of Mecklenburg, Germany, FAMED 18th-CENTURY WEIGHT LIFTER —COULD HURL SILVER COINS THE SIZE OF A SILVER DOLLAR AT AN OAK TREE FROM A DISTANCE OF 20 FEET *WITH SUCH FORCE THEY HAD TO BE PRIED OUT WITH A CHISEL!*

THE ELUSIVE WATERFALL
LOCH CON WATERFALL in Scotland IS 1,000 FEET HIGH, YET FEW PEOPLE HAVE SEEN IT BECAUSE IT FALLS FOR LESS THAN 30 MINUTES AT A TIME *AND ONLY AFTER A VERY HEAVY RAIN*

THE FORCEPS USED BY DENTISTS IN INDIA 2,500 YEARS AGO *WERE SHAPED LIKE BIRDS*

THE CHURCH OF RENAISON in France, WHILE CROWDED WITH 200 WORSHIPERS, WAS SET AFIRE BY A BOLT OF LIGHTNING AND DESTROYED —YET ALTHOUGH EVERY PERSON IN THE CHURCH WAS INJURED, NOT A SINGLE PARISHIONER WAS KILLED AND ALL 200 RECOVERED AND WERE DISCHARGED FROM THE HOSPITAL 2 MONTHS LATER ON THE SAME DAY (June, 1760)

THE OLDEST CARPET IN THE WORLD
A CARPET, found in an ancient burial mound in Pazyryk, Siberia, WAS IN PERFECT CONDITION BECAUSE IT HAD BEEN COATED WITH ICE FOR 2,400 YEARS

THE STRANGEST LEASE IN ALL HISTORY!
THE ANNUAL RENTAL of the Castle of Keralio, in France, FOR A PERIOD OF 350 YEARS PRIOR TO 1789, CONSISTED OF A SINGLE EGG— BUT IT HAD TO BE TRANSPORTED TO THE NEIGHBORING CASTLE OF SEREAC IN A CART PULLED BY 4 OXEN AND THEN DELIVERED INTO THE LANDLORD'S HAND FROM A LITTER CARRIED ON THE BACKS OF 4 MEN

Ripley's Believe It or Not!

THE DOG THAT SAVED 92 LIVES!

THE S.S. ETHIE, A COASTAL STEAMER OF 414 TONS, AGROUND ON MARTIN'S POINT OFF CURLING, NEWFOUNDLAND, AND BREAKING UP IN A VIOLENT STORM AND HEAVY SEAS, WAS UNABLE TO FIRE A LIFELINE OR LAUNCH ITS BOATS, AND *NO MEMBER OF THE CREW DARED ATTEMPT TO SWIM ASHORE*

A NEWFOUNDLAND DOG MADE THE SWIM WITH A LIFELINE GRIPPED IN ITS TEETH AND ALL 92 PASSENGERS AND CREW MEMBERS WERE PULLED TO SAFETY ON A BOATSWAIN'S CHAIR (Dec. 10, 1919)

THE SOVIET LEGATION
in Helsinki WAS HIT BY THE FIRST BOMB DROPPED BY SOVIET AIRCRAFT WHEN THEY ATTACKED FINLAND ON NOV. 30, 1939

A FEMALE MAGPIE WHOSE MATE HAS DIED IS COURTED IMMEDIATELY BY OTHER MALES *WHO ASSEMBLE PROMPTLY NEAR THE BODY OF THE DEAD MAGPIE*

THE "KISSING" SYCAMORES
in Fife, Scotland

PINGUICALA VULGARIS CATCHES INSECTS BY IMPRISONING THEM *WITH ITS LEAVES*

SUSUMU HORI,
of New York City, IN A SINGLE ROUND OF GOLF AT THE RIVER VALE COUNTRY CLUB, New Jersey, **MADE 2 HOLE-IN-ONES** 8th AND 17th HOLES August 2, 1964

RAILWAY CARS ON THE FIRST RAIL LINE from Paris to Orleans, France, WERE LIFTED FROM THE AXLES AT THE SOUTHERN TERMINUS AND, WITH THEIR PASSENGERS STILL IN PLACE, WERE PLACED ON THE UNDERCARRIAGE OF A STAGECOACH SO THE FINAL JOURNEY *COULD BE COMPLETED ON HIGHWAYS* (1843)

ONEY WITH A HEART

FRENCH COINS IN
Martinique ONCE WERE
UNCHED THROUGH THE CENTER
THE SHAPE OF A HEART
E TINY HEART STAMPED
T OF EACH COIN WAS
ED AS SMALL CHANGE

THE SACRED IBIS

WAS WORSHIPED
AND PROTECTED IN
ANCIENT EGYPT AS
THE MESSENGER OF
THE GOD OSIRIS
-YET IT IS NOW EXTINCT

THE SCALP

OF A RED-HEADED
WOODPECKER WAS
USED BY THE KAROK
INDIANS OF THE
KLAMATH RIVER DISTRICT
of Northern Calif.
AS MONEY

T. REUBEN RUSSELL

f Edinburg, Ohio,
SKED BY ANDREW B.
ADER FOR THE HAND
F HIS DAUGHTER,
NN, INSISTED THAT
THE YOUNG MAN
FIRST DEMONSTRATE
HIS CHARACTER BY
ACCOMPANYING HIM ON
WHALING TRIP THAT
STED 54 MONTHS
ANOTHER 3 YEARS
PASSED BEFORE THE
CAPTAIN FINALLY
GAVE THE COUPLE
HIS BLESSING

THE STRANGEST SERIES OF DUELS IN HISTORY!

HENRI TRAGNE of Marseilles, France,
FOUGHT 5 DUELS
IN THE FIRST 4 EACH OF HIS OPPONENTS FELL DEAD
BEFORE A SINGLE SHOT WAS FIRED – AND IN THE 5th
TRAGNE HIMSELF WAS FATALLY STRICKEN
IN THE SAME MANNER (1861-1878)

ST. JOHN'S WORT

a weed in
the Hebrides
IS
CONSIDERED
A POWERFUL
REMEDY
AGAINST THE
EVIL EYE

THE STRANGEST VERDICT IN ALL HISTORY!

CONSUL CALPURNIUS PISO of Rome
SENTENCED A ROMAN SOLDIER TO
DEATH FOR THE MURDER OF A COMRADE
-BUT THE EXECUTION WAS HALTED WHEN
THE SUPPOSED VICTIM REAPPEARED
ALIVE AND UNHARMED!
PISO THEN SENT THE 2 SOLDIERS
AND THE EXECUTIONER TO THEIR DEATH
- ONE SOLDIER BECAUSE HE WAS
DOOMED BY THE ORIGINAL
SENTENCE, THE SECOND BECAUSE
HE WAS RESPONSIBLE FOR HIS
COMRADE'S DEATH, AND THE
EXECUTIONER FOR FAILING TO
CARRY OUT AN ORDER! (7 B.C.)

The LARGEST ANTIQUE VASE EVER FOUND was excavated near Vix, France, in 1929 – A GREEN BRONZE JAR WEIGHING 460 POUNDS AND MEASURING 5' IN HEIGHT AND 5½' IN WIDTH IT HAD BEEN BURIED FOR 2,600 YEARS

THE WEAPON THAT WAS GUEST OF HONOR AT NEARLY 230,000 BANQUETS!

THE BATTLE-AXE WIELDED BY WELSH KNIGHT SIR HYWEL OF THE AXE WAS SO DEVASTATING TO THE ENEMY IN THE BATTLE OF POITIERS IN 1356 THAT HIS ENGLISH COMMANDER, THE BLACK PRINCE, ORDERED THAT 8 YEOMEN PAID BY THE CROWN MUST SERVE SUMPTUOUS MEALS TO THE WEAPON 3 TIMES EACH DAY FOREVER AFTER!

FOR 210 YEARS THE FOOD WAS PLACED BEFORE THE AXE EVERY DAY IN THE CASTLE OF CRICCIETH, WALES – AND THEN GIVEN TO THE POOR

THE MAN WHOSE HAIR TURNED WHITE INSTANTLY!

Duke Ludwig II (1228-1294) of Bavaria, WHO HAD HIS WIFE EXECUTED FOR INFIDELITY, WAS ONLY 28 YEARS OF AGE

YET WHEN HE DISCOVERED PROOF THAT SHE HAD BEEN INNOCENT, HIS HAIR TURNED COMPLETELY WHITE WITHIN A FEW MOMENTS! FOR THE NEXT 38 YEARS HE VAINLY SOUGHT DEATH IN A HUNDRED BATTLES

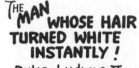

THE CHURCH OF MÖGGERS in Austria

WAS BUILT BESIDE AN ANCIENT ROMAN WATCH TOWER SO IT COULD USE THE 1,100-YEAR-OLD LOOKOUT POST AS ITS BELFRY

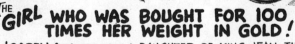

THE GIRL WHO WAS BOUGHT FOR 100 TIMES HER WEIGHT IN GOLD!

ISABELLA (1348-1372) DAUGHTER OF KING JEAN THE GOOD, OF FRANCE, AS A MEANS OF RAISING THE RANSOM NEEDED TO FREE HER FATHER FROM THE ENGLISH, WAS SOLD BY THE KING AT THE AGE OF 12 TO DUKE GALEAZZO II, RULER OF MILAN, FOR $1,452,000

THE GIRL, WHO BECAME THE BRIDE OF THE DUKE'S YOUNG SON, WEIGHED 78 POUNDS – AND THE PRICE PAID WAS 7,800 POUNDS OF GOLDEN FLORINS

THE OLDEST LATIN INSCRIPTION

WRITTEN IN THE ALPHABET ON WHICH OURS IS BASED – CARVED ON A CLASP 2,600 YEARS AGO

IN THOSE DAYS LATIN WAS WRITTEN FROM RIGHT TO LEFT

Believe It or Not!

THE HOODOO ENGINE

ENGINE 37 of the Central Railway of Peru HAD ITS NUMBER CHANGED TO 33 IN AN ATTEMPT TO IMPROVE ITS LUCK AFTER IT **HAD BEEN DERAILED 5 TIMES** THEN, PULLING A WORK TRAIN OVER CHAUPICHACA GORGE, IT COLLIDED WITH A CRANE-**CAUSING THE ENTIRE BRIDGE TO COLLAPSE INTO THE RIVER FAR BELOW**

A **REPLICA** OF THE ROUEN CATHEDRAL, France,

WITH EVEN ITS INTERIOR FURNISHINGS AND LIGHTING FAITHFULLY REPRODUCED Constructed by Lucien Dussaussay

THE NEWEST ALPHABET
A COMPLETE ALPHABET AND A SET OF NUMERALS WERE COMPILED BY KISIMI KAMARA IN 1936 FOR THE MENDE TRIBE, of Sierra Leone, Africa -WHICH PREVIOUSLY HAD NO WRITTEN LANGUAGE

PIERRE MOUCHON (1733-1797) of Geneva, Switzerland, MEMORIZED THE ENTIRE FRENCH ENCYCLOPEDIA - 17 VOLUMES COMPRISING 18,000,000 WORDS

Sultan **YKSHID** of Egypt WAS SO FEARFUL OF ASSASSINATION THAT HE SLEPT PART OF EACH NIGHT IN 3 DIFFERENT HOUSES OR TENTS FOR THE LAST 45 YEARS OF HIS LIFE— HE NEVER SLUMBERED MORE THAN 3 HOURS IN ONE PLACE - AND NEVER REVEALED HIS NOCTURNAL DESTINATIONS

THE "PALACE" DESIGNED BY A DREAM
PALAIS IDEAL, Hauterive, France, A STRUCTURE OF ROCKS AND CONCRETE, WAS BUILT BY FERDINAND CHEVAL, A RURAL LETTER CARRIER, IN HIS SPARE TIME AND WITHOUT ASSISTANCE **EXACTLY AS HE SAW IT IN A DREAM** HE LABORED FOR 33 YEARS AFTER COMPLETING HIS DAILY 20-MILE ROUNDS AS A POSTMAN

A **NESTING ROBIN** IS DEPICTED ON A COLUMN OF THE CHURCH OF CHRIST, IN Victoria, B.C., TO COMMEMORATE A PAIR OF ACTUAL ROBINS THAT NESTED THERE WHILE THE STRUCTURE WAS BEING BUILT -THE FIRST LIVING THINGS TO SEEK SANCTUARY IN THE CATHEDRAL

"Sandy" A RED HEN LAYS GREEN EGGS Owned by W.Y. STEWART, Lake Wales, Fla.

Ripley's Believe It or Not!

MELLIA TESSELLATA
A CRAB DEFENDS ITSELF BY CARRYING IN EACH CLAW A *RED SEA ANEMONE* THAT PACKS A PAINFUL STING

THE **BAY SCALLOP**
HAS ON ITS SHELL A ROW OF BLUE EYES THAT ARE SENSITIVE TO LIGHT

THE MALAY APPLE
WHICH HAS RED FLOWERS GROWING DIRECTLY FROM ITS STEM *IS THE ONLY HAWAIIAN FRUIT THAT WAS NOT INTRODUCED TO THE ISLANDS BY EUROPEANS*

THE **SOLVERENUS**
A FISH THAT HAS *HAIR INSTEAD OF SCALES*

THE **ARCH OF TRAJAN**
IN ANCONA, ITALY, WAS BUILT WITHOUT MORTAR OF ANY KIND —YET IT HAS ENDURED FOR NEARLY *1,900 YEARS*

THE **GILDED KEYS**
GIVEN TO NAPOLEON I UPON HIS ARRIVAL AT ELBA TO SYMBOLIZE THE KEYS TO THE CITY OF PORTOFERRAIO, *ACTUALLY WERE THE KEYS TO THE LOCAL TAVERN* 1814

THE**MOST** **ASTOUNDING FEAT OF SEAMANSHIP IN HISTORY!**
HENRY BLOGG, COXSWAIN OF A BOAT AT NORFOLK, ENGLAND, UNABLE TO PULL ALONGSIDE THE FOUNDERING S.S. OXSHOTT, BREAKING UP IN HEAVY SEAS WITH 16 SAILORS LASHED TO ITS FUNNEL, *CAREFULLY GAUGED A MONSTROUS WAVE AND RODE IT ONTO THE DECK OF THE GROUNDED FREIGHTER!*
THEN WITH THE OXSHOTT'S CREW ABOARD HIS LIFEBOAT *BLOGG USED ANOTHER WAVE TO WASH HIS CRAFT BACK INTO THE SEA – WITHOUT LOSS OF A SINGLE LIFE* (Aug. 5, 1941)

THE OXARÁ WATERFALL
IN Iceland
WAS CREATED ARTIFICIALLY 1,030 YEARS AGO *TO SERVE AS BACKDROP FOR A MEETING OF THE ISLAND'S PARLIAMENT*

A **PETITION** IN PICTURE WRITING
FORWARDED TO THE U.S. GOVERNMENT BY 7 INDIAN TRIBES – REQUESTING OWNERSHIP OF 4 SMALL LAKES, (IN lower left corner) THE WATERS OF WHICH FLOW INTO LAKE SUPERIOR

THE "BANDAGE" THAT PROVED TO BE A STRANGE PROPHECY!

LYSIMACHUS (356-282 B.C.) A GENERAL SERVING ALEXANDER THE GREAT, WAS WOUNDED IN THE HEAD BY AN ARROW, AND KING ALEXANDER STANCHED THE FLOW OF BLOOD BY **PLACING HIS CROWN ON THE HEAD OF LYSIMACHUS!**

AFTER ALEXANDER'S DEATH LYSIMACHUS BECAME KING AND RULED THRACE FOR 28 YEARS

EMPEROR HADRIAN
(76-138) of Rome
COULD WRITE, DICTATE AND ENGAGE IN A CONVERSATION **ALL AT THE SAME TIME**

HE COULD GIVE THE NAME, RANK, AGE AND PLACE OF RESIDENCE OF EVERY PENSIONER IN THE ENTIRE EMPIRE

THE STRANGE EXODUS FROM A CITY THAT WAS CONDEMNED TO DEATH !

Delhi, now the capital of India, BECAUSE ONE OF ITS INHABITANTS HAD SENT EMPEROR MOHAMMED TOUGHLAQ AN ANONYMOUS LETTER OF COMPLAINT, WAS ORDERED ABANDONED BY EVERY LIVING SOUL— ITS 60,000 MEN, WOMEN AND CHILDREN WERE FORCED TO WALK 600 MILES TO THE NEW CAPITAL CITY OF DAULATABAD –A MARCH THAT LASTED 40 DAYS AND CAUSED THE DEATH OF HUNDREDS FROM STARVATION AND FATIGUE

1339

THE LARGEST POSTAGE STAMP
A 25-CENT STAMP ISSUED IN THE U.S. IN SEPTEMBER, 1865, 3.6 INCHES LONG AND 2 INCHES WIDE

COUNT ALEKSANDR KONSTANTINOVICH BENCKENDORFF
(1849-1917)
RUSSIAN AMBASSADOR IN LONDON FROM 1903 TO 1917

COULD NOT SPEAK, READ OR WRITE RUSSIAN

THE HOLY GRAIL

AN AGATE CHALICE DISPLAYED IN THE CATHEDRAL OF VALENCIA, SPAIN, SINCE 1437, IS BELIEVED TO BE THE ONE USED BY CHRIST DURING THE LAST SUPPER

THE COLLEGE THAT WAS BUILT OF JELLYFISH

Wolsey's College of Ipswich, England, WAS CONSTRUCTED OF LIMESTONE NODULES CALLED SEPTARIA —WHICH ARE THE REMAINS OF FOSSILIZED JELLYFISH

ELECTRIC LIGHT BULB

USED REGULARLY FOR 39 YEARS

Owned by Mrs. Marcus Curle, Campbellford, Ont.

THE MOST POWERFUL POTENTATE IN ALL HISTORY!

CALIPH ALI IBN ABI TALIB (602-661) HAVING LOST HIS SHIELD WHILE LEADING THE ARABS IN THE BATTLE OF KHAIBAR, IN ARABIA IN WRENCHED THE HUGE GATE OF THE FORTRESS FROM ITS HINGES **AND CARRIED THE 850-LB. DOOR AS A SHIELD!**

AFTER THE CALIPH'S VICTORY, SEVEN OF HIS STRONGEST FOLLOWERS EACH ATTEMPTED TO LIFT THE GATE — AND FAILED

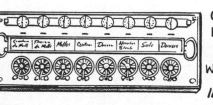

THE FIRST CALCULATING MACHINE

BLAISE PASCAL, THE CELEBRATED FRENCH MATHEMATICIAN, WHILE WORKING AS A BOOKKEEPER AT THE AGE OF 19, INVENTED A CALCULATING MACHINE IN 1642

Antonio PIGAFETTA (1491-1534)

IN A PILGRIMAGE OF THANKSGIVING FOR BEING ONE OF THE FEW SURVIVORS OF MAGELLAN'S CIRCUMNAVIGATION OF THE EARTH, CLAD ONLY IN A NIGHTSHIRT AND CARRYING A LIGHTED CANDLE, WALKED FROM LISBON, PORTUGAL TO SEVILLE, SPAIN —A DISTANCE OF 200 MILES

HE PLACED THE CANDLE ON THE ALTAR IN THE CATHEDRAL OF SEVILLE (1522)

THE FIRST SHOCK THERAPY

THE SNAKE HOUSE of ancient Epidaurus, Greece, WAS VISITED BY MENTAL CASES WHOSE PHYSICIANS FELT THE SIGHTS THERE COULD CURE BY THE POWER OF SHOCK

Ripley's Believe It or Not!

THE FISH THAT WORE A COLLAR
A STEELHEAD caught by Virgil Franceschi in the Eel River, Mendocino County, Calif., WAS WEARING A RED RUBBER BAND THAT HAD BECOME IMBEDDED IN ITS GILLS

THE DAY THE FATE OF THE WORLD WAS DECIDED BY FISH!
THE NAVAL BATTLE OF ACTIUM, IN WHICH MARC ANTONY AND CLEOPATRA LOST THEIR BID FOR MASTERY OF THE ROMAN EMPIRE, WAS WON BY GAIUS OCTAVIANUS BECAUSE ANTONY'S FORCES WERE THROWN INTO CONFUSION WHEN THEIR LEADER WAS FORCED TO ABANDON HIS FLAGSHIP -RENDERED INOPERABLE BY A HUGE MASS OF SUCKER FISH THAT HAD BECOME ATTACHED TO ITS KEEL!

PRIMEVAL CORN
FROM WHICH OUR PRESENT CORN IS DESCENDED HAD EVERY KERNEL ENCASED IN ITS OWN CAPSULE

IT IS STILL CULTIVATED IN BOLIVIA -WHERE IT IS BELIEVED TO HAVE MAGIC MEDICINAL PROPERTIES

THE MYSTERIOUS VANISHING LAKE OF AMRAOTI, India
BAIRAM GHAT
IS ALTERNATELY FILLED WITH WATER FOR ONE YEAR -AND DRY FOR EXACTLY 2 YEARS

THE MAN WHO WAS KILLED BY A METEORITE!
MANFREDO SETTALA (1600-1680) famed Italian physicist WAS THE FIRST PERSON IN ALL HISTORY FATALLY INJURED BY AN AEROLITE!

THE CLOCK of KING LOUIS XIV in the Monarch's Chamber at Versailles STOPPED AT 8:15 A.M. ON SEPT. 1, 1715 THE MOMENT OF HIS DEATH - AND HAS NEVER RUN AGAIN

TORSO ROCK
NATURAL STONE FORMATION (Canada)

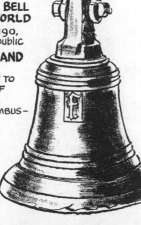

THE FIRST CHURCH BELL IN THE NEW WORLD Santo Domingo, Dominican Republic
KING FERDINAND of Spain PRESENTED IT TO THE COLONY OF ISABELLA -FOUNDED BY COLUMBUS- IN 1493

IT WAS BURIED BY AN EARTHQUAKE FOR 300 YEARS

Ripley's — Believe It or Not!

PETRARCH'S TOMB in Arqua, Italy, WHEN IT WAS OPENED IN 1883 WAS FOUND TO HAVE BEEN INVADED BY A SWARM OF BEES WHICH HAD PENETRATED INTO THE FAMED POET'S COFFIN AND BUILT A HONEYCOMB **DIRECTLY OVER HIS HEART**

THE **WHITE GOBY** (Aphya Pellucida) HAS THE SHORTEST LIFE SPAN OF ANY VERTEBRATE
IT IS SPAWNED IN JULY, HATCHES IN AUGUST, AND ALWAYS DIES THE FOLLOWING JULY

THE **OAK LEAF INSECT** LOOKS AMAZINGLY LIKE THE SCALLOPED LEAF OF THE OAK TREE -AND *EACH AUTUMN ITS COLOR BROWNS AT THE SAME TIME AS THE LEAVES*

THE **FISH** THAT KEPT 900 SENATORS DEBATING ALL NIGHT
EMPEROR DOMITIAN of Rome
HAVING RECEIVED A HUGE TURBOT AS A GIFT CONVENED THE ENTIRE SENATE IN AN EMERGENCY NIGHT SESSION *TO DECIDE HOW IT SHOULD BE COOKED!*
AFTER HOURS OF DEBATE OVER WHETHER THE FISH SHOULD BE CUT UP TO FIT IN EXISTING VESSELS - THE SENATORS VOTED TO ORDER A NEW POT LARGE ENOUGH TO HOLD IT

THE **CENTERPIECE** OF EVERY BANQUET PREPARED BY CAREME, THE GREAT FRENCH CHEF,
WAS A CAKE SHAPED LIKE A ROMAN RUIN

THE SWIMMERS WHO WERE SAVED FROM DROWNING BY A WHALE
2 MAORI WOMEN, THE ONLY SURVIVORS WHEN A CANOE SANK IN COOK STRAIT, NEW ZEALAND, WERE SAVED WHEN THEY FOUND FLOATING IN THE WATER **THE CARCASS OF A WHALE**
A HARPOON WAS IMBEDDED IN THE WHALE, AND THE WOMEN PULLED THEMSELVES ABOARD THE CARCASS BY A LINE TRAILING FROM THE WEAPON *--AND FLOATED MORE THAN 80 MILES TO SAFETY* (1834)

THE WOODPECKER FINCH

OF THE GALAPAGOS ISLANDS IN THE PACIFIC, HAS DEVELOPED THE LONG BILL OF A WOODPECKER--BUT BECAUSE IT DOES NOT HAVE THE WOODPECKER'S LONG TONGUE, IT PRIES INSECTS OUT OF TREE CREVICES WITH A TWIG

THE MISTLETOE BIRD of Australia

FEEDS ITS YOUNG WHILE *HANGING UPSIDE DOWN*

THE CALOPOGON ORCHID

DUMPS TO THE GROUND ANY INSECT THAT ALIGHTS ON IT *THEN SPILLS ITS POLLEN ON THE INSECT'S BACK*

THE MOUNTAIN OF THE MONKS

near Kayseri, Turkey
60 CHURCHES - MONASTERIES AND CHAPELS HAVE BEEN DUG OUT OF ITS ROCKS AND *WERE USED BY REFUGEE CHRISTIAN MONKS FOR 300 YEARS*

A GRAVESTONE

in the Holy Land BEARING THE NAME JESUS *-AS IT WAS WRITTEN WHEN THE SAVIOUR LIVED*

THE CHIPMUNK

CAN EAT THE DEADLY POISONOUS AMANITA MUSHROOM - KNOWN AS THE DEATHCUP- WITHOUT SUFFERING ILL EFFECTS

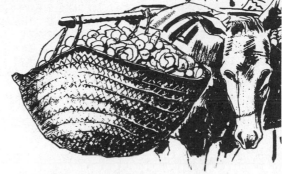

SULTAN IBN AMI AMRAN of Tripoli

TO WIN FAVOR AMONG HIS PEOPLE AS A HUMBLE MONARCH *PEDDLED FRUIT AND VEGETABLES THROUGHOUT HIS KINGDOM FOR 20 YEARS* (1349-1369)

THE CHATEAU OF LASSAY in France

WAS BUILT BY ARMAND de MADAILLAN AS A WEDDING PRESENT FOR HIS BRIDE *IN 35 DAYS* (1676)

FLUTES

THE MOST POPULAR MUSICAL INSTRUMENT OF THE MAORIS, OF NEW ZEALAND, *WERE MADE FROM THE WINGBONES OF THE ALBATROSS*

FERDINAND RAIMUND

(1790-1836) FAMED AUSTRIAN ACTOR AND PLAYWRIGHT COMMITTED SUICIDE BY SHOOTING HIMSELF WHEN HE BECAME PANIC-STRICKEN AFTER *BEING BITTEN ON THE FINGER BY A SMALL DOG*

THE CHURCH THAT STOOD BUT A MINUTE!

OWING TO A FAULTY CORNERSTONE THE CHURCH OF ST. JOHN in Barmouth, Wales, *CRASHED IN RUINS A MINUTE AFTER IT WAS FINISHED* IT WAS REBUILT AND THE NEW EDIFICE HAS ENDURED TO THE PRESENT DAY

THE STRANGEST INHERITANCE IN ALL HISTORY

ROBERT FALLON of NORTHUMBERLAND, ENGLAND, AFTER WINNING $600 IN A POKER GAME IN SAN FRANCISCO'S BELLA UNION SALOON, *WAS ACCUSED OF CHEATING AND SHOT DEAD!*

CONSIDERING MONEY WON BY CHEATING TO BE UNLUCKY, THE OTHER PLAYERS CALLED IN THE FIRST PASSERBY TO SIT IN FOR THE DEAD MAN -- CONFIDENT THE YOUTH WOULD SOON LOSE THE $600.

THE STRANGER HAD INCREASED THE SUM TO $2,200 BY THE TIME THE POLICE ARRIVED, AND WHEN THEY DEMANDED THE ORIGINAL $600 FOR THE DEAD MAN'S NEXT OF KIN *THE YOUTH PROVED HE WAS THE UNLUCKY GAMBLER'S SON -- WHO HAD NOT SEEN HIS FATHER FOR 7 YEARS* (1858)

MONUMENT TO A COW

THIS MONUMENT, ERECTED BY THE BUTCHERS OF TOKYO IN 1931, MARKS THE SPOT ON WHICH THE FIRST COW IN JAPAN WAS SLAUGHTERED IN 1858 FOR HUMAN CONSUMPTION Temple Yard, Shimoda

A TORTOISE

STILL ALIVE IN THE GARDEN OF THE QUEEN'S PALACE, AT NUKU'ALOFA, IN THE TONGA ISLANDS, WAS A GIFT FROM CAPTAIN COOK -- *WHO LEFT IT THERE 193 YEARS AGO*

THE OLDEST DOORKNOCKER IN THE WORLD!

A BRONZE HEAD OF DIANA NOW A DOORKNOCKER AT 12 Portman Street, London, WAS ORIGINALLY USED IN THE DOOMED CITY OF POMPEII WHERE IT HAD BEEN BURIED FOR NEARLY 1900 YEARS

THE PINE SLASH BEETLE

HAS FROM 3 TO 8 MATES AND BUILDS *SEPARATE NESTS FOR EACH OF HIS FAMILIES* THE MALES ARE POLYGAMISTS BECAUSE THEY DIE YOUNG -WEARING THEMSELVES OUT DIGGING HOMES- WHICH RESULTS IN AN OVERSUPPLY OF FEMALES

STAR-SHAPED SAND DUNES

FORMED IN THE SAHARA DESERT BY CONFLICTING WINDS

THE STRANGEST FAMILY TREE IN ALL HISTORY

DOMINIQUE DOMINIQUE, a French farmer IN 1911 MARRIED IN MARSEILLE A WAITRESS NAMED **DOMINIQUE DOMINIQUE**

HIS FATHER AND GRANDFATHER ALSO WERE OLDEST SONS NAMED DOMINIQUE DOMINIQUE AND MARRIED WAITRESSES NAMED DOMINIQUE DOMINIQUE- YET NONE OF THE GIRLS HAD PREVIOUSLY BEEN RELATED

Ripley's — "Believe It or Not!"

FRANCOIS FOUQUET (1587-1640) of France, WAS THE FATHER OF A PRIEST, 2 BISHOPS AND 6 NUNS

The **FIRST METAL-LINED BATHTUB** WAS CONSTRUCTED BY ADAM THOMPSON OF CINCINNATI, OHIO, IN 1840, AND WEIGHED *NEARLY A TON*

PRINCESS JACUBA (1401-1436) OF HAINAUT, BELGIUM, WAS MARRIED TO JEAN, SON OF KING CHARLES VI, of France, *WHEN SHE WAS 5 YEARS OF AGE—* SHE ONLY LIVED TO BE 35, BUT SHE HAD A TOTAL OF **4 HUSBANDS**

A **PERSON** STANDING UNDER AN OAK TREE IS 60 TIMES MORE LIABLE TO BE HIT BY LIGHTNING THAN IF HE HAD TAKEN REFUGE FROM A STORM BENEATH A BEECH TREE *THE OAK TREE HAS VERTICAL ROOTS WHICH PROVIDE A MORE DIRECT ROUTE TO GROUND WATER*

The **CACTUS WREN** STATE BIRD OF ARIZONA, HAS A "SONG" THAT SOUNDS LIKE A TIN BUCKET ROLLING DOWN A HILL

THE **MYRIANID WORM** MULTIPLIES *BY DIVISION* IT BREAKS IN HALF AND THE BACK SECTION IMMEDIATELY GROWS A NEW HEAD

THE **WATER-BUG FROG** of Australia SURVIVES DROUGHTS OF AS LONG AS **18** MONTHS BY ABSORBING SO MUCH WATER DURING RAINY SEASONS THAT *IT LOOKS LIKE AN ORANGE*

THE **AMERICAN GIRL WHO COULD HAVE BEEN QUEEN OF FRANCE** ABIGAIL WILLING, DAUGHTER OF THOMAS WILLING, A PRESIDENT OF THE BANK OF THE U.S., *REJECTED A PROPOSAL FROM LOUIS PHILIPPE, THE DUKE OF ORLEANS, WHILE HE WAS TEACHING IN A PHILADELPHIA GIRLS' SCHOOL AS A REFUGEE FROM THE FRENCH REVOLUTION* HER FATHER TOLD LOUIS PHILIPPE: "IF YOU HAVE NO CHANCE FOR THE THRONE OF FRANCE, YOU ARE NO MATCH FOR MY DAUGHTER, AND IF YOU SHOULD BECOME KING, MY DAUGHTER WILL BE NO MATCH FOR YOU" *LOUIS PHILIPPE BECAME KING OF FRANCE AND RULED FOR 18 YEARS*

Ripley's Believe It or Not!

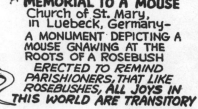

A MEMORIAL TO A MOUSE
Church of St. Mary, in Luebeck, Germany—
A MONUMENT DEPICTING A MOUSE GNAWING AT THE ROOTS OF A ROSEBUSH ERECTED TO REMIND PARISHIONERS, THAT LIKE ROSEBUSHES, ALL JOYS IN THIS WORLD ARE TRANSITORY

THE FLOWER BUG
THE GEOMETRID CATERPILLAR of So. America, AS A DISGUISE, COVERS ITSELF WITH FLOWER BUDS

A SHOE ONCE WORN BY ST. BRIDGET, IS ENSHRINED IN THE NATIONAL MUSEUM OF DUBLIN **IN A SILVER CASKET**

SENPEN FROM THE ARNOLD WINICK STABLE, AT DELRAY BEACH, FLA., HAS OUTLINED ON ITS FOREHEAD A **LARGE SEAHORSE**

JUDGE GEORGE GREEN
(1817-1880) of Cedar Rapids, Iowa, WAS A LAWYER, GEOLOGIST, TEACHER, LEGISLATOR, NEWSPAPER PUBLISHER, SUPREME COURT JUSTICE, MAYOR, HOTEL OWNER, NURSERY OWNER, STEAMBOAT BUILDER AND **PRESIDENT OF 6 BANKS, 17 COMPANIES, 10 RAILROADS AND 3 COLLEGES**

THE LEOPARD FROG
CAN LEAP OUT OF THE WATER AND SLAY A FLYING BIRD

THE ·CASTLE OF THE CAVE
IN SLOVENIA, YUGOSLAVIA, A FORTRESS CONSTRUCTED BY THE KOBENZL FAMILY IN 1570, IS LOCATED **IN A LARGE CAVE AT THE FOOT OF A 426-FOOT CLIFF.** IT IS NOW A WORLD WAR II MUSEUM

THE BOAT THAT PERFORMED A RESCUE WITHOUT HUMAN ASSISTANCE!
ADOLPHE PONS, A FRENCH TRADER, FELL OVERBOARD FROM HIS MOTOR LAUNCH, OFF NEW CALEDONIA, AND A NATIVE ASSISTANT UNTHINKINGLY DIVED TO AID HIM, THEIR CRAFT CONTINUING ON UNDER FULL POWER--**LEAVING THE 2 MEN 8 MILES FROM THE NEAREST LAND AND IN WATERS INFESTED WITH SHARKS.**
BOTH MEN WOULD HAVE BEEN DEAD IN MINUTES--**BUT THEIR UNATTENDED MOTORBOAT SUDDENLY TURNED ABOUT AND CAME BACK FOR THEM, AND THEY CLIMBED BACK ABOARD UNHARMED** (DECEMBER 24, 1923)

THE OLDEST HOUSE IN CANADA

A MUSEUM, in Sillery, near Quebec, ORIGINALLY WAS A JESUIT RESIDENCE BUILT IN 1637

THE MAN WHO OUTFOUGHT A LION WITH HIS BARE FIST!

E. CRONJE WILMOT
WHOSE RIFLE JAMMED ON A HUNTING TRIP IN BECHUANALAND, AFRICA
WAS WOUNDED 23 TIMES BY A FULL-GROWN LION
BUT SAVED HIS LIFE BY JAMMING HIS FIST DEEP INTO THE ATTACKING BEAST'S THROAT (Nov. 2, 1947)

A SHARP MACHETE

WAS THE SYMBOL BEFORE WHICH ALL OFFICIALS OF VITORIA, SPAIN, TOOK THEIR OATH OF OFFICE FOR CENTURIES-- A REMINDER THAT IF THEY VIOLATED THEIR OATH, THEY WOULD DIE BY THAT SAME MACHETE

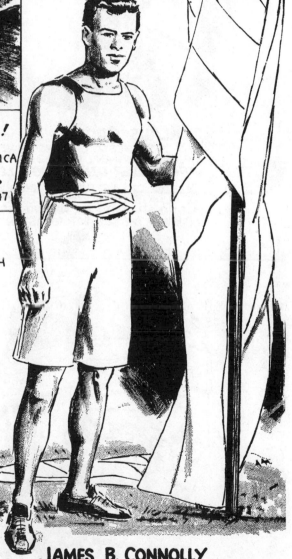

JAMES B. CONNOLLY

an American runner
BECAME THE FIRST OLYMPICS WINNER IN MODERN TIMES
- COMPETING IN AN EVENT FOR WHICH HE HAD NOT EVEN TRAINED

NO AMERICAN HAD ENTERED THE HOP, STEP AND JUMP CONTEST WHICH WAS THE FIRST EVENT WHEN THE OLYMPICS WERE REVIVED IN ATHENS IN 1896, SO CONNOLLY VOLUNTEERED TO COMPETE
AND WON WITH A MARK OF 45 FEET

THE MOUNTAIN RESORT THAT IS ALWAYS IN MOTION

GROSSGMEIN, A RESORT VILLAGE IN AUSTRIA, BUILT ON A ROCKY BASE, IS CONSTANTLY SHIFTING BECAUSE IT RESTS ON A BED OF SALT 1,000 FEET THICK

THE SIEGE THAT WAS RELIEVED BY A PHANTOM ARMY

GENERAL DU BELLAY SAVED THE BESIEGED AND STARVING GARRISON OF LANDRECIES, FRANCE, BY **TYING 600 BAGS OF FLOUR ON 600 HORSES, EQUIPPING THEM WITH LANCES, SWORDS AND HELMETS—AND LEADING THEM ON A DARK AND FOGGY NIGHT THROUGH A FORCE OF 40,000 ENEMY SOLDIERS**

THE FLOUR BAGS LOOMED OUT OF THE GLOOM AS GIANT SOLDIERS AND SO TERRIFIED THE FOE THAT THEIR PASSAGE WAS NOT CHALLENGED AND THE CITY WAS SAVED (1543)

KLAUS GROTH (1819-1899)

WAS A PROFESSOR AT THE UNIVERSITY OF KIEL, GERMANY, FOR 33 YEARS *WITHOUT EVER DELIVERING A LECTURE*

HE HAD ONE LECTURE PLANNED WHICH HE ALWAYS LISTED ON THE BLACKBOARD — BUT NO STUDENT EVER WAS INTERESTED ENOUGH IN THE SUBJECT TO LISTEN TO IT

TREE STUMP

on Vargas Island, off Vancouver, B.C. SHAPED LIKE A HUMAN EAR

SWIFT ARROW (1788-1917)

A CHIPPEWA INDIAN CHIEF *LIVED TO THE AGE OF 129*

PROSPERITY PAGODAS

LINE THE BANKS OF THE YANGTZE RIVER IN CHINA

IN THE BELIEF THAT THEY WILL PREVENT THE REGION'S WEALTH FROM BEING WASHED DOWNSTREAM

U.S. SUPREME COURT JUSTICE JOHN A. CAMPBELL

(1811-1889) of Alabama IS THE ONLY MEMBER OF THE COURT IN ITS ENTIRE HISTORY WHOSE *APPOINTMENT WAS REQUESTED BY HIS FELLOW JURISTS*

HIS APPEARANCES BEFORE THE COURT SO IMPRESSED THE JURISTS THEY RECOMMENDED HIM TO PRESIDENT PIERCE

Ripley's Believe It or Not!

THE LANTERN FISH
THE DEEP SEA ANGLER FISH (galatheathauma axeli) LIES AT THE BOTTOM OF THE SEA AND LURES ITS FOOD TO IT BY *A LIGHT THAT GLOWS FROM ITS OPEN MOUTH*

A **NEWSPAPER** MAILED TO MARY C. FELTON, IN SYRACUSE, N.Y., IN 1847, CREATED A CASE THAT WENT THROUGH 5 COURTS BECAUSE SOMEONE HAD SCRAWLED AN INITIAL ON THE WRAPPER AND A POSTMASTER INSISTED ON COLLECTING *FIRST CLASS POSTAGE* MARY SUED FOR POSSESSION OF HER PAPER AND THE U.S. SUPREME COURT *AWARDED HER 6 CENTS FOR THE PAPER, PLUS COSTS*

THE **QUEEN** WHO WALKED THROUGH FIRE!
RICHARDE, Queen of the Franks, SUSPECTED OF INFIDELITY BY HER HUSBAND, KING LOUIS THE STOUT (839-888) TO PROVE HER INNOCENCE WAS FORCED TO WALK *THROUGH A ROARING FIRE-WHILE WEARING A GOWN SATURATED WITH WAX* THE QUEEN PASSED THE ORDEAL-BUT LEFT HER HUSBAND AND ENTERED A CONVENT

THE CHURCH OF THE HOLY TRINITY
In Toronto, Ontario, WAS BUILT WITH A $25,000 DONATION IN 1845 *FROM A WOMAN IN RIPON, ENGLAND, WHO NEVER REVEALED HER IDENTITY*

THE **TURBAN** WORN BY SYED SIBGHATULLA, RULER OF THE HURS OF INDIA, WHEN HE WAS EXECUTED FOR MUTINY IN 1943, HAD BEEN WORN AS THE EMBLEM OF OFFICE BY SUCCESSIVE GENERATIONS *FOR 1,232 YEARS*

OUR "ARABIC" NUMERALS EVOLVED FROM ARAB NUMBERS CREATED IN THE 6th CENTURY

1	2	3	4
6	7	8	9

Ripley's® Believe It or Not!

A **SKETCH** BY FRENCH AUTHOR VICTOR HUGO OF THE TOWER OF THE CHATEAU COLLART, IN SCHENGEN, LUXEMBOURG, WHICH HAS BEEN REPRODUCED IN HUNDREDS OF THOUSANDS OF PRINTS, WAS ORIGINALLY DRAWN DURING A LUNCHEON PARTY **WITH A MATCH AND COFFEE GROUNDS**

THE **CHURCH** of **SANTA CLARA VELHA** in Coimbra, Portugal, HAS STOOD FOR 600 YEARS, BUT FOR SEVERAL CENTURIES IT HAS BEEN ABANDONED BECAUSE THE CHANGING COURSE OF THE MONDEGO RIVER HAS **FILLED THE INTERIOR OF THE CHURCH TO THE LEVEL OF ITS WINDOWS WITH SAND**

DR. **FREDERICK LIST** (1789-1846) WHO RETURNED TO HIS NATIVE GERMANY AS AMERICAN CONSUL TO LEIPZIG WAS SO DESPONDENT OVER HIS INABILITY TO WIN APPROVAL OF HIS PLANS FOR A SYSTEM OF RAIL LINES IN SAXONY THAT HE **COMMITTED SUICIDE.** A FEW YEARS AFTER HIS DEATH HIS PLAN WAS ADOPTED AND THE RAILROAD WAS BUILT EXACTLY AS HE HAD SUGGESTED

THE **OWL MONKEY** *SLEEPS ALL DAY AND FEEDS ONLY AT NIGHT*

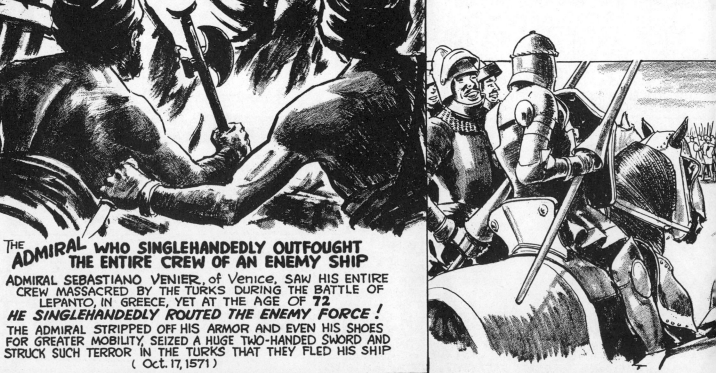

THE **ADMIRAL** WHO SINGLEHANDEDLY OUTFOUGHT THE ENTIRE CREW OF AN ENEMY SHIP

ADMIRAL SEBASTIANO VENIER, of Venice, SAW HIS ENTIRE CREW MASSACRED BY THE TURKS DURING THE BATTLE OF LEPANTO, IN GREECE, YET AT THE AGE OF **72** **HE SINGLEHANDEDLY ROUTED THE ENEMY FORCE!** THE ADMIRAL STRIPPED OFF HIS ARMOR AND EVEN HIS SHOES FOR GREATER MOBILITY, SEIZED A HUGE TWO-HANDED SWORD AND STRUCK SUCH TERROR IN THE TURKS THAT THEY FLED HIS SHIP (Oct. 17, 1571)

THE ÉLYSÉE PALACE in Paris, France, *OFFICIAL RESIDENCE OF THE PRESIDENT* WAS PURCHASED IN 1805 BY NAPOLEON I AS A GIFT FOR HIS BROTHER-IN-LAW, JOACHIM MURAT, **FOR $180,000**

THE EMPEROR NEVER LEARNED THAT MURAT SECRETLY RECEIVED A KICKBACK OF $40,000 FROM ITS ORIGINAL OWNER

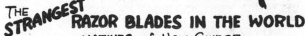

SKUNK CABBAGE EACH SPRING PUSHES UP THROUGH THE FROZEN GROUND *ROLLED UP LIKE A CIGAR* THE TEMPERATURE INSIDE THE PLANT IS 25 DEGREES WARMER THAN THE OUTSIDE AIR

THE **STRANGEST RAZOR BLADES IN THE WORLD** NATIVES of New Guinea SHAVE WITH STRING-LIKE AND AMAZINGLY SHARP *BLADES OF GRASS*

GEOGRAPHICAL LICHENS WHICH ENCRUST ROCKS IN GERMANY'S BLACK FOREST WERE GIVEN THAT NAME BECAUSE THEY LOOK LIKE *CAREFULLY DRAWN MAPS*

THE **JACANA** of Africa, WHICH CAN BALANCE ON FLOATING LEAVES, HAS THE *BIGGEST FEET OF ANY BIRD* ITS FEET ARE AS LONG AS ITS BODY

THE **RABBIT** THAT SAVED THOUSANDS OF LIVES!

THE BATTLE OF BUIRONFOSSE, in France, WHICH HISTORICALLY IS REGARDED AS ONE OF THE OPENING ENGAGEMENTS OF THE HUNDRED YEARS' WAR BETWEEN FRANCE AND ENGLAND, ACTUALLY NEVER TOOK PLACE, BECAUSE AS THE ARMIES WERE ABOUT TO CLASH A *FRIGHTENED RABBIT DASHED BETWEEN THE 2 LINES OF ARMED MEN*

THE SIGHT WAS SO HILARIOUS THAT THE SOLDIERS OF BOTH ARMIES ROARED WITH LAUGHTER – AND *WITHDREW WITHOUT STRIKING A BLOW* (Mar.26,1339)

THE **BARONESS de MERE** (1751 - 1829) IN HER 30-YEAR CAREER AS A NOVELIST *PUBLISHED 320 VOLUMES*

THE HORSE THAT WALKED A TIGHTROPE!

FRANK CORRADINI, AN ITALIAN TRAINER WHO DIED IN 1899, STAGED CIRCUS EXHIBITIONS THROUGHOUT EUROPE *IN WHICH A HORSE ACTUALLY BALANCED HIGH ABOVE THE ARENA ON A TIGHTROPE*

ALFRED H. REED, IN LESS THAN 7 MONTHS, WALKED FROM NORTH CAPE TO BLUFF, N.Z. —A DISTANCE OF 1,700 MILES – AND CLIMBED 7,515-FOOT MT. NGAURUHOE ON THE WAY *AT THE AGE OF 85* AT 90 HE WALKED 630 MILES FROM SYDNEY TO MELBOURNE, AUSTRALIA

EGG SHAPED LIKE A BOWLING PIN

from a hen owned by Mrs. EDNA HULLIHEN Baltimore, Md.

THE FEAT THAT WAS CELEBRATED IN EVERY PARISIAN PAWNSHOP

SANTOS - DUMONT PIONEER FRENCH BALLOONIST WHO WON A $25,800 PRIZE IN 1901 BY FLYING A DIRIGIBLE IN A TIGHT CIRCLE AROUND THE EIFFEL TOWER GAVE $10,000 TO HIS AIDES AND DONATED THE REMAINING $15,800 TO *REDEEM EVERY TOOL HOCKED BY FRENCH WORKMEN IN THE PAWNSHOPS OF PARIS*

LEON GAMBETTA (1838-1882) a Prime Minister of France, MEMORIZED EVERY WORD OF THE NOTABLE SPEECHES BY LEADERS OF THE FRENCH REVOLUTION, EVERY WORD WRITTEN BY RABELAIS, AND *COULD REPEAT FROM MEMORY THE ENTIRE FRENCH BUDGET OF ANY YEAR – NEVER ERRING IN ANY OF ITS THOUSANDS OF COLUMNS OF FIGURES*

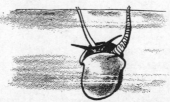

THE SNORKEL SNAIL

WHILE UNDERWATER BREATHES AIR THROUGH **2 TUBES IT** EXTENDS TO THE SURFACE

Ripley's—® Believe It or Not!

KAATERSKILL FALLS
IN THE CATSKILL MOUNTAINS, N.Y.,
260 FEET HIGH,
IS MARKED BY A MEMORIAL
TABLET *TO A MONGREL
TERRIER THAT LEAPED TO
ITS DEATH OVER THE FALLS*-
THE DOG'S MASTER HAD TOSSED
A STONE INTO THE WATER
AND THE TERRIER, TRAINED
TO RETRIEVE ANYTHING ITS
OWNER THREW, UNHESITATING-
LY PLUNGED AFTER IT

THE BIGGEST HORSE RACE IN ALL HISTORY!
CALIPH HISHAM (688-743)
WHO RULED A GREAT MOHAMMEDAN EMPIRE FOR 19 YEARS,
SEVERAL TIMES A YEAR STAGED A HORSE RACE IN
WHICH **4,000 PURE ARABIAN STALLIONS FROM HIS
OWN STABLE COMPETED OVER A 112-MILE COURSE**

THE **WATER
FLEA**
*IS NOT
A FLEA
AT ALL.*
IT IS A
MINUTE
CRUSTACEAN
-AND THERE
ARE 1,000,000
FEMALES
FOR EACH
MALE

A **WHITE CARNEAU
PIGEON**
HATCHED BLIND
AT A SUMTER,
S.C. HATCHERY
**COULD ONLY FLY
BACKWARDS**

THE BANDIT WHO WAS BRANDED BY A BOLT OF LIGHTNING!
Paris, France
A ROBBER, REVIVED BY DR. FELIX MARSANNE, JR., IN 1872
AFTER HE HAD BEEN KNOCKED UNCONSCIOUS BY LIGHTNING,
WAS FOUND AT THE HOSPITAL TO HAVE BRANDED ON HIS
CHEST- Ⓓ Ⓕ Ⓜ
THREE MONTHS EARLIER HE HAD ROBBED AND KILLED
DR. FELIX MARSANNE SR. AND WHEN HIT BY
LIGHTNING WAS CARRYING IN HIS BREAST POCKET
THE WALLET OF HIS VICTIM — WITH Dr. F.M.
EMBOSSED ON A STEEL PLATE

3-17

Ripley's Believe It or Not!

THE HUGE ORGAN
in the Church of St. Florian, Austria, **SERVES AS A MEMORIAL TO COMPOSER ANTON BRUCKNER**

BRUCKNER BEGAN HIS CELEBRATED CAREER AS A CHURCH ORGANIST ON THIS ORGAN – AND **IS BURIED AT ITS BASE**

The MOST EXPENSIVE MEDICAL POTION IN HISTORY

RAJAH GHIYATH-ud-din (1448-1528) of Malwa, India, DURING AN ILLNESS, WAS ASKED BY HIS PHYSICIAN TO DRINK A POTION BREWED FROM **300** INGREDIENTS - *AT A COST OF $40,000*

THE RAJAH, A TEETOTALLER, SPILLED IT ON THE GROUND WHEN HE LEARNED THAT IT CONTAINED *⅛ OF AN OUNCE OF NUTMEG, AN INGREDIENT USED IN INDIA TO FLAVOR WINE*

A **GOLDEN RECEPTACLE**
now in the Museum of Ancient Art, Lisbon, Portugal, WAS MADE FROM THE FIRST GOLD BROUGHT BACK FROM INDIA IN 1498 BY VASCO DA GAMA

AUGUSTUS HILL GARLAND
(1832-1899) of ARKANSAS, REFUSED A NOMINATION TO THE U.S. SUPREME COURT ON THE GROUNDS THAT HE DID NOT HAVE *A LIFE EXPECTANCY FOR THE COURT OF 20 YEARS*

HE DIED THIRTEEN YEARS LATER – WHILE ARGUING A CASE BEFORE THAT COURT

EQUATIONS THAT CARRY ALL 9 DIGITS TWICE –

$51,249,876 \times 3 = 153,749,628$
$32,547,891 \times 6 = 195,287,346$
$16,583,742 \times 9 = 149,253,678$

CUCUMBER
GROWN BY JOHN BUNCE, OF HAVERHILL, N.H., *REACHED A LENGTH OF 10 FEET, 10 INCHES* (182

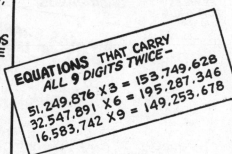

ALFRED DEACON
(1856-1919) WAS ATTORNEY GENERAL OF AUSTRALIA FROM 1901 TO 1903 AND 3 TIMES SERVED AS PRIME MINISTER, *BUT HE REFUSED CABINET POSTS 9 TIMES AND 3 TIMES DECLINED THE PREMIERSHIP*

STREET LIGHTS
in Graz, Austria, WERE PROTECTED IN 1728 BY A LAW THAT PUNISHED ANY PERSON WHO DAMAGED ONE 3 TIMES—BY CUTTING OFF HIS RIGHT HAND

A *WATCH* CREATED BY MICHEL BUMEL, IN GERMANY IN 1625 IS SQUARE, HINGED IN THE MIDDLE AND *DESIGNED TO LOOK LIKE A BOOK*

THE STATUE OF CHRIST
in the Cathedral of Burgos, Spain, HAS ACTUAL HUMAN HAIR, EYEBROWS, FINGERNAILS, TOENAILS AND A BEARD —*THOSE OF THE ANONYMOUS SCULPTOR*

THE MONARCH WHO WAS HIS OWN BODYGUARD
KING ALEXANDER I (1078-1124) of Scotland, WHO WAS CALLED "THE FIERCE", WAS ATTACKED ONE NIGHT IN HIS BEDCHAMBER BY 6 HEAVILY ARMED ASSASSINS

THE MONARCH AWAKENED FROM A DEEP SLEEP, SEIZED HIS SWORD **AND KILLED ALL 6!**

WEDDING RINGS
in old England, TO EMPHASIZE THAT LOVE IS AS STRONG AS DEATH, *FEATURED A DEATH'S-HEAD*

THE FISH WITH HEAD AND TAIL LIGHTS
HEMIGRAMMUS OCELLIFER HAS RED EYES THAT REFLECT THE LIGHT AND A COPPER SPOT ON ITS TAIL THAT *ACTS AS A REAR REFLECTOR*

THE WEATHER THISTLE
FORECASTS RAIN BY CLOSING ITS GOLDEN BLOSSOMS AND ANNOUNCES THE COMING OF FAIR WEATHER BY OPENING THEM

THE MOST AMAZING MUSICIAN IN ALL HISTORY!
KARL HERMANN UNTHAN, BORN IN PRUSSIA IN 1848 WITHOUT ARMS, BECAME A CONCERT STAR AND SOLOIST WITH MANY ORCHESTRAS, *PLAYING THE VIOLIN WITH HIS FEET*

HE ALSO WAS A NOTED MARKSMAN, SWIMMER AND HORSEMAN—COULD TYPE, WRITE WITH A PEN, WIND HIS WATCH, SHAVE HIMSELF AND PLACE STUDS IN HIS COLLAR

THE MONASTERY OF SAN JUAN de la PEÑA near Jaca, Spain, BUILT IN A DEEP GORGE BETWEEN 2 SHEER CLIFFS *CAN BE REACHED ONLY BY EXPERT MOUNTAIN CLIMBERS*

THE **5 STARS** of the **FLAG** of Yemen SYMBOLIZE THE 5 DOGMAS OF THE MOHAMMEDAN RELIGION AND THE 5 PRAYER PERIODS OBSERVED BY MOSLEMS EACH DAY

THE **CAT** THAT SAVED A QUEEN !

FRANÇOISE d'AUBIGNÉ (1635-1719) 3-YEAR-OLD DAUGHTER OF THE FRENCH GOVERNOR OF MARIE-GALANTE, WAS PRONOUNCED DEAD AT SEA ON A VOYAGE TO THE ISLAND AND HER BODY WAS SEWN UP IN A SACK – *TO BE DROPPED OVERBOARD*

WHEN A MEOWING DURING THE FUNERAL SERVICE REVEALED THE CHILD'S PET HAD CRAWLED INTO THE BAG, THE CAPTAIN RECALLED THAT CATS SHUN CORPSES, RE-EXAMINED THE GIRL – AND *FOUND HER STILL ALIVE*

THE CHILD RECOVERED, EVENTUALLY BECAME THE WIFE OF KING LOUIS XIV of France – AND LIVED TO THE AGE OF 84, KNOWN TO HISTORY AS THE MARQUISE DE MAINTENON

CERCOPAGIS TENERA a crustacean of the Sea of Azov *HAS A TAIL 6 TIMES AS LONG AS ITS BODY*

THE **ARAUCARA TREES** of Chile, WHICH FURNISH WOOD FAMED FOR ITS HARDNESS, *ARE NEVER FELLED FOR LUMBER UNTIL THEY HAVE BEEN GROWING FOR 500 YEARS*

ARCHDUKE KARL LUDWIG (1833-1896) BROTHER OF THE AUSTRIAN EMPEROR WAS A MAN OF SUCH PIETY THAT ON A TRIP TO THE HOLY LAND HE INSISTED ON DRINKING FROM THE RIVER JORDAN DESPITE WARNINGS THAT IT WOULD MAKE HIM FATALLY ILL – *HE DIED WITHIN A FEW WEEKS*

THE COAT OF ARMS of Bar, France, DISPLAYS 2 FISH AND 3 PANSIES – THE FRENCH WORD FOR PANSY ALSO MEANS "THOUGHT" – AND FISH ARE SILENT – SO THE COAT OF *ARMS DEPICTS THE MOTTO :* "Think more and talk less"

PLVS PENSER — QVE DIRE

THE **WATERLOO WAR MEDAL** AWARDED TO ALL SOLDIERS WHO PARTICIPATED IN THAT DEFEAT OF NAPOLEON, DEPICTS VICTORY SEATED ON A PEDESTAL – *A REPRODUCTION OF A GREEK COIN MINTED 2,265 YEARS EARLIER*

Ripley's Believe It or Not!

THE GIRLS WHO ARE
GUARANTEED A HUSBAND
BABY GIRLS
of the Tiwi Tribe of Australia
**ARE MARRIED AS SOON
AS THEY ARE BORN**
*MOREOVER, A WIDOW MUST
REMARRY AT THE FUNERAL
OF HER HUSBAND*

THE SHIPWRECKED SAILORS WHO WERE SAVED
BY A SPRING – 1,500 MILES AT SEA!
THE **CREW** OF THE SAILING SHIP "LARA",
DRIFTING IN 3 LIFEBOATS IN THE PACIFIC OCEAN WEST OF THE
COAST OF MEXICO, AFTER THE VESSEL HAD BEEN DESTROYED
BY FIRE, WAS SAVED WHEN THE CAPTAIN NOTICED THAT THE
WATER HAD CHANGED FROM BLUE TO GREEN –AND FOUND
THAT THE BOATS WERE OVER *A FRESH-WATER SPRING*
7 OF THE CREWMEN WERE UNCONSCIOUS FROM THIRST, BUT
ALL SURVIVED AND THE CREW FINALLY REACHED MEXICO
23 DAYS AFTER THE SHIPWRECK   (1881)

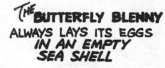

A **GRIFFIN VULTURE**
at the
Vienna Menagerie
in Austria
*LIVED TO THE AGE
OF 118 YEARS*

THE **SEA FERN
CATERPILLAR,**
WHICH FEEDS ON
THE SWEET FERN,
*LOOKS EXACTLY LIKE THE
SERRATED LEAVES OF THE FERN*

THE **BUTTERFLY BLENNY**
ALWAYS LAYS ITS EGGS
IN AN EMPTY
SEA SHELL

DENONCIE SEGRETT

A **SCULPTURED LION'S HEAD**
ON THE WALL OF A FARMHOUSE
at Vescovana, Italy,
HAS AN OPEN MOUTH INTO WHICH
TOWNSPEOPLE WERE INVITED TO DROP
SECRET DENUNCIATIONS OF LOCAL OFFICIALS
*BUT THE DEPOSITORY HAS NEVER BEEN
USED BECAUSE BIRDS HAVE ALWAYS
BUILT NESTS IN THE LION'S MOUTH*

GRAND DUKE ADOLF
(1817-1905) RULER OF
NASSAU AND LUXEMBOURG,
CONVINCED THAT 7th SONS
ALWAYS BROUGHT GOOD FORTUNE,
WAS GODFATHER TO THE 7th
CONSECUTIVE SON BORN TO ANY
MOTHER IN HIS COUNTRY
*AND ALWAYS GAVE THE
CHILD HIS NAME AND
A PURSE OF GOLD*

Ripley's Believe It or Not!

A TINY CRAB (Hapalocarcinus marsupialis) PROTECTS ITSELF AGAINST ENEMIES ON THE BARRIER REEF, AUSTRALIA, *BY IMPRISONING ITSELF FOR LIFE* SOON AFTER BIRTH IT TAKES UP ITS HOME IN THE FORK OF 2 CORAL BRANCHES WHICH GROW INTO A CAGE WITH OPENINGS JUST LARGE ENOUGH TO PERMIT ENTRANCE OF SEA WATER CARRYING THE CRAB'S NOURISHMENT

THE BED ON WHICH EMPEROR CHARLES V of Germany DIED IN 1558 IS PRESERVED IN THE MONASTERY OF YUSTE, SPAIN, *WITH ITS ORIGINAL BEDDING AND COVER*

THE MEN NO WHIP CAN SCAR!

THE SEERS of the Raj Gonds of Hyderabad, India, ONCE A YEAR PROPHESY THE FUTURE FOR EACH VILLAGE -*BUT ONLY AFTER THEY HAVE BEEN WHIPPED FOR HOURS* EACH SEER IS LASHED ACROSS HIS BARE BACK BY THREE HUSKY TRIBESMEN -*YET THEY FEEL NO PAIN AND THE WHIPS NEVER RAISE A WELT*

THE REV. **CHRISTIAN FRANZ WERLEMAN** PASTOR OF THE CHURCH OF REPELEN, GERMANY, FROM 1803 TO 1832 DEVELOPED SUCH A FEAR OF SPEAKING FROM THE PULPIT THAT *HE DID NOT DELIVER A SINGLE SERMON DURING THE ENTIRE 29 YEARS*

THE **STRANGEST TREASURE HUNT IN ALL HISTORY** PRINCE MELCHIOR von MECKAU, ruler of Brixen, Austria, DIED IN 1509 DURING A TRIP TO ROME, AND WHILE HIS BODY WAS LYING IN STATE **ONE OF THE HONOR GUARDS DREAMT THE DEAD MAN HAD BEEN CARRYING A FORTUNE** THE CORPSE WAS SEARCHED AND IN THE CUFF OF ONE SLEEVE WAS FOUND A RECEIPT FOR 300,000 GOLD PIECES THE PRINCE HAD DEPOSITED IN A GERMAN BANK- *A PIECE OF PAPER WORTH $2,000,000*

THE GRAVE of MUNGO PIR, a Mohammedan holy man, LOCATED ON THE INDUS RIVER NEAR KARACHI, PAKISTAN, HAS BEEN GUARDED FOR 50 YEARS BY 4 CROCODILES DESCENDED, NATIVES INSIST, FROM 4 PET CROCODILES THAT WERE IN HIS FUNERAL PROCESSION

THE MAN WHO KILLED A BEAR WITH HIS BARE HANDS!

MOSE ROBINSON of Craighead County, Ark., HAVING WOUNDED A HUGE BEAR WITH HIS SINGLE-SHOT RIFLE AND LOST HIS KNIFE IN THE THICK BRUSH, SUDDENLY FOUND HIMSELF *WITHOUT WEAPONS FACING AN ENRAGED BEAR* HE PUNCHED THE ANIMAL WITH HIS FISTS AND WAS HIMSELF BADLY MANGLED -BUT FINALLY SUCCEEDED IN CHOKING THE BEAR TO DEATH

THE OAK CEILING OF THE CHURCH OF SHEPTON MALLET, ENGLAND, HAS 350 CARVED PANELS, 396 FOLIAGE-TYPE ORNAMENTS AND 1,400 CARVED LEAVES -YET NO 2 ARE EXACTLY ALIKE

THE OLD TOWER of GREVENMACHER in Luxembourg

A PART OF THE TOWN WALL ERECTED IN 882, WAS THE ONLY STRUCTURE *NOT DEMOLISHED IN AN AIR RAID AGAINST THE TOWN IN 1944-* YET 34 YEARS EARLIER THE TOWER HAD BEEN ORDERED RAZED AS UNSAFE

THE UNHAPPY WOMAN TO WHOM LOVE ALWAYS BROUGHT DEATH!

ANTONIA (35-65) DAUGHTER OF EMPEROR CLAUDIUS of Rome, SAW HER TWO HUSBANDS EXECUTED, AND WHEN SHE REFUSED THE ARDENT MARRIAGE PROPOSAL OF EMPEROR NERO, *WAS HERSELF EXECUTED BY THE SPURNED RULER!*

LAPP SKIERS
OFTEN LEAP CHASMS
125 FEET WIDE

A **ROMAN WINE BOTTLE**
DUG UP IN THE GERMAN PALATINATE STILL HAD ITS WINE INTACT AFTER **1,700 YEARS**

LANTERN
in the West Indies
COMPRISING A PERFORATED GOURD
FILLED WITH HUNDREDS OF FIREFLIES

The **MEMORIAL TO AN AMAZING LABOR OF LOVE**
AMITHA A MONK of Polonnarua, Ceylon, CONSTRUCTED A FENCE AROUND THE LOCAL SANCTUARY IN THE 14th CENTURY UNAIDED -*ALTHOUGH HE WAS BLIND AND HAD NO HANDS*
WHEN THE ORIGINAL FENCE DISINTEGRATED THE KING OF LANKA HAD IT REPRODUCED IN STONE ON THE SAME SPOT AND IT STILL STANDS AS A MEMORIAL TO THE MONK'S ACHIEVEMENT

The **PAPAYA TREE**
CAN BE "MILKED" BY MAKING AN INCISION *EITHER IN THE FRUIT OR THE TREE ITSELF*
THE MILK COAGULATES QUICKLY ON CONTACT WITH THE AIR AND SEALS THE OPENING

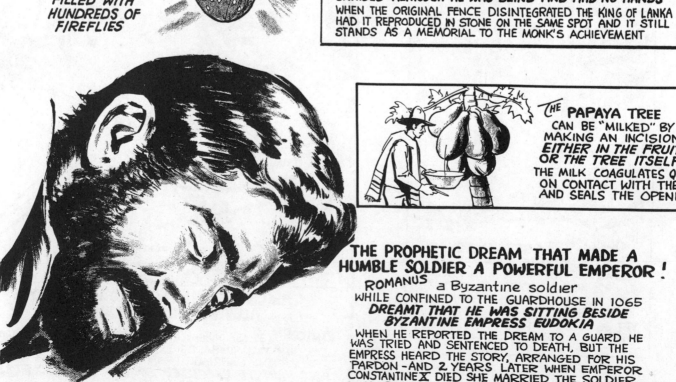

THE PROPHETIC DREAM THAT MADE A HUMBLE SOLDIER A POWERFUL EMPEROR !
ROMANUS a Byzantine soldier
WHILE CONFINED TO THE GUARDHOUSE IN 1065 *DREAMT THAT HE WAS SITTING BESIDE BYZANTINE EMPRESS EUDOKIA*
WHEN HE REPORTED THE DREAM TO A GUARD HE WAS TRIED AND SENTENCED TO DEATH, BUT THE EMPRESS HEARD THE STORY, ARRANGED FOR HIS PARDON -AND 2 YEARS LATER WHEN EMPEROR CONSTANTINE X DIED SHE MARRIED THE SOLDIER, *WHO BECAME EMPEROR ROMANUS IV DIOGENES !*

Ripley's Believe It or Not!

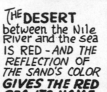

A **SINGLE EAR OF CORN** GROWN BY LEONARD E. CLORE, OF Franklin County, Indiana, WAS SOLD AT A CORN EXHIBIT IN CHICAGO IN 1893 *FOR $250*

THE **DESERT** between the Nile River and the sea IS RED - AND THE REFLECTION OF THE SAND'S COLOR *GIVES THE RED SEA ITS NAME*

THE STRANGEST COURTSHIP IN ALL HISTORY!

DUKE HENRI de GUISE (1614-1664) of France EACH MONTH FOR A YEAR, SENT HIS BELOVED ANNE DE GONZAGUE BY COURIER A PARCHMENT BEARING HIS SOLEMN OATH THAT HE WOULD MARRY HER - *EACH OF THE 12 MESSAGES WRITTEN IN HIS OWN BLOOD!* YET WHEN HE WAS FREE TO MARRY, HE MARRIED SOMEONE ELSE

THE **PARTRIDGE PLANT** GROWS EACH BERRY FROM A COMBINATION OF 2 BLOSSOMS

A **FEMALE PLATYPUS** WEIGHING 2 POUNDS DURING THE 11 WEEKS SHE IS NURSING HER YOUNG *EATS 1¾ POUNDS OF FOOD EACH DAY*

DR. CHRISTIAN von GLUECK (1755 - 1831) PROFESSOR OF ROMAN LAW AT THE UNIVERSITY OF ERLANGEN, GERMANY, FOR 47 YEARS, WAS SO DEVOTED TO HIS PROFESSION THAT DURING HIS VACATIONS HE DELIVERED LECTURES TO A STUDENT WHOM *HE HIRED TO LISTEN TO HIM*

BOUNDARY MARKERS in Thailand ARE SHAPED LIKE *MINIATURE TEMPLES*

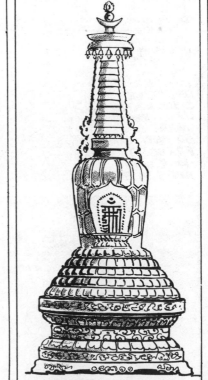

THE **BOTTLE PAGODA** of Jehol, China **22 FEET HIGH** AND PATTERNED AFTER A BUDDHIST BURIAL URN, IS SHAPED LIKE A BOTTLE AND *COVERED WITH BLUE GLASS*

RIPLEY's Believe It or Not!

THE STRANGEST SUICIDE IN ALL HISTORY!

COCCEIUS NERVA DISTINGUISHED LAWYER AND FRIEND OF EMPEROR TIBERIUS OF ROME, BECAME SO DESPONDENT THAT THE EMPEROR, AWARE THAT COCCEIUS WAS CONTEMPLATING SUICIDE, INSISTED THAT HIS FRIEND ATTEND EVERY COURT BANQUET – SO THE EMPEROR COULD WATCH OVER HIM

COCCEIUS PRETENDED HE WAS EATING – *BUT COMMITTED SUICIDE BY STARVATION WHILE ATTENDING SCORES OF BANQUETS* (33 A.D.)

M. CUSTERS WHO JOINED THE UNIVERSITY OF NEW MEXICO, IN ALBUQUERQUE, AS A JANITOR, *BECAME A MEMBER OF THE FACULTY – TEACHING SURVEYING AND TRIGONOMETRY* LATER HE BECAME BLIND AND SERVED AS THE SCHOOL'S LIBRARIAN – AND COULD RECOGNIZE EACH STUDENT IN THE SCHOOL BY HIS OR HER VOICE

THE ANNUAL DONATION BY THE RESIDENTS OF SPEZET, FRANCE, TO OUR LADY OF CRANN ON A FESTIVE HOLIDAY *IS A TUB OF BUTTER SURMOUNTED BY A WREATH MADE OF 50 AND 100-FRANC NOTES – WORTH $10 AND $20 EACH*

THE INSECT ATLAS THE CICADA (Sphongophorous inflatus) BEARS ON ITS SHOULDERS A HUGE SPHERE

FLOWERS WERE IN SUCH DEMAND FOR THE FUNERAL OF ASSASSINATED FRENCH PRESIDENT SADI CARNOT IN 1894 THAT THE SMALLEST ROSES *SOLD FOR $30 EACH*

THE DOG SOLDIERS

GREAT MASTIFFS in medieval warfare WERE SENT AGAINST THE ENEMY WITH A LEATHER COAT OF "ARMOR," A SHARP SPEAR AND A BURNING SPONGE SET IN ALCOHOL *SO THEY WOULD SET FIRE TO ANYTHING IN THEIR PATH*

AN ALPHABET WAS CREATED FOR THE MIAOTSE NATIVES OF South China BY THE BRITISH BIBLE SOCIETY SO *THE BIBLE COULD BE TRANSLATED FOR THEIR*

ISCHIA, an island off Italy, HAS 6 VOLCANOES WHICH, WHILE THEY HAVE NOT ERUPTED SINCE 1302, STILL RUMBLE MENACINGLY. IT HAS BEEN SHAKEN BY MANY EARTHQUAKES' – ONE OF WHICH ON JULY 28, 1883, DESTROYED 3 TOWNS AND KILLED 2,300 MEN, WOMEN AND CHILDREN

WHITE CARROTS ARE GROWN IN FRANCE AS ANIMAL FODDER

THE OCTAGONAL STREET LAMPS in Trafalgar Square, London, ORIGINALLY WERE USED AS LANTERNS ON ADMIRAL NELSON'S FLAGSHIP *IN THE BATTLE OF TRAFALGAR*

AUGUSTIN THIERRY (1795-1856) the French historian DICTATED THE CONTENTS OF 20 HIGHLY REGARDED VOLUMES OF FRENCH HISTORY *AFTER HE HAD BECOME BLIND AND A BEDRIDDEN PARALYTIC*

THE RIVER THAT CROSSES OVER ITSELF
THE GARONNE RIVER, near Agen, France, HAS A 2,000-FOOT LONG IRRIGATION AQUEDUCT THAT CARRIES WATER FROM THE GARONNE *ACROSS THE RIVER*

THE STRANGEST PARALLEL IN ALL HISTORY!
KING UMBERTO I (1844-1900) of Italy HAD A DOUBLE NAMED UMBERTO SANTINI AND THEY LOOKED EXACTLY ALIKE. THEY WERE BORN IN TORINO ON THE SAME DAY, UMBERTO BECAME A RESTAURATEUR ON THE DAY UMBERTO BECAME KING, BOTH HAD WIVES NAMED MARGHERITA, EACH HAD A SON NAMED VITTORIO AND BOTH DIED IN MONZA, ITALY, OF GUNSHOT WOUNDS ON THE SAME DAY
-THE MONARCH BY ASSASSINATION, AND HIS DOUBLE BY A GUN ACCIDENT!

THE FRUIT OF THE BEAD TREE of India FEEDS SHEEP, GOATS AND BIRDS - YET IT IS **HIGHLY POISONOUS TO MAN**

BENT'S FORT BUILT BY TRADER WILLIAM BENT BETWEEN LAS ANIMAS AND LA JUNTA, KANSAS, WAS OFFERED TO THE U.S. GOVERNMENT FOR $16,000, BUT THE GOVERNMENT REFUSED TO PAY MORE THAN $12,000, ALTHOUGH IT WAS THE LARGEST STRUCTURE WEST OF THE MISSISSIPPI. *BENT PROMPTLY REMOVED THE FORT'S FURNISHINGS AND SUPPLIES AND BURNED IT TO THE GROUND*

ELIZABETH, COUNTESS OF KENT FOR VIOLATING A PLEDGE THAT SHE WOULD NEVER REMARRY AFTER HER HUSBAND'S DEATH IN 1360, WAS SENTENCED TO PERFORM A 40-MILE WALK ONCE EACH YEAR, TO READ 22 PSALMS EVERY DAY AND TO EAT ONE DAY EACH WEEK *ONLY BREAD AND SOUP*

THE RED STEM FIG TREE (Ficus variegata) of Malaya *BEARS AS MANY AS 6 CROPS OF FIGS ON ITS TRUNK EACH YEAR*

AEGER TIBULARIUS a prehistoric crayfish *HAD TENTACLES 6 TIMES AS LONG AS ITS BODY*

THE MAN FATE SAVED FROM HANGING 3 TIMES!

SPORES of the HORSETAIL FERN ARE ENVELOPED BY 4 RIBBONS WHICH SHRINK IN DRY WEATHER, *BUILDING UP PRESSURE THAT EJECTS THE SPORES WHEN THE RIBBONS ARE DAMPENED BY RAIN*

JOSEPH M. AIGNER (1818-1886) famed Viennese portrait painter ATTEMPTED TO HANG HIMSELF IN VIENNA IN 1836 AND AGAIN IN BUDAPEST IN 1840 - *BUT EACH TIME WAS SAVED BY THE TIMELY ARRIVAL OF A CAPUCHIN MONK WHOSE NAME AIGNER NEVER LEARNED* IN 1848 AIGNER WAS SENTENCED TO THE GALLOWS AS A REBEL LEADER - BUT WAS SAVED WHEN THE SAME MONK RECOGNIZED THE PAINTER AND OBTAINED A REPRIEVE FOR HIM! AT THE AGE OF 68 AIGNER COMMITTED SUICIDE BY SHOOTING HIMSELF - AND *THE SAME MONK OFFICIATED AT HIS FUNERAL*

THE **COAT OF ARMS** of Chelles, France, COMMEMORATES THE FACT THAT IN ANCIENT TIMES **2 LADDERS** LASHED TOGETHER SERVED THE TOWN AS ITS GALLOWS

Ripley's — Believe It or Not!

CONSECUTIVE **LICENSE PLATES** ISSUED IN ILLINOIS TO MRS. MARGARET ALEXANDER AND MR. AND MRS. VERN FARTHING -*NEXT DOOR NEIGHBORS IN MT. VERNON, ILL.* THEY APPLIED FOR THE PLATES BY MAIL - AT DIFFERENT TIMES

THE **SOLID SILVER TOMB** of St. Francis Xavier, in the Cathedral of the Good Jesus, in Goa, India, WAS DONATED BY GRAND DUKE FERDINAND II OF TUSCANY IN 1655 -*IN EXCHANGE FOR A PILLOW ON WHICH THE SAINT HAD SLEPT*

THE **MOST BIZARRE ACT OF PROOF IN ALL HISTORY!** *SAID,* ASSASSIN OF CALIPH HAKIM of Egypt (996-1021), WHEN CHALLENGED TO PROVE HOW HE HAD COMMITTED THE MURDER, CRIED; "*THUS*" -AND PLUNGED HIS DAGGER DEEP INTO HIS OWN HEART!

THE STRANGEST SHIPWRECK IN ALL HISTORY

THE "*GEM*" A CUTTER CARRYING 6 CREWMEN, 4 PASSENGERS AND 500 BAGS OF WHEAT SAILED SERENELY INTO SHELTERED SOUTH BAY, AT ROTTNEST ISLAND, AUSTRALIA, ON MAY 17, 1876, **AND SUDDENLY VANISHED!** DIVERS LOCATED THE WRECKAGE, WITH ALL SAILS STILL SET, BUT COULD DISCOVER NO REASON FOR THE SHIP'S SINKING -*AND NO TRACE OF THE CREW AND PASSENGERS HAS EVER BEEN FOUND*

DEER WITH 78-POINT ANTLERS SHOT NEAR BRADY, TEXAS, 1892 Buckhorn Museum, San Antonio, Texas

CHARLOTTE YONGE (1823-1901) the English novelist BEGAN TEACHING SUNDAY SCHOOL IN Otterbourne, England, **AT THE AGE OF 7** SHE CONTINUED CONDUCTING CLASSES WEEKLY FOR **71 YEARS**

A **BIRD** OF A FISH STORY A SWALLOW FLYING LOW OVER THE RIVER LEA, ENGLAND, WAS CAUGHT IN JULY, 1824 *BY A PIKE*

A **HAT** OF SOLID GOLD FOUND BURIED IN COUNTY TIPPERARY IN 1692 *HAD BEEN USED AS A CROWN BY THE ANCIENT KINGS OF IRELAND*

Ripley's ® Believe It or Not!

THE **PAGODA BRIDGE** on the Grand Canal, in An Hwei, China, HAS ON IT A TEMPLE PAGODA AT WHICH EVERY PEDESTRIAN CROSSING THE SPAN PAUSES TO **PRAY FOR SAFETY FROM TRAFFIC ACCIDENTS**

THE **HUMAN GARDEN**

RAMDAS BODHANO of Dakor, India, PLANTED A SWEET BASIL SEED IN HIS PALM AND A **4**-INCH PLANT **GREW FROM HIS HAND!**

DE-GRASSE · POP. 1

OKA-SUR-LE-LAC POPULATION 1

2 TOWNS in Quebec— EACH HAS ONLY **ONE INHABITANT**

THE **MOST ILL-STARRED BRIDE IN ALL HISTORY** Torino, Italy

THE WEDDING DAY OF PRINCESS MARIA VITTORIA, WHO MARRIED THE DUKE D'AOSTA, THE SON OF THE KING OF ITALY, ON MAY 30, 1867, WAS MARRED BY THESE EVENTS:

THE BRIDE'S WARDROBE MISTRESS HANGED HERSELF, THE GATEKEEPER OF THE ROYAL PALACE CUT HIS THROAT, THE COLONEL LEADING THE WEDDING PROCESSION SUCCUMBED TO SUNSTROKE, THE STATIONMASTER DIED UNDER THE WHEELS OF THE HONEYMOON TRAIN – THE KING'S AIDE WAS KILLED IN A FALL FROM HIS HORSE, AND THE BEST MAN SHOT HIMSELF

SQUIDS and OCTOPUSES HAVE **2 GILLS, 2 KIDNEYS** and **3 HEARTS**

PORTABLE HUTS ARE USED BY THE SOMALI TRIBE OF AFRICA WHICH MAKES ITS HOMES OUT OF GRASS MATS **THAT DOUBLE AS PACK SADDLES**

THEFT OF A GERANIUM BUSH IS STILL PUNISHABLE IN ENGLAND *BY 5 YEARS IN PRISON*

WOODEN NICKELS ISSUED IN Vancouver, B.C., in 1955 TO PAY BLOOD DONORS WERE STAMPED *BLOOD MONEY*

THE **HUT** THAT IS A MEMORIAL TO A MARTYRED PRESIDENT

THE GARFIELD HUT in Long Branch, N.J., IS BUILT WITH THE TIES USED ON A SPECIAL RAILROAD SPUR CONSTRUCTED BY 2,000 RESIDENTS OF THE COMMUNITY SO THE FATALLY WOUNDED PRESIDENT GARFIELD COULD TRAVEL OVER IT FROM THE REGULAR RAIL LINE TO THE PRESIDENTIAL COTTAGE

THE SPUR, 5/8ths OF A MILE IN LENGTH, WAS BUILT BETWEEN 6 P.M. ON SEPT. 4, 1881, AND 1 P.M. THE FOLLOWING DAY

John E. HEARN of Cotulla, Texas, TRAPPED OR SHOT **25,000 COYOTES, 10,000 BOBCATS, 1,100 WOLVES AND 129 MOUNTAIN LIONS**

GLOVES PLACED ON THE HANDS OF MUMMIES OF NOBLES BY THE ANCIENT INCAS OF PERU *WERE SOLID GOLD*

THE **ENGLISHMAN** WHO SPEN 40 YEARS BEHIND BAR ALTHOUGH HE WAS NEVE ACCUSED OF A CRIME

MAJOR JOHN BERNARDI (1657-17 IMPRISONED IN 1696 ON SUSPICION THAT HE WAS PLOTTING TO ASSASSINATE KING WILLIAM III, WAS NEVER FORMALLY CHAR WITH CRIME -YET HE REMAINED IN NEWGA PRISON, IN LONDON, UNTIL HIS DEATH AT THE AGE OF 79 -A *PERIOD OF 40 YEAR*

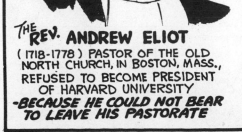

THE **REV. ANDREW ELIOT** (1718-1778) PASTOR OF THE OLD NORTH CHURCH, IN BOSTON, MASS., REFUSED TO BECOME PRESIDENT OF HARVARD UNIVERSITY -*BECAUSE HE COULD NOT BEAR TO LEAVE HIS PASTORATE*

ADELIE PENGUINS DRINK ONLY SALT WATER *11 MONTHS A YEAR* DURING THEIR MONTH OF COURTSHIP THEY ALWAYS CHANGE TO FRESH WATER -WHICH THEY OBTAIN BY EATING THE ANTARCTIC SNOW

THE JEWEL OF THE SEA
LYCOTHEUTIS DIADEMA, A SQUID, HAS ULTRAMARINE BLUE EYES LINED WITH 5 LUMINOUS SPOTS *WHICH GLOW RUBY RED, BLUE AND WHITE*

THE WAR THAT WAS CAUSED BY A COW!

Lord Jean de Gosnes, ruler of Jallet, Belgium, INCENSED BECAUSE ONE OF HIS PEASANTS WAS SUMMARILY HANGED IN CONDROZ, BELGIUM, FOR STEALING A COW, *INVADED THE TOWN, MASSACRED ALL OF ITS INHABITANTS AND TOUCHED OFF A WAR THAT RAVAGED 4 PRINCIPALITIES AND CAUSED 15,000 DEATHS* (1275)

THE RAILROAD BRIDGE
OVER THE Kuhmatt Ravine, Switzerland, **146** FEET LONG BECAUSE OF THE HAZARDS OF WINTER AVALANCHES *IS DISMANTLED EVERY YEAR IN THE FALL AND REBUILT EACH SPRING*

A **LOVE BIRD**
THAT WOULD SHRED PAPER AND MAKE ITSELF AN *ARTIFICIAL TAIL*
Owned by George Conklin, Torrance, Calif.

THE **PITCHER PLANT**
(Sarracenia Variolaris)
LURES CREEPING INSECTS TO THEIR DEATH BY A TRAIL *OF SWEET HONEY*
BUGS FOLLOWING THE TRAIL OF HONEY TO THE TOP OF THE PLANT FALL INTO A POOL CONTAINING A NARCOTIC THAT FIRST DRUGS AND THEN KILLS THEM

THE **NEW GUINEA STARFISH**
(Culcita novaeguineae)
WHICH HAS NO ARMS, *LOOKS LIKE AN OVERSTUFFED PILLOW*

THE **SCEPTER**
of the King of Loango, Africa, WAS A NOTCHED KNIFE CONSIDERED SO SACRED *THAT IT WAS PUNISHABLE BY DEATH FOR A COMMONER EVEN TO GAZE UPON IT*

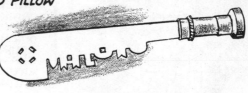

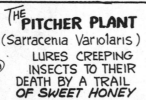

WINE GRAPES
ARE GROWN ON THE SHORES OF THE ADRIATIC SEA IN ITALY *BY STRINGING VINES ON POPLAR TREES*

THE **BLOOD** OF EVERY MAMMAL HAS A SALT CONTENT *EXACTLY THE SAME AS THAT OF THE OCEANS, WHEN THE FIRST MAMMALS EMERGED MILLIONS OF YEARS AGO*

Ripley's Believe It or Not!

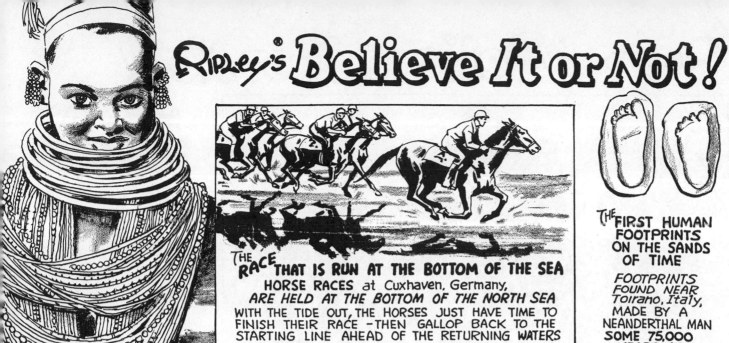

THE RACE THAT IS RUN AT THE BOTTOM OF THE SEA
HORSE RACES at Cuxhaven, Germany, ARE HELD AT THE BOTTOM OF THE NORTH SEA WITH THE TIDE OUT, THE HORSES JUST HAVE TIME TO FINISH THEIR RACE — THEN GALLOP BACK TO THE STARTING LINE AHEAD OF THE RETURNING WATERS

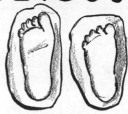

THE FIRST HUMAN FOOTPRINTS ON THE SANDS OF TIME
FOOTPRINTS FOUND NEAR Toirano, Italy, MADE BY A NEANDERTHAL MAN SOME 75,000 YEARS AGO

CHUA, A RYE THAT GROWS IN THE HIMALAYAS AND IS USED AS A BREAKFAST FOOD, COVERS EVERY FIELD WITH A DAZZLING BLANKET OF BRILLIANT YELLOW, RED ORANGE AND PURPLE

THE ONLY FEMALES WHO NEVER HIDE THEIR AGE
GIRLS of the Bondo Tribe in the eccan, India, ADVERTISE THEIR AGING **BY ADDING ANOTHER NECKLACE EACH MONTH**
GIRL OF 15 WEARS 180 NECKLACES ADDING ANOTHER EVERY MONTH UNTIL SHE IS MARRIED

THE LILY LEAF CATERPILLAR
SEWS ITSELF A COAT BY STITCHING TOGETHER, WITH STRANDS OF SILK, 2 SECTIONS OF A LILY PAD

1666
IN EARLIER TIMES WAS EXPECTED TO **BE THE END OF THE WORLD** IN ROMAN NUMBERS THE YEAR REPRESENTED ALL THE DIGITS IN **DESCENDING ORDER** - MDCLXVI

WOMEN of Oberstdorf, Germany, WEAR 10-POUND FUR HATS **EVEN ON THE HOTTEST DAYS OF SUMMER**
DURING THE WARM SEASON THEY ADD A STIFF STRAW HAT ON TOP OF THE FUR

THE PILGRIMAGE THAT WAS MADE OVER A ROAD PAVED WITH GOLD!
KHALIL DHAHERI master of the Egyptian Mint, DURING AN 800-MILE PILGRIMAGE TO MECCA HAD SERVANTS STREW GOLD COINS IN HIS PATH SO THAT **HIS CAMEL WALKED ON GOLD EVERY FOOT OF THE WAY!** OTHER SERVANTS PICKED UP THE COINS AFTER THE CARAVAN HAD PASSED AND $2,000,000 WORTH OF THEM WERE GIVEN TO THE POOR IN MECCA (1455)

Ripley's—®Believe It or Not!

from an old print

THE MOST INHUMAN EXECUTION IN HISTORY!
THE DUKE de NEMOURS (1437-1477)
WHO THREE TIMES BROKE HIS PROMISE NOT TO CONSPIRE AGAINST KING LOUIS XI, OF FRANCE, WAS BEHEADED IN PARIS ON AUG. 4, 1477
-WITH HIS THREE SONS, 4 TO 10 YEARS OF AGE, FORCED TO CROUCH BENEATH THE SCAFFOLD

PROFESSOR ALPHEUS S. PACKARD (1798-1884)
SERVED ON THE FACULTY OF BOWDOIN COLLEGE, BRUNSWICK, ME., **CONTINUOUSLY FOR 65 YEARS**

LOVE ON THE INSTALLMENT PLAN
WOODEN TABLETS ON THE KEI ISLANDS, INDONESIA, RECORD PAYMENTS MADE FOR A BRIDE
-WHICH BEGIN WHEN THE GIRL IS ONLY 8 AND CONTINUE UNTIL SHE IS 16

MORTON ST. HUDSON ST
ONE WAY
ONE WAY
SNOW REMOVAL STREET

HUDSON MORTON
of Ann Arbor, Mich., STROLLING THROUGH MANHATTAN *FOUND HIMSELF AT THE INTERSECTION OF HUDSON AND MORTON STREETS*

THE ELECTRIC CATFISH
SHOCKS SMALLER FISH TO DEATH
-ONLY TO EAT THE FOOD THEY HAVE SWALLOWED BUT NOT YET DIGESTED

A HANK OF RICE
CONTAINING **673** SPIKES OF RICE
-GROWN FROM A SINGLE GRAIN
Submitted by Jean Reville
Brisbane, Australia

OPTICAL ILLUSION
IS THE MAN LOOKING DOWN
-OR AT THE CARD HE IS HOLDING?

2 ONE-DOLLAR BILLS
BRAND NEW AND CONSECUTIVELY NUMBERED, USED BY HARRY D. RANSIER TO PAY A GROCERY BILL WERE *RETURNED TO HIM AS CHANGE IN ANOTHER PURCHASE 4 DAYS LATER*
San Antonio, Texas

THE LAKE THAT GETS LOST
LAKE LOUGHAREEMA in County Antrim, No. Ireland, FROM TIME TO TIME SUDDENLY VANISHES *THROUGH AN UNDERGROUND CHANNEL*

AN ASPEN TREE
in Tauranga, New Zealand,
WHICH GREW FROM A RIDING CROP
SHOVED INTO THE GROUND BY A
BRITISH SOLDIER **104** YEARS AGO

THE MOST HOLY RIVER IN THE WORLD
THE SIPRA RIVER in India
IS SO REVERED BY THE HINDUS
*THAT MERELY THINKING OF IT IS
BELIEVED TO ASSURE FORGIVENESS OF SINS*
NO FISH MAY BE TAKEN FROM ITS WATERS
AND NO FISH OR ANIMAL IS HARMED
WITHIN 10 MILES OF ITS SHORES

THE COAL HOUSE
ERECTED AS AN OFFICE FOR THE CHAMBER
OF COMMERCE OF MIDDLESBOROUGH, KY.,
WAS BUILT FROM 40 TONS OF COAL

THE PEACOCK
WAS INTRODUCED TO
EUROPE IN 331 B.C. BY
ALEXANDER THE GREAT
WHO WAS SO SMITTEN
BY THE BIRD'S BEAUTY
THAT HE CONSIDERED
IT THE MOST SUITABLE
MEMORIAL TO HIS
CONQUEST OF INDIA

THE PETTICOAT PALM
THE WASHINGTONIA
PALM of Calif.
SHIELDS ITS TRUNK
FROM THE SUN'S RAYS
*BY WRAPPING IT
IN A PROTECTIVE
COVERING OF
LEAVES*

THE SHOTGUN PROPOSALS
AN ENGAGEMENT IS NOT OFFICIAL
IN RURAL AREAS OF VALENCIA, SPAIN,
UNTIL THE YOUNG MAN HAS POKED
A SHOTGUN THROUGH THE OPEN
WINDOW OF THE GIRL'S BEDROOM
*AND FIRED BOTH BARRELS OF
BUCKSHOT INTO THE CEILING*

HYPSA MONYCHA CATERPILLARS
BY THEIR
COLORING AND BY
GROUPING THEMSELVES
IN TIGHT FORMATION
ON THE TIP OF A STEM
*CONVINCE THEIR ENEMIES
THEY ARE A FLOWER*

A GLASS BOWL
IN THE CHURCH OF ALBA de TORMES, SPAIN,
IN WHICH THE HEART OF ST. THERESA
IS ENSHRINED, HAS BEEN KEPT
AIRTIGHT SINCE 1582 – YET IT
STILL FOGS OVER ON THE INSIDE

THE DEEPEST SWIMMER IN THE SEA
BASSOGIGAS, A FISH
CAUGHT AT A DEPTH OF
23,400 FEET

A **TOTEM POLE** in Old Kasaan,
on Prince of Wales Island
WAS SPLIT IN HALF
*BY A TREE THAT GREW
INSIDE THE POLE*
Submitted by Emery F. Tobin,
Ketchikan, Alaska

LOTTE FRUTIGER
CLIMBED MOUNT ALLALINHORN,
Switzerland
13,234 FEET HIGH AND ALWAYS
COVERED WITH ICE, IN **8 HOURS**
– WHEN SHE WAS ONLY
8 YEARS OF AGE (Sept. 27, 1927)

THE **HEART** OF A **SHARK**
STILL BEATS STRONGLY HOURS AFTER
ITS REMOVAL FROM THE BODY

SILVER
found in the
Genderbach Mine,
near Laasphe, Germany,
*IN THE SHAPE
OF NATURAL
SILVER CROSSES*

**GOETHEA
CAULIFLORA**
of Brazil
GROWS
FLOWERS
**DIRECTLY FROM
ITS BARK**

THE **GOLD CROWN**
of the statue of
Our Lady of Valencia,
in Valencia, Spain,
IS ENCRUSTED WITH
4,835 WHITE
DIAMONDS
3,082 ROSE
DIAMONDS
656 PEARLS
16 EMERALDS
7 AMETHYSTS
8 TOPAZES
60 HALF PEARLS
4 OPALS
5 SAPPHIRES

GARCILASO de la **VEGA**
(1533 - 1616)
who was born in Cuzco, Peru,
*WAS THE NEW WORLD'S
FIRST NATIVE AUTHOR
AND HISTORIAN*
HIS MOTHER WAS AN
INCA PRINCESS

THE **CITY THAT WAS SENTENCED TO DEATH !**
LYONS, BECAUSE IT WAS ROYALIST,
WAS ORDERED EXPUNGED BY THE FRENCH REVOLUTIONARY TRIBUNAL
ITS BUILDINGS WERE CONDEMNED TO THE LAST TIMBER AND 35,000
INHABITANTS WERE HANGED OR CUT DOWN **WITH GRAPE SHOT** (1793)

Ripley's — ® Believe It or Not!

A NEGATIVE FIGURE MULTIPLIED BY A PLUS EQUALS A NEGATIVE
-BUT TWO NEGATIVES MULTIPLIED BY EACH OTHER YIELD A PLUS

$$-3 \times 4 = -12$$
$$-3 \times -4 = 12$$

ANTONIO de CANEVALI
of Lugano, Switzerland,
WAS APPOINTED TAX COLLECTOR OF THE CITY
2 MONTHS BEFORE HE WAS BORN

HIS FATHER ACTED AS HIS REPRESENTATIVE UNTIL ANTONIO WAS OLD ENOUGH TO SERVE

THE TITOKI BERRY
of New Zealand
TAKES A FULL YEAR TO RIPEN, SO THE TREE SIMULTANEOUSLY BEARS FRUIT AND THE FLOWERS OF THE FOLLOWING YEAR'S BERRIES

THE HIGHEST PLANT IN THE WORLD
Stellaria decumbens
A CUSHION PLANT, GROWS IN THE HIMALAYA MOUNTAINS
AT A HEIGHT OF 20,130 FEET

THE CHURCH OF NOSSA SENHORA de CONCEICAO da PRAIA
in Bahia, Brazil,
WAS CONSTRUCTED IN LISBON, PORTUGAL, IN 1550, THEN TAKEN APART AND SHIPPED IN SEVERAL CARAVELS TO BRAZIL
-A JOURNEY OF 5,000 MILES

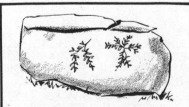

A ROCK on the Sinai Peninsula, Egypt,
STILL BEARS THE IMPRESSION OF 2 FRAIL SPRIGS OF MYRTLE WHICH FELL ON THE ROCK DURING ITS PROCESS OF FORMATION, 1,000,000 YEARS AGO

THE MAN WHO WAS KILLED BY A CORPSE!
ETIENNE BONNESTABLE
FIGHTING A PISTOL DUEL WITH JULES de CASIAS IN PARIS, FRANCE, FIRED BY ERROR BEFORE THE SECONDS GAVE THEIR SIGNAL, AND **HIS OPPONENT WAS KILLED INSTANTLY**

AS BONNESTABLE LEANED OVER THE DEAD MAN, A MUSCULAR REFLEX TIGHTENED THE CORPSE'S FINGER ON HIS STILL-LOADED PISTOL
-AND BONNESTABLE FELL DEAD WITH A BULLET THROUGH HIS HEART! (1889)

Ripley's Believe It or Not!

THE OLDEST PRINTED BOOK A SCROLL OF INDIAN SACRED WRITINGS PRINTED WITH WOODEN TYPE 1,559 YEARS AGO

THE BLOSSOMS OF THE FIG TREE **ARE NEVER VISIBLE** THE BLOSSOMS ARE INSIDE THE FIG, WHERE THEY DEVELOP INTO SEEDS

A **CACTUS** on Reunion Island in the Indian Ocean, BLOOMS ONLY ONCE EVERY **50 YEARS**

FELIX MARTINI A WAITER IN THE CAFÉ HELDER, in Paris, France, MEMORIZED THE ENTIRE FRENCH MILITARY YEAR-BOOK FOR 1856 - CONTAINING 1,171 PAGES OF STATISTICS, INCLUDING THE NAME, RANK, POST AND BIRTHDATE OF 26,208 OFFICERS

ARCHIBALD CAMPBELL Earl of Argyll **SACRIFICED 6 SONS TO GAIN A DAUGHTER-IN-LAW** HE KIDNAPED MURIEL CAWDOR, WHOM HE MARRIED TO HIS SON - AFTER A PITCHED BATTLE IN WHICH **6 OF THE EARL'S SONS WERE SLAIN** (1499)

THE WAR THAT WAS WON BY A HERD OF GOATS! THE **WOMEN** of Gruyere, Switzerland, FINDING THEIR TOWN BESIEGED BY A BERNESE ARMY WHILE ALL THEIR MEN WERE ENGAGED IN BATTLE ELSEWHERE, AFFIXED BLAZING TORCHES TO THE HORNS OF A HERD OF GOATS AND DROVE THEM DOWN THE MOUNTAINSIDE TOWARD THE ATTACKING TROOPS

THE BERNESE FLED - CONVINCED THEY WERE BEING PURSUED BY DEMONS (1499)

THE PARLIAMENT HOUSE in Sydney, Australia, WAS BUILT IN 1811, BY 3 CONTRACTORS WHO IN PAYMENT WERE GRANTED **EXCLUSIVE RIGHTS TO SELL RUM IN THE COLONY**

COOKIES SHAPED LIKE EXPLODING FIREWORKS ARE BAKED ANNUALLY IN VALENCIA, SPAIN, TO OBSERVE THE ANNIVERSARY OF KING JAIME'S TRIUMPHAL ENTRY INTO THE CITY 628 YEARS AGO

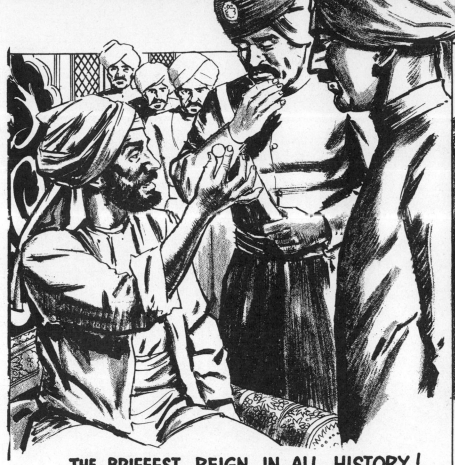

THE BRIEFEST REIGN IN ALL HISTORY!

NIZAM, A WATER CARRIER OF AJMER, INDIA, HAVING SAVED MOGUL EMPEROR HUMAYUN FROM DROWNING, WAS REWARDED BY BEING NAMED EMPEROR OF INDIA *FOR A PERIOD OF 6 HOURS*

ALL HIS RULINGS WERE BINDING AND HE COMMEMORATED HIS REIGN BY ORDERING THE MINTING OF SPECIAL COINS MADE FROM LEATHER INSTEAD OF THE USUAL SILVER (1555)

THE CATHEDRAL OF AJACCIO
in Corsica
WAS BUILT BY BISHOP GIUSEPPE MASCRADI WHO TURNED OVER TO THE BUILDING FUND HIS OFFICIAL FOOD ALLOWANCE FOR THE 5-YEAR PERIOD THE STRUCTURE WAS UNDER CONSTRUCTION (1582-1587)

THE SHIP THAT BECAME AN ISLAND
A SAILING SHIP, ABANDONED IN THE MARONI RIVER BETWEEN FRENCH AND DUTCH GUIANA, FILLED WITH SOIL AND SPROUTED TREES AND PLANTS *—ALL IN A PERIOD OF 36 YEARS*

A **NEW MOSQUE** near Ismailia, Egypt, TO EMPHASIZE ITS MODERNISTIC CONSTRUCTION, *HAS A MINARET SHAPED LIKE A ROCKET MISSILE*

BENJAMIN SCHULZE
(1689-1760)

COPIED THE BIBLE IN LONGHAND 3 TIMES *—EACH TIME IN A DIFFERENT HINDU LANGUAGE*

HE KNEW **100** FOREIGN ALPHABETS AND COULD RECITE THE LORD'S PRAYER IN **215** LANGUAGES

NATURE'S THERMOMETER

THE MALLEE BIRD of Australia LEAVES ITS EGGS TO INCUBATE IN A CAVITY FILLED WITH DECAYING VEGETATION — AND *REGULARLY CHECKS THE TEMPERATURE WITH ITS TONGUE*

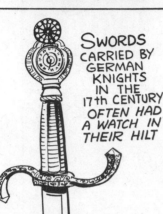

SWORDS CARRIED BY GERMAN KNIGHTS IN THE 17th CENTURY OFTEN HAD A WATCH IN THEIR HILT

THE "OTHELO" FIRST OFFICIAL LIFEBOAT of Barfleur, France, IN ITS FIRST RESCUE EFFORT, SAVED 28 MEMBERS OF THE CREW OF AN AMERICAN SHIP *NAMED THE "OTHELO"* (Dec. 4, 1872)

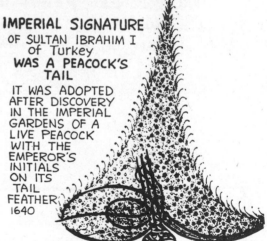

IMPERIAL SIGNATURE

OF SULTAN IBRAHIM I of Turkey **WAS A PEACOCK'S TAIL**

IT WAS ADOPTED AFTER DISCOVERY IN THE IMPERIAL GARDENS OF A LIVE PEACOCK WITH THE EMPEROR'S INITIALS ON ITS TAIL FEATHER 1640

THE FIRST CHRISTIAN KING

ABGAR, pagan ruler of Armenia, *BECAME A CHRISTIAN IN 32 A.D.* IN GRATITUDE FOR HIS RECOVERY FROM A SERIOUS ILLNESS

THE *PULPIT* of St. Leonard's-on-Sea Church, England, MOST OF THE PARISHIONERS OF WHICH ARE FISHERMEN, IS SHAPED *LIKE THE PROW OF A BOAT*

THE NEWE ZEITUNG

FOUNDED AS A MONTHLY IN RORSCHACH, SWITZERLAND, IN 1597 *WAS THE WORLD'S FIRST REGULAR PERIODICAL*

Ripley's Believe It or Not!

THE LIVING BRIDGES OF INDIA
THE AERIAL ROOTS of Indian fig trees GRAFT TOGETHER SO FIRMLY AND FAST THAT LINKING THE ROOTS OF TREES ON OPPOSITE BANKS OF A RIVER *CREATES BRIDGES OF GREAT STRENGTH*

THE MOST ORNATE UNIFORM IN ALL HISTORY
THE MARQUIS de la ENSENADA (1702-1781) Spanish statesman FOR A PERIOD OF 20 YEARS ALWAYS ORNAMENTED HIS UNIFORM WITH DIAMONDS- BEGINNING EACH WEEK WITH $100,000 WORTH OF GEMS AND ADDING MORE EACH DAY UNTIL ON SATURDAYS HE *DISPLAYED DIAMONDS VALUED AT $700,000*

THE OLD SOLDIER!
ANVAR-UD-DIN
(1642-1749) Nabob of Arcot, India, LED HIS TROOPS INTO THE BATTLE OF AMBOUR MOUNTED ON AN ELEPHANT *AT THE AGE OF 107!* HE WAS SLAIN IN THAT BATTLE WHEN HE WAS HIT BY 2 BULLETS (July 23, 1749)

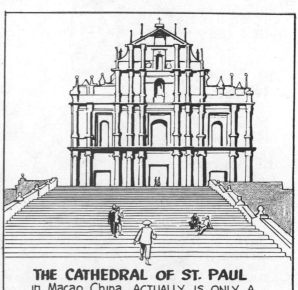

THE CATHEDRAL OF ST. PAUL
In Macao, China, ACTUALLY IS ONLY A MAJESTIC STAIRWAY AND A FACADE BECAUSE THE REMAINDER OF THE STRUCTURE WAS DESTROYED BY FIRE *131 YEARS AGO*

Ripley's — Believe It or Not!

2-FACED KITTEN
SIAMESE KITTEN BORN WITH **2 NOSES, 2 MOUTHS** AND **4 EYES**
Submitted by June A. Weikel, Coopersburg, Pa.

NESTOR'S BATHTUB
A BATHTUB EXCAVATED IN NESTOR'S PALACE, in Pylos, Greece, IS MENTIONED IN THE THIRD BOOK OF HOMER'S ODYSSEY AND IS **3,400** YEARS OLD – *ANTEDATING THE FALL OF TROY*

CHILDREN
BORN IN ITALY IN 1348, THE YEAR OF EUROPE'S GREAT PLAGUE, *GREW ONLY 22 TO 24 PERMANENT TEETH INSTEAD OF THE NORMAL 32*

THE RAINBOW FALLS
A SECTION OF THE MIGHTY VICTORIA FALLS, IN RHODESIA, *IS FAMOUS FOR ITS VIVID RAINBOW*

"LADY PREMIER"
A RACING HOMING PIGEON HATCHED IN CHICAGO, IN 1939, *HAD 4 LEGS*

THE MONARCH WHOSE PEN WAS AS MIGHTY AS HIS SWORD
KING CHARLES XII (1682-1718) of Sweden WHILE IN EXILE IN TURKEY, BY MERELY WRITING LETTERS TO THE SULTAN, PERSUADED HIM TO CHANGE THE TURKISH GOVERNMENT 4 TIMES AND TO DECLARE WAR ON RUSSIA 3 TIMES - ALL IN A PERIOD OF 2 YEARS

THE SWEET CIRCLE
A SPRING OF SWEET WATER off Taranto, Italy, WHICH APPEARS IN THE FORM OF A WHITE CIRCLE - *RISING FROM THE BOTTOM OF THE SALTY SEA*

THE FISH THAT MOO
THE EAGLE FISH, WHICH REACHE A LENGTH OF 7 FEET AND A WEIGHT OF 440 POUNDS, *HAS A VOICE THAT SOUNDS LIKE THE LOWING OF CATTLE*

THE **BELTED WRASSE**
A FISH- APPEARS TO BE WEARING A WHITE BELT AROUND ITS MIDDLE

AN **ARCTIC TERN**
TAGGED ON JULY 5, 1955, in Murmansk, Russia, WAS RECAPTURED ON MAY 15, 1956, IN FREEMANTLE, AUSTRALIA, AFTER A FLIGHT OF 14,000 MILES

THE **SKI** RESCUE
STAGED 762 YEARS AGO!
KING HAAKON HAAKONSSON (1204-1263) of Norway ENDANGERED BY A CIVIL WAR WHEN HE WAS ONLY AN INFANT OF 2, WAS SAVED BY TWO FOLLOWERS, THORSTEIN SKEVLA AND SKERVALD SKRUKA, WHO CONCEALED THE CHILD IN THEIR CLOTHING IN THE BITTER COLD OF A SEVERE WINTER AND CARRIED HIM 230 MILES ON SKIS!

THE **GECKO**
A LIZARD - IS SO NAMED BECAUSE IT CROAKS THAT NAME REPEATEDLY

THE LITTLE GIANT!
MAX SICK, A GERMAN WEIGHT LIFTER, WEIGHED ONLY 147 POUNDS, YET USING THE PRESS METHOD, HE LIFTED A MAN 40 POUNDS HEAVIER THAN HIMSELF ABOVE HIS HEAD WITH ONE HAND 16 TIMES -WHILE HOLDING IN HIS OTHER HAND A FULL GLASS OF BEER FROM WHICH HE DID NOT SPILL A SINGLE DROP

THE **GUILLEMOT** LAYS A SINGLE EGG AMONG THOUSANDS OF OTHERS OF THE SAME SPECIES -BUT SHE CAN ALWAYS IDENTIFY HER OWN BECAUSE NO TWO EGGS ARE EVER ALIKE IN EITHER COLOR OR MARKINGS

THE FIRST FOUNTAIN PEN
A GOOSE QUILL, ENCASED IN A METAL TUBE, WITH A SUPPLY OF INK SEALED IN THE TUBE, WAS CONSTRUCTED IN LEIPZIG, GERMANY, IN 1781

THE **STRANGEST COURTSHIP IN HISTORY**
FRANZ GRILLPARZER (1791-1872)
AUSTRIAN NATIONAL POET, NEVER MARRIED- YET HE WAS ENGAGED TO KATHI FRÖHLICH FOR 50 YEARS
THE WEDDING DATE WAS SET 50 TIMES -BUT WAS CANCELLED EACH TIME BECAUSE OF A LOVERS' QUARREL

THE MOST AMAZING SWIMMING FEAT IN ALL HISTORY!
GENERAL QUINTUS SERTORIUS THE ONLY SURVIVOR OF A MASSACRE OF AN ENTIRE ROMAN ARMY BY THE GERMANS IN 105 B.C., ESCAPED BY SWIMMING ACROSS THE RAGING WATERS OF THE RHONE RIVER, *ALTHOUGH HE WAS CRITICALLY WOUNDED AND BURDENED BY A HEAVY COAT OF ARMOR, HIS SHIELD AND SWORD!*

AN APARTMENT HOUSE
in Beirut, Lebanon, AT ONE END IS ONLY *5 FEET WIDE*

FRANC
THE BASIC FRENCH COIN *MEANS "FREE"*

THE FIRST FRANC WAS A GOLD COIN MINTED IN THE 14th CENTURY FOR A RANSOM TO FREE KING JOHN II OF FRANCE, WHO WAS HELD PRISONER BY THE ENGLISH FOR 8 YEARS

THE CENTENNIAL WHITE OAK
of Salem, N.J., WHICH WAS PLANTED IN 1875, *OWNS THE LAND ON WHICH IT GROWS.* TITLE TO THE GROUND WAS VESTED IN THE TREE BY JOHNSON HUBBELL

A GOLD MEDAL
CREATED BY JERONIMO SCOTTO, AN ITALIAN MAGICIAN, WHO SAID HE HAD COINED IT FROM A BASE METAL CONVERTED *BY ALCHEMY* (1580)

THE AIR MAIL STAMP
of Sierra Leone, Africa, IS SHAPED LIKE AN EAGLE

THE MOST CO-OPERATIVE STUDENT IN HISTORY
KING HENRY VI (1421-1471) of England, WHO ASCENDED THE THRONE AT THE AGE OF 9 MONTHS, HAD A WOODEN SIGNATURE STAMP WITH WHICH EACH TIME HE HAD MISBEHAVED AS A CHILD, *HE WOULD APPROVE A SPECIAL LAW PERMITTING HIS TUTOR TO WHIP HIM*

THIS WAS THE FIRST KNOWN USE OF A SIGNATURE STAMP

THE HUMAN FLAG
8 WOMEN of Wessington Springs, S.D., TO CELEBRATE THE 100th ANNIVERSARY OF THE CREATION OF THE SOUTH DAKOTA TERRITORY, WORE DRESSES WHICH, WHEN THEY STOOD IN LINE, *FORMED AN AMERICAN FLAG*

THE CHINESE LETTERED GOLDFISH IS COVERED WITH CHINESE CHARACTERS -ACHIEVED BY YEARS OF CROSSBREEDING

AUGUSTIN BÉGIN
(1825-1908)
CHOIR LEADER OF THE PARISH CHURCH OF WOTTON, CANADA, BECAME A CHOIR BOY AT THE AGE OF 10 AND NEVER MISSED A SERVICE *FOR 73 YEARS*

THE **WOOD SWALLOWS** of Australia CLING TO EACH OTHER BENEATH THE BRANCHES OF A TREE LIKE A HUGE *SWARM OF BEES*

BLUE WHALES IN INFANCY GAIN WEIGHT AT THE RATE OF 10 POUNDS AN HOUR

BARRISTERS -English trial lawyers-
ARE FORBIDDEN TO SUE FOR THEIR FEES
THEIR PAYMENT IS CONSIDERED AN HONORARIUM AND ITS COLLECTION CANNOT BE ENFORCED IN A COURT OF LAW

PI TING JUI
PAINTED ON ANCIENT PORCELAIN BY THE CHINESE, WAS A REBUS DEPICTING A BRUSH, A CAKE OF INK AND A JADE SCEPTER *WHICH ALSO MEANS:"MAY IT HAPPEN AS YOU WISH "*

THE HOTTEST DANCE IN ALL THE WORLD!
THE SANGHYANG IS PERFORMED BY 2 BALINESE YOUNGSTERS WHO, AFTER BEING LULLED INTO A TRANCE BY A MUSICAL MONOTONE, *DANCE IN BARE FEET FOR 90 MINUTES ON GLOWING EMBERS!*

A MESSAGE
"WRITTEN" ON PERU'S COASTAL DESERT IN LETTERS FORMED BY THE MOSSLIKE TILLANDSIA PLANT *HAS REMAINED CLEARLY VISIBLE FOR 50 YEARS* THE PLANT HAS NO ROOTS, NEEDS NO WATER AND REMAINS FIRMLY IN PLACE IN THE SAND

Ripley's — Believe It or Not!

THE DICHEA ORCHID of Brazil HAS A HUMAN FACE

BILLY PEIRSE
(1764-1839)
an English jockey
READ ONLY 2 BOOKS IN HIS ENTIRE LIFETIME
-THE BIBLE AND ADAM SMITH'S "WEALTH OF NATIONS"- YET HE READ BOTH OF THOSE FROM COVER TO COVER **30 TIMES**

PHILIP REIDEL of Chardon, Ohio, WAS CONSIDERED SO CRITICALLY WOUNDED WHEN A BULLET LODGED IN HIS RIGHT LUNG THAT SURGEONS REFUSED TO RISK REMOVING IT - *YET A FEW DAYS LATER HE COUGHED UP THE SLUG*

THE CATHEDRAL OF ST. BASIL
in Moscow, Russia,
WAS BUILT WITH 8 CUPOLAS TO COMMEMORATE THE 8 DAYS IVAN THE TERRIBLE FOUGHT TO CAPTURE THE CITY OF KAZAN- TO MAKE CERTAIN THAT ITS ARCHITECTS, BARNA AND POSTNIK, NEVER AGAIN BUILT SO MAGNIFICENT A STRUCTURE, IVAN DEPRIVED THEM *OF THEIR EYES, ARMS AND TONGUES.*

THE STRANGEST CUNEIFORM EVER FOUND
A FRAGMENT OF CLAY THE SIZE OF A QUARTER ON WHICH AN ANCIENT BABYLONIAN SCRIBE *INSCRIBED 144 WORDS OF PRAYER IN 30 LINES.*

SINCE MAGNIFYING GLASSES WERE NOT INVENTED 3,500 YEARS AGO, THE SCRIBES WORKED BY PEERING THROUGH A HOLLOW REED

THE BACKSTROKE BUG
Buena Margaritacea, an insect, *SWIMS ON ITS BACK AND USES ITS HIND LEGS AS OARS*

THE ORIGINAL GOVERNMENT HOUSE of Auckland, N.Z., *WAS BUILT IN ENGLAND, TAKEN APART AND TRANSPORTED BY SHIP TO NEW ZEALAND - WHERE IT WAS REASSEMBLED IN 1840* THE STRUCTURE, WHICH MEASURED 120 FEET BY 50 FEET AND WEIGHED 250 TONS, WAS A REPLICA OF THE HOUSE BUILT FOR NAPOLEON ON ST. HELENA

THE FIRST HOUSES IN THE WORLD WITH IDENTIFYING NUMBERS

THE NOTRE DAME BRIDGE in Paris, France, FOR A PERIOD OF 380 YEARS HAD ON IT 78 THREE-STORY HOUSES, WHICH WERE MARKED BY NUMBERS IN 1512 -214 YEARS BEFORE ANY OTHER HOME WAS NUMBERED

THE WORLD'S MOST AMAZING WATCH

IT TOOK 5 YEARS TO CREATE, AND WHEN A BUTTON IS PRESSED IT *REVEALS THE EXACT HOUR AND MINUTE BY BELLS AT ANY TIME* - IT NORMALLY STRIKES THE HOURS AND QUARTER HOURS, SERVES AS AN ALARM CLOCK, PERPETUAL CALENDAR, SHOWS THE POSITION OF THE STARS AND THE TIME OF EACH SUNRISE AND SUNSET

THE PLANT THAT IS ALL SEED

BRYOPHYLLUM RE-CREATES ITSELF WHEN ANY FRAGMENT OF ITS LEAF OR STEM FALLS TO THE GROUND

THE DUCHESS de LONGUEVILLE

(1619-1679) A MEMBER OF THE FRENCH ROYAL FAMILY, HEARTBROKEN OVER THE DEATH OF HER SON IN BATTLE, *VOWED SHE WOULD NEVER AGAIN SIT DOWN FOR THE REMAINDER OF HER LIFE* FOR 7 YEARS SHE STOOD ALL DAY, SLEPT AT NIGHT ON THE BARE GROUND- *SHE DIED ON HER FEET*

THE MOST AMAZING MILITARY VICTORY IN ALL HISTORY !

EMPEROR CONSTANTINE V, LEADING A BYZANTINE ARMY OF 80,000 SOLDIERS, FOUGHT AND DEFEATED A BULGARIAN ARMY OF EQUAL STRENGTH *WITHOUT A SINGLE BYZANTINE SOLDIER BEING KILLED OR WOUNDED* -YET 20,000 BULGARIANS WERE SLAIN! (774)

SCHUYLER COLFAX
(1823-1885)
BECAME THE FIRST AMERICAN TO PRESIDE OVER BOTH HOUSES OF CONGRESS
HE WAS ELECTED VICE-PRESIDENT OF THE U.S. IN 1868 WHILE SERVING AS SPEAKER OF THE HOUSE OF REPRESENTATIVES

THE **TOMB**
of the 13th Dalai Lama of Tibet, in Lhasa, IS COVERED WITH 300,000 OUNCES OF SOLID GOLD - **VALUED AT $10,500,000**

THE **"88" BUTTERFLY** ALWAYS DISPLAYS THAT NUMBER ON ITS WINGS

A **WEDDING BAND** LOST BY MRS. VICTOR GRIMEAU IN HER BARN AT WHITEWOOD, SASKATCHEWAN, IN **1922**, WAS FOUND A MILE AWAY IN A STRAWBERRY PATCH BY HER GRANDSON **45 YEARS LATER**

A **TREE** GROWING IN THE SHAPE OF A CROSS ON A MOUNTAIN PEAK near Oberammergau, Bavaria, SITE OF THE FAMOUS PASSION PLAYS

REPUBLIQUE FRANÇOISE 500
ASSIGNAT DE CINQ CENTS

SILK MONE
ISSUED BY FRANCE IN 179 DURING THE REVOLUTION COULD NOT BE COUNTERFEITE BECAUSE IT WAS WOVEN ON THE ONLY MACHINES OF THEIR KIND

THE **DEAL FISH** DURING ITS GROWTH ASSUMES AT VARIOUS PERIODS THE FORM OF **3 DIFFERENT FISHES**

THE **STRANGE PROPHECY THAT WAS FULFILLED BY A VIOLENT DEATH!**
WALTER INGRAM, of London, England, BROUGHT BACK FROM EGYPT IN 1884 THE MUMMIFIED HAND OF AN ANCIENT EGYPTIAN PRINCESS, WHICH WAS FOUND TO BE CLUTCHING A GOLD PLAQUE INSCRIBED:
"WHOEVER TAKES ME AWAY TO A FOREIGN COUNTRY WILL DIE A VIOLENT DEATH AND HIS BONES WILL NEVER BE FOUND!"
4 YEARS LATER INGRAM WAS TRAMPLED TO DEATH BY A ROGUE ELEPHANT NEAR BERBERA, SOMALILAND, AND HIS REMAINS WERE BURIED IN THE DRY BED OF A RIVER BUT AN EXPEDITION SENT TO RECOVER HIS BODY FOUND A FLOOD HAD WASHED IT AWAY

Ripley's — Believe It or Not!

THE CROOKED RIVER
THE RAAB RIVER IN BURGENLAND, AUSTRIA, OVERFLOWS ITS BANKS EACH YEAR - *EACH TIME ADDING ANOTHER LOOP TO ITS COURSE*

SINGLE GIRLS
of Nazaré, Portugal, FROM THE AGE OF 3 WEAR **7 PETTICOATS**

FEMALE WATER FLEAS
ARE TWICE THE SIZE OF THE MALE -AND OUTNUMBER THEM A MILLION TO ONE

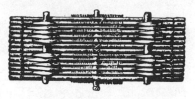

A GUITAR
USED BY NATIVES of Dahomey, Africa, HAS A WOODEN FRAME AND STRINGS MADE OF **BARK** -IT PRODUCES PLEASANT MUSIC

THE HUMAN CALCULATOR
JUDGE SAMUEL E. PERKINS (1811-1879) WHILE PRESIDENT OF THE STATE BANK OF INDIANA, REGULARLY COUNTED ITS KEGS OF SILVER *BY MERELY HEFTING EACH BARREL*

EACH KEG HELD $500 IN SILVER COINS, YET ONCE HE NOTED *A SHORTAGE OF ONLY 25 CENTS*

GOLDEN SCALES
WERE PLACED IN THE GRAVES OF EGYPTIAN PRINCESSES WHO HAD DIED WHILE THEY WERE STILL VERY YOUNG, *IN THE BELIEF THAT THEY COULD AFFORD TO WEIGH THEIR GOOD DEEDS AGAINST THEIR SINS*

HUNTING DOGS
in 16th-century Spain *WERE DRESSED IN STEEL ARMOR*

THE PEEK-A-BOO CITY OF PETRA
Jordan
ITS MAIN ENTRANCE IS A CHASM 450 FEET LONG WHICH TWISTS AND TURNS BETWEEN TWO WALLS OF SOLID ROCK **350 FEET HIGH**
THE CHASM IS SO NARROW THAT IN MANY PLACES THE TWO WALLS TOUCH OVERHEAD

THE SEA LAMPREY
a relic of prehistoric times, CANNOT BE CAUGHT WITH A ROD AND HOOK BECAUSE *IT HAS NEITHER RIBS NOR JAWS-* IT IS A PARASITE THAT ATTACHES ITSELF TO A FISH BY SUCTION AND THEN DRAWS OUT ITS VICTIM'S BLOOD

RIPLEY's Believe It or Not!

THE MAN WHO BROKE A BEAR TO THE PLOW!

MARINUS, founder of the Republic of San Marino, CAPTURED A BEAR THAT HAD KILLED HIS MULE AND FORCED THE BEAR TO TAKE ITS VICTIM'S PLACE - *PULLING A PLOW!*

MARY D. JONES
HIS PERFECT
FIRST WIFE
(1838-1868)

LUCY TALBOT
HIS SWEET
2ND WIFE
(1839-1872)

MARY E. BRIGGS
HIS HEALTHFUL
3RD WIFE
1862 -

TOMBSTONE
OF THEODORE MANNING
IN WARRENVILLE, Ill.,
ERECTED BY HIS THIRD
WIFE, WHO SURVIVED HIM

THE WORLD'S HIGHEST TIDAL WAVE

A TIDAL WAVE THAT STRUCK CAPE LOPATKA ON THE SOUTHERN TIP OF KAMCHATKA, SIBERIA, IN 1737, ATTAINED A HEIGHT **OF 210 FEET**

DON'T WAIT
OUTSIDE
BETTER WEIGHT
INSIDE

SIGN IN A BUTCHER'S WINDOW
in Newcastle, Australia

THE FIRST STATION
on the Sierra Leone Railroad, in Africa,
WAS MERELY A HUGE COTTON TREE
-THE BRANCHES OF WHICH SHELTERED
WAITING PASSENGERS (1908)

CHARLES BOYINGTON
HANGED IN MOBILE, ALA., IN 1835
FOR THE MURDER OF HIS FRIEND,
*PREDICTED THAT AS PROOF OF HIS
INNOCENCE AN OAK TREE WOULD
SPRING FROM HIS GRAVE*
AN OAK TREE DID GROW
OUT OF THE GRAVE

HALOSTACHYS CASPICA
WHICH GROWS IN THE ARID CASPIAN DESERT
HAS ROOTS 14 TIMES AS LONG AS THE PLANT ITSELF

ANTONIO PERSIO
(1550-1608)

AN ITALIAN COLLEGE PROFESSOR, TAUGHT THEOLOGY FOR **3** YEARS, PHYSICS FOR **4** YEARS, MATHEMATICS FOR **5** YEARS, MEDICINE FOR **6** YEARS, JURISPRUDENCE FOR **7** YEARS **AND WAS RETIRED FOR JUST 8 YEARS BEFORE HIS DEATH**

MRS. CORINNE JOLY of St. Paul, Alberta, WAS THE SISTER OF **4** PRIESTS AND MOTHER OF **4** NUNS, THE AUNT OF **6** PRIESTS AND THE GRANDMOTHER OF **3** PRIESTS

ESQUI REDEGRAY
RECOMMANDÉ A MONSIEUR LE COMTE DE VERGENNES PAR LE COMTE DE VALMONT AMBASSADEUR DE FRANCE A LONDRES.

THE WREATH ON A CARD OF INTRODUCTION, ISSUED BY THE FRENCH MINISTRY OF FOREIGN AFFAIRS TO FOREIGN DIGNITARIES IN THE 18th CENTURY, REVEALED IN AN INTRICATE CODE SUCH DATA AS ITS *BEARER'S MARITAL STATUS, RELIGION, GAMBLING HABITS, EDUCATION, DISCRETION AND POLITICAL AFFILIATION*

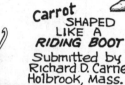

THE LION'S MOUTH an African plant PRODUCES A FRUIT THAT *CLIMBS THE PLANT'S STEM*

Carrot SHAPED LIKE A *RIDING BOOT* Submitted by Richard D. Carney, Holbrook, Mass.

THE WAR THAT WAS WON WITH SHOVELS!

KING FERGANISH of the Ephtalites, DEFEATED A HUGE ARMY OF PERSIANS IN 484 **BY MERELY DIGGING A VAST DITCH!**

KING PEROZ II of Persia, 29 OF HIS SONS AND HIS ENTIRE ARMY WERE MASSACRED WHEN THEY PLUNGED INTO A DITCH CAMOUFLAGED WITH TREE BRANCHES — *AND THE EPHTALITES COLLECTED* **$100,000,000 IN BOOTY**

THE INSECT THAT FISHES WITH A NET **THE LARVA** of the CADDIS FLY CATCHES THE SMALL ORGANISMS ON WHICH IT FEEDS BY SPREADING OVER THE WATER OF STREAMS *A NET IT SPINS OF SILK*

THE CHILDREN OF THE SEA

2 INFANTS, STRAPPED INSIDE A GREEN CRADLE, WERE FOUND ON THE BEACH OF WYCK, GERMANY, IN 1825 — *HAVING SURVIVED A GREAT FLOOD THAT KILLED HUNDREDS AND LEVELED SCORES OF VILLAGES*

WITH THEIR IDENTITIES A MYSTERY, THEY WERE ADOPTED BY A SHIPOWNER, GREW UP TO BECOME CAPTAINS OF THEIR OWN VESSELS *—AND BOTH WERE LOST AT SEA!*

THE HEART BLOOM
A STAR-SHAPED PLANT in the Sahara IS GAZED AT INTENTLY BY BEDOUIN GIRLS IN THE BELIEF IT WILL MAKE THEM *STARRY EYED*

HOWARD HILL FAMED AMERICAN ARCHER ARMED ONLY WITH A CONVENTIONAL BOW KILLED A 12-FOOT THRESHER SHARK WITH A SINGLE ARROW **WHILE UNDER WATER AT A DEPTH OF 40 FEET** THE SHARK WAS ONLY 15 FEET AWAY BUT HILL MASTERED HITTING A TARGET UNDER WATER AT A DISTANCE OF 60 FEET

A PINTAIL DUCK
BANDED BY THE BEAU RIVER REFUGE, IN UTAH, SET A NEW LONGEVITY RECORD FOR WATERFOWL WHEN IT WAS CAUGHT IN MEXICO **13 YEARS LATER**

THE LARGEST LOAF OF BREAD IN THE WORLD

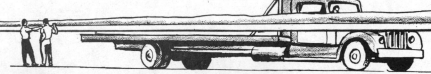

A LOAF OF FRENCH BREAD, 50 FEET LONG AND WEIGHING 120 POUNDS, WAS BAKED IN ST. CHARLES, Ill., IN 1963, *IN A DRAINSPOUT* - Submitted by Margaret Gilkison, Chicago, Ill.

WILLIAM LEGGETT
(1802-1875)
ATTENDED SERVICES DAILY AT BOTH THE ST. GEORGE AND ETON COLLEGE CHAPELS IN ETON, ENGLAND, FOR 50 YEARS - WITHOUT ONCE BEING ABSENT OR TARDY *HE HAD MEMORIZED THE ENTIRE BIBLE - YET HE COULD NEITHER READ NOR WRITE*

EASTER CAVE
near Kallmunz, Germany, DISPLAYS ON AN IRIDESCENT WALL *A NATURAL OUTLINE OF THE MADONNA AND CHILD*

A **CANARY** OWNED BY HARRY CHAMBERS, of Moorestown, N.J., WHICH LIVED TO THE AGE OF 25, WAS GIVEN A PUBLIC FUNERAL IN 1918 *ATTENDED BY THE ENTIRE POPULATION OF THE TOWN*

Ripley's Believe It or Not!

IBRAHIM PASHA
(1798-1848) AN EGYPTIAN COMMANDER IMPRESSED BY THE COURAGE OF ABDALLAH IBN SAUD, COMMANDER OF THE SAUDI ARABIAN ARMY HE HAD JUST DEFEATED IN BATTLE, OFFERED TO SUPPLY THE SAUDI ARMY WITH FOOD, ARMS AND AMMUNITION SO THEY COULD CONTINUE TO FIGHT

ABDALLAH DECIDED TO SURRENDER INSTEAD (1818)

PROFESSOR WILHELM EDINGER
of Berne, Switzerland
WHOSE NOSE WAS SLICED OFF IN A SABER DUEL *REPLACED IT WITH A PROBOSCIS OF CLAY WHICH WAS HELD IN PLACE BY HIS SPECTACLES* WHEN HE MOVED HIS GLASSES UP ON HIS FOREHEAD, HIS NOSE WOULD ALSO RISE

THE **OECOPHYLLA ANT** OF W. AFRICA, CREATES ITS NEST BY SEWING TOGETHER LEAVES WITH SILK THREADS. THE THREADS ARE PROVIDED BY THEIR LARVAE, WHICH ARE CARRIED ABOUT BY THE WORKERS —AS LIVING SHUTTLES

COPPER COINS
WORTH 3 CENTS EACH, MINTED BY THE VILLAGE OF FROHNLEITEN, AUSTRIA, IN 1719 WERE SQUARE

THE **FIRST MEDAL FOR VALOR** WARRIORS WERE HONORED FOR BRAVERY BY THE EGYPTIAN PHARAOHS BY HAVING A GOLDEN BEE PINNED ON THEIR TUNICS 3,500 YEARS AGO

THE **SWEET-AFTER-DEATH PLANT** HAS NO FRAGRANCE WHILE IT IS ALIVE, BUT AFTER ITS LEAVES HAVE DIED AND WITHERED THEY HAVE THE SWEET SMELL OF VANILLA

THE **ENTRANCE** of the Manor House of Visborggaard, in Denmark, FOR GENERATIONS HAS BEEN BELIEVED TO BE UNDER A SPELL CAST BY A FRENCH GOVERNESS, SPURNED IN LOVE, WHO VOWED THAT NO FUTURE MISTRESS OF THE MANOR *WILL EVER BE DRIVEN THROUGH THE ARCHWAY TO HER GRAVE*

WHEN THE NEXT MISTRESS OF THE MANOR DIED, THE HORSES REFUSED TO PASS THROUGH THE ARCH—*AND EVER SINCE EVERY COFFIN HAS BEEN CARRIED OUT BY HAND*

THE **LARGEST DRUMS IN THE WORLD** THE NAGAS of Assam, India, COVER HOLLOWED-OUT TREE TRUNKS WITH SKIN TO BUILD DRUMS SO LARGE EACH CAN BE BEATEN BY 50 DRUMMERS SIMULTANEOUSLY

Ripley's Believe It or Not

THE STRANGEST WHALING SHIP DISASTER IN HISTORY
AN ENTIRE WHALING FLEET COMPRISING **29 SHIPS** WAS CRUSHED TO SPLINTERS BY ICEBERGS OFF ICY CAPES, IN THE ARCTIC, IN SEPTEMBER, 1871 - YET ALTHOUGH MANY WIVES AND CHILDREN WERE ABOARD **NOT A SINGLE LIFE WAS LOST**

WOMEN of the Aures Mountain region of Algeria **NEVER HAVE TO SEW A GOWN** THE CLOTH IS WOVEN IN A SIZE AND SHAPE THAT MAKES IT **READY TO WEAR**

NICHOLAS ZOGRAPHOS (1886-1953) A PROFESSIONAL GAMBLER LEFT AN ESTATE OF **$14,000,000** *EVERY DOLLAR OF IT WON PLAYING BACCARAT*

THE CANINE MOUNTAIN CLIMBER
"TSCHINGEL," A DOG OWNED BY ALPINIST WILLIAM A.B. COOLIDGE, DURING A PERIOD OF 11 YEARS, CLIMBED **30 PEAKS AND 36 ALPINE PASSES** *MOST OF THEM MORE THAN 12,000 FEET HIGH* THE DOG WAS NAMED FOR THE TSCHINGEL PASS, IN SWITZERLAND - 9,265 FEET HIGH - WHICH SHE ASCENDED IN 1865 AS A PUPPY

IF A HANDFUL OF SALT IS DROPPED INTO HALF A GLASS OF WATER, WILL IT CHANGE THE LEVEL OF THE WATER? **YES- THE WATER LEVEL WILL DROP**

THE ALFALFA PALACE in Fallon, Nevada,
BUILT IN 1915 TO HOUSE THE AGRICULTURAL EXHIBIT AT THE STATE FAIR WAS CONSTRUCTED ENTIRELY FROM **54 TONS OF HAY**

THE LUSH GREEN LEAVES
OF THE GABOR BUSH of the Sahara Desert *FATALLY POISON ANY ANIMAL THAT EATS THEM*

AN **IMPRESSIONIST PAINTING**
ENTITLED "And the sun went to sleep over the Adriatic" EXHIBITED IN 1910 IN THE SALON DES INDEPENDENTS, IN PARIS, FRANCE, **WON HIGH PRAISE**
IT WAS SUBSEQUENTLY REVEALED THAT IT HAD BEEN PAINTED BY A DONKEY - **WITH A BRUSH TIED TO ITS TAIL**

THE MAN WHO OUTWRESTLED A TIGER!
SIR EDWARD WINTER   (1622-1686)
ENGLISH COMMANDER OF FORT ST. GEORGE, IN MADRAS, INDIA, **STRANGLED A FULLY GROWN TIGER WITH HIS BARE HANDS!**

A **MEDAL**
DEPICTING THE CAPTURE BY THE DUTCH OF A SPANISH FLEET CARRYING $54,000,000 IN SILVER, WAS ISSUED BY THE SPANISH GOVERNMENT IN 1628 - **TO DRAMATIZE THE NEED FOR NEW TAXES TO REPLACE THE LOSS**

THE **SHELL** of the beach crab of the North Sea IS PITTED WITH SMALL CRAYFISH -WHICH HAVE NO MEANS OF MOVEMENT AND USE THEIR MOLLUSK HOST AS PERMANENT TRANSPORTATION

LAW and **JUSTICE**
TEACH THE SAME GRADES IN THE Greenmont School, in Vienna, West Va.
Submitted by Linda Pitner, Vienna, West Va.

ALLSPICE
GETS ITS NAME FROM THE FACT THAT ITS BERRY COMBINES THE MINGLED FRAGRANCE OF **CLOVES, NUTMEG AND CINNAMON**

REUBEN ELIYAHU ISRAEL
WAS THE **12th** DESCENDANT OF THE SAME FAMILY TO SERVE AS RABBI OF THE ISLAND OF RHODES, GREECE- **A CONTINUOUS SUCCESSION FOR 232 YEARS**

PARUMA, a village in Venezuela, IS DESTROYED BY THE FLOODING OF THE ORINOCO RIVER **EVERY YEAR**
THE VILLAGERS REBUILD ON THE SAME SPOT BECAUSE THOUSANDS OF TURTLES APPEAR ON THE RIVER BANK AFTER EACH FLOOD

A PERFECT DIAMOND IS CALLED A STONE "OF THE FIRST WATER" BECAUSE IT IS INVISIBLE IN WATER

A POSTAGE STAMP ISSUED BY GREECE IN 1954 REPRODUCES THE ENTIRE TEXT OF A DEBATE ON THE STATUS OF CYPRUS IN THE BRITISH PARLIAMENT —A TOTAL OF 746 WORDS

THE NIGHTMARE THAT WAS A FATAL PROPHECY!

JEAN PETION de VILLENEUVE (1756-1794) ONE OF THE LEADERS OF THE FRENCH REVOLUTION, WAS PLAGUED FROM CHILDHOOD BY A RECURRING DREAM IN WHICH *HE AND A COMPANION WERE DEVOURED BY A PACK OF WILD ANIMALS.* IN JUNE, 1794, PETION AND A FRIEND WERE ATTACKED AND KILLED BY A PACK OF RAVENOUS WOLVES!

THE OLDEST PAYROLL A CUNEIFORM RECORD FOUND IN UR OF THE CHALDEES, HOME OF THE PATRIARCH ABRAHAM, LISTS 1,197 SLAVES AND THE DAILY ALLOWANCE THEY RECEIVED 5,000 YEARS AGO

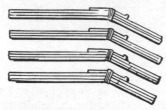

4 GOLD RODS FOUND IN THE TOMB OF KING TUT WERE CONSTRUCTED AT AN ANGLE OF 26½ DEGREES BECAUSE THAT IS THE ANGLE OF THE REFRACTION OF LIGHT —AND THE ANCIENTS EXPECTED THEIR MONARCH'S SOUL TO RISE TO HEAVEN ON A RAY OF SUNLIGHT THE GREAT PYRAMID IS ALSO CONSTRUCTED AT AN ANGLE OF 26½ DEGREES

PAUL MORPHY (1837-1884) American chess wizard MEMORIZED THE 535-PAGE LOUISIANA CIVIL CODE AND PASSED HIS BAR EXAMINATION AT THE AGE OF 19 HE WAS ADMITTED TO THE BAR WITH THE STIPULATION THAT HE COULD NOT PRACTICE LAW UNTIL HE BECAME 21

"H.M.S. BOUNTY" CONSTRUCTED FOR A MODERN MOVIE AS AN EXACT DUPLICATE OF THE SHIP ON WHICH THE HISTORIC MUTINY WAS STAGED, COST $750,000. 174 YEARS EARLIER THE ORIGINAL "BOUNTY" COST $9,750

THE FIRST POVERTY PROGRAM THE CORONATION OF EVERY BYZANTINE EMPEROR WAS CELEBRATED BY DISTRIBUTION OF 10,000 LOAVES OF BREAD —WITH 3 GOLD COINS DISPLAYING THE HEAD OF THE NEW RULER BAKED INSIDE EACH LOAF

FISH AND REPTILES CONTINUE TO GROW AS LONG AS THEY LIVE

Ripley's Believe It or Not!

THE FIRST COUNTERFEIT COIN
"GOLD" COINS CONSISTING OF SOLID LEAD WITH A THIN COATING OF GOLD WERE MINTED BY POLYCRATES, RULER OF THE GREEK ISLAND OF SAMOS IN 535 B.C.

IDOL
CARVED BY NATIVES OF THE Marquesas Islands, IN THE Pacific FROM A HUMAN THIGH BONE

A LABOR OF LOVE
THE CATHEDRAL OF ST. GEORGE in Ferrara, Italy WAS DESIGNED BY AN ARCHITECT NAMED WILIGELMO AND WHEN THE PHILANTHROPIST WHO WAS FINANCING IT DIED SUDDENLY THE ARCHITECT COMPLETED THE STRUCTURE AT HIS OWN EXPENSE
(1135)

A 3-LEAF CLOVER
A 4-LEAF CLOVER AND
A 5-LEAF CLOVER
ALL GROWING ON A SINGLE STEM
Submitted by Jeanette Ross, Albuquerque, N. Mexico

CHURCH OF TRÉHORENTEUC, France,
WAS BUILT IN 1516 ENTIRELY FROM STONES DONATED BY RESIDENTS IN AN AREA OF 50 MILES EACH OF WHOM REMOVED A ROCK FROM THE WALLS OF HIS HOUSE

MOTHER OF PEARL
FOUND BY SHARON GRAY IN HER GARDEN IN LOMPOC, CALIF., BEARING THE PERFECT OUTLINE OF A MAN'S HEAD

THE FIGHT THAT WAS WON BY A CORPSE!
ARRACHION -famed Greek athlete-BEING SLOWLY STRANGLED IN A WRESTLING MATCH IN WHICH NO HOLDS WERE BARRED - STAMPED ON HIS OPPONENT'S FOOT WITH SUCH FORCE THAT HIS ADVERSARY TAPPED ARRACHION'S SHOULDER IN THE TRADITIONAL GESTURE OF SURRENDER
A MOMENT LATER ARRACHION SANK TO THE GROUND IN DEATH -BUT THE JUDGES RULED THAT THE DEAD MAN HAD WON THE FIGHT!

Ripley's® Believe It or Not!

THE
SASSAFRAS
TREE
BEARS 3
DIFFERENT-
SHAPED LEAVES
ON THE SAME
BRANCH

MONARCH
BUTTERFLIES
(Danaus plexipus)
WHICH BREED IN
CANADA AND THE
NORTHERN U.S.
MIGRATE IN THE FALL
TO THE GULF STATES
IN FORMATIONS SO
LARGE THEY COVER
AN AREA 432 MILES
IN LENGTH AND 40
MILES IN WIDTH
-17,280 SQ. MILES
OF BUTTERFLIES

PINE
TREE
SHAPED BY
NATURE
LIKE THE   Submitted by
LETTER   Fred E. King,
"S"   Haydenville,
           Mass.

THE BATTLE THAT WAS LOST BY AN ACT OF CHIVALRY
BARON de la GARDE
COMMANDING A FORCE OF ONLY 6 FRENCH SHIPS AND FACING A
POWERFUL FORCE OF 24 SPANISH GALLEYS, SENT WORD TO THE
SPANISH COMMANDER THAT HE HAD AS A GUEST THE QUEEN OF
BOHEMIA AND HUNGARY-WHO WAS SISTER TO THE SPANISH KING-
*THE CHIVALROUS SPANIARDS FIRED A SALUTE TO THE QUEEN FROM
ALL THEIR BATTERIES - THE FRENCH SANK MOST OF THE
SPANISH FLEET BEFORE THE CREWS COULD RELOAD THEIR GUNS*
off Corsica, 1551,

MELONS
growing in the Sahara
Desert ARE SO
BITTER THEY ARE
FED TO THIEVES
AS PUNISHMENT
-YET CAMELS AND
GAZELLES CONSIDER
THEM A DELICACY

THE FEMALE
DEEP-SEA ANGLER
ALWAYS CARRIES WITH HER
3 HUSBANDS

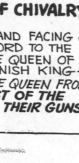

THE
MOST
POPULAR
DESSERT
AT ALL
BANQUETS
IN ANCIENT
ROME
WAS A
SWEET
ONION

THE SUBIACO BRIDGE   Italy
BUILT IN 1358 AS A MEMORIAL TO 1,456
SUBIACO SOLDIERS WHO DEFEATED AN INVADING
ARMY, IS EXACTLY 1,456 INCHES LONG

BYRON KILBOURN AND   MOSES M. STRON
TO SECURE A GRANT OF 1,000,000 ACRES OF
WISCONSIN LAND FOR THEIR RAILROAD,
DISTRIBUTED $862,000 IN BRIBES AMONG TH
GOVERNOR, LIEUTENANT GOVERNOR,
STATE SENATORS, ASSEMBLYMEN, A SUPREM
COURT JUSTICE, THE GOVERNOR'S
SECRETARY, AND THE CHIEF CLERK AND
ASSISTANT CLERK OF THE ASSEMBLY (185

KING PTOLEMY II WHO RULED EGYPT FROM 285 TO 246 B.C. IS HISTORICALLY CALLED "PHILADEPHUS" -WHICH MEANS "LOVER OF HIS BROTHERS" *HE KILLED 2 OF HIS BROTHERS*

KING PTOLEMY IV WHO RULED EGYPT FROM 221 TO 203 B.C. WAS CALLED "PHILOPATOR" -MEANING "LOVER OF HIS FATHER" *HE KILLED HIS FATHER*

THE WARSHIP THAT TORPEDOED ITSELF ! THE "TRINIDAD," A BRITISH CRUISER, FIRED A TORPEDO AT A GERMAN DESTROYER IN THE ARCTIC IN WORLD WAR II *BUT THE TORPEDO CIRCLED BACK AND HIT THE CRUISER -DAMAGING IT SERIOUSLY* (MARCH 29, 1942)

EMPEROR ROMANUS IV WHO RULED BYZANTIUM FROM 1068 TO 1071 COULD LEAP FROM THE GROUND TO THE BACK OF HIS HORSE *-WHILE WEARING FULL ARMOR*

HATS WORN BY NATIVES of Halmahera, Indonesia, ARE MADE FROM DRIED PETALS OF ORCHIDS *WHICH RETAIN THEIR FRAGRANCE FOR MONTHS*

THE **SILVERY SCALES** COVERING THE SAVALO - A COLOMBIAN FISH - ARE EACH *3 INCHES WIDE*

THE JINX SHIP PÈRE MARQUETTE #3 a Lake Michigan steamer WAS WRECKED IN 1888, SANK IN 1890, WAS REFLOATED AND WENT AGROUND IN 1893, IN 1902 AND IN 1916, COLLIDED WITH A BRIDGE IN 1917, BECAME CAUGHT IN AN ICE FIELD IN 1920 *-AND WAS FINALLY JUNKED AS A "HOODOO SHIP" IN 1921*

VAUCLUSE HOUSE in Woollahra, Australia, BUILT IN 1802 BY SIR HARRY BROWN HAYES, OF IRELAND, WAS INFESTED WITH VENOMOUS SNAKES UNTIL SIR HARRY SURROUNDED THE HOUSE WITH 500 TONS OF EARTH IMPORTED FROM COUNTY CORK *IT WAS NEVER AGAIN BOTHERED BY SERPENTS OF ANY KIND*

JAN DRIESCHE (1588-1609) of Leyden, Holland, WHO BECAME COURT PREACHER FOR KING JAMES I of England AT THE AGE OF 17, *MASTERED BOTH HEBREW AND GREEK WHEN HE WAS ONLY 5*

"I" IN SIAMESE IS EXPRESSED BY **9** DIFFERENT WORDS

THE AMAZING PROPHECY THAT WAS FULFILLED BY THE PROPHET'S OWN CORPSE!

BARON VILANEUF, French alpinist, ONLY A FEW DAYS BEFORE HE WAS KILLED BY AN AVALANCHE WHILE ASCENDING THE ALETSCH GLACIER IN THE SWISS ALPS ON JUNE 14, 1854, PREDICTED THAT IF A MEMBER OF HIS PARTY WERE ENGULFED BY THAT GLACIER *HIS BODY WOULD EMERGE ABOUT 32 YEARS LATER* THE BARON'S BODY WAS FOUND AT THE FOOT OF THE GLACIER, COMPLETELY PRESERVED, IN 1887 - **33 YEARS LATER**

THE BIRD THAT LAYS EGGS IN "MATCHING COLORS" THE HAWK CUCKOO, WHICH SMUGGLES ITS EGGS INTO THE NESTS OF OTHER BIRDS, *LAYS BROWN EGGS OR BLUE EGGS - ALWAYS MATCHING THE EGGS IN THE NEST IT HAS INVADED*

THE LUCKIEST WAR FLYER IN ALL HISTORY! LIEUTENANT BOHRLE, of the German Air Force, RIDING AS OBSERVER OVER THE FRENCH LINES IN WORLD WAR I, WHEN THE PLANE'S MOTOR SUDDENLY STOPPED, *WAS HURLED OUT OF THE CRAFT AT AN ALTITUDE OF 13,000 FEET—* AS THE PLANE PLUMMETED DOWN, ITS PILOT, LIEUT. ROSENGART, FELT A BUMP AND DISCOVERED *THAT BOHRLE HAD BEEN HURLED BACK INTO HIS SEAT BY A WIND SQUALL—* ROSENGART MANAGED TO GET THE ENGINE STARTED AGAIN AND THEY LANDED SAFELY BEHIND THEIR OWN LINES (1917)

Ripley's Believe It or Not!

SHE WAS GOOD
BUT NOT BRILLIANT
USEFUL BUT
NOT GREAT

Epitaph of MARY KEITH MARSHALL (1737-1807) THE MOTHER OF CHIEF JUSTICE MARSHALL IN THE FAMILY GRAVEYARD NEAR WASHINGTON, KY.

THE **IRON FIDDLE**
A VIOLIN CONSTRUCTED OF IRON PLATES BY JOHN BUNYAN, THE ENGLISH WRITER AND TINKER, WHO NEVER PLAYED IT BECAUSE HE *FELT THAT PRODUCING MUSIC FOR PLEASURE WOULD BE SINFUL*

THE **FIRST MAN TO KILL A RHINOCEROS WITH BOW AND ARROW**
ROBERT N. SWINEHART of *Emmaus, Pa.* ON A HUNTING TRIP IN S.E. ANGOLA, PORTUGUESE W. AFRICA, *STALKED AND KILLED A 3-TON BLACK RHINOCEROS WITH A SINGLE ARROW* THE FIBERGLASS ARROW, TIPPED WITH STEEL, PENETRATED THROUGH THE INCH-THICK HIDE TO A DISTANCE OF NEARLY 2 FEET

LIVING JEWELRY
A LIVE TORTOISE
FORGOTTEN ON A PARIS TO LONDON PLANE IN 1929, WAS FOUND TO HAVE A SHELL STUDDED WITH *EMERALDS, RUBIES AND DIAMONDS* IT WAS RECLAIMED BY ITS OWNER 2 DAYS LATER

A **COIN** MINTED IN GREECE IN 43 B.C. TO COMMEMORATE CAESAR'S ASSASSINATION BEARS THE DATE OF THE IDES OF MARCH AND DISPLAYS **2 DAGGERS**

TREE TRUNK WHICH FORMED THE LIKENESS OF *A HUMAN MASK* Lake Garda, Italy

THE **COUNT de TENDE** (1507-1586) WAS CHIEF COUNCIL TO THE KING OF FRANCE, CHAMBERLAIN OF THE ROYAL COURT, GOVERNOR OF PROVENCE, LIEUT. GENERAL OF THE FRENCH ARMY AND GRAND ADMIRAL OF THE FRENCH NAVY *AT THE AGE OF 13*

THE **GREATEST DON JUAN**
ANTOINE DUBOIS (1716-1775) AN ACTOR AT THE COMEDIE-FRANCAISE in Paris, France, COURTED A TOTAL OF **16,527 WOMEN** *HE CATALOGUED EACH DATE IN HIS DIARY*

OYSTERS EATEN BY RICH BURGHERS IN 16th CENTURY ANTWERP, BELGIUM, WERE SERVED *WITH THEIR SHELLS GOLD PLATED -ON PLATES EDGED WITH GENUINE ORIENTAL PEARLS*

Ripley's ® Believe It or Not!

THE VIKING
WHO HAD LEGS LIKE STEEL SPRINGS
GUNNAR HAMUNDARSON (910-960) of Iceland COULD JUMP HIGHER THAN HIS HEIGHT *WEARING FULL ARMOR*

HE ALSO COULD LEAP AS FAR BACKWARD AS FORWARD

THE KOARA
A NEW ZEALAND FISH, SWIMS IN SUMMER IN HOT SPRINGS -- AND IN WINTER HIBERNATES IN *DRY UNDERGROUND CAVES*

THE MOUNTED KNIGHT
SHRUBBERY TRIMMED IN THE SHAPE OF A *HORSE AND RIDER*
SUBMITTED BY LAEL LYONS, ALEXANDRIA, VA.

THE CASA de CORDERO in Madrid, Spain, WAS ACQUIRED BY SANTIAGO ALONSO CORDERO IN 1860 BY WINNING **THE GRAND PRIZE IN A NATIONAL LOTTERY**
THE SPANISH GOVERNMENT DID NOT HAVE THE $900,000 IN CASH WHICH CORDERO WON AS HIS LOTTERY PRIZE, *SO HE DEMANDED AND GOT THE BUILDING IN THE CENTER OF MADRID*

THE TENDER-HEARTED TYRANT
THE TURKISH PASHA HAFIZ ALI (1732-1818) ruler of Vidin BOASTED THAT HE HAD KILLED ONE ENEMY OF STATE FOR EVERY WAKING HOUR OF HIS 20-YEAR REIGN - A TOTAL OF MORE THAN 70,000 PERSONS -YET HE DIED OF A BROKEN HEART *MOURNING THE DEATH OF A PET STARLING*

The TIPPLER COIN

EMPEROR JAHANGIR (1569-1627) of India ALTHOUGH FORBIDDEN ALCOHOLIC DRINKS BY HIS MOSLEM FAITH WAS SO FOND OF WINE THAT HE CREATED GOLD COINS DEPICTING HIM RAISING A WINE CUP TO HIS LIPS

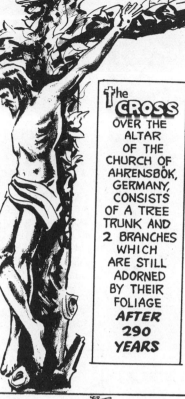

The CROSS

OVER THE ALTAR OF THE CHURCH OF AHRENSBÖK, GERMANY, CONSISTS OF A TREE TRUNK AND 2 BRANCHES WHICH ARE STILL ADORNED BY THEIR FOLIAGE **AFTER 290 YEARS**

A TOADSTOOL

GREW THROUGH THE TILES OF A BATHROOM FLOOR IN A 2d-FLOOR APARTMENT Submitted by Mrs. Louise Kormann Baltimore, Md.

TOY BOATS

MADE BY YOUNGSTERS IN THE NETHERLANDS *FROM WOODEN SHOES*

MOST AMAZING GESTURE OF BENEVOLENCE IN ALL HISTORY!

HERODES ATTICUS, A PRIVATE CITIZEN OF GREECE, PERSONALLY FINANCED THE FIRST SYSTEM OF SOCIAL SECURITY--*WILLING AN ANNUAL PENSION EQUIVALENT TO $525 TO EVERY ATHENIAN CITIZEN FOR LIFE*

THE ANNUAL COST TO HIS ESTATE WAS $21,000,000--*WHICH TODAY WOULD AMOUNT TO $2,100,000,000 A YEAR*

THE ART MUSEUM

IN Santa Fe, New Mexico, HAS ONE FAÇADE COPIED FROM A CHURCH IN LAGUNA, N.M., ANOTHER FACADE RESEMBLING THE TWO TOWERS OF ACOMA, N.M., A BALCONY PATTERNED AFTER THAT OF THE SAN FELIPE PUEBLO CHURCH, AND AN AUDITORIUM COPIED FROM THE CHURCHES OF PECOS AND ACOMA

MONARCH WHO RULED FROM THE CRADLE TO THE GRAVE

EMPEROR OJIN-TENNO (201-310) *RULED JAPAN FOR 109 YEARS* HE BECAME EMPEROR AT BIRTH AND OCCUPIED THE THRONE UNTIL HIS DEATH

DURING HIS MINISTRY HE ENJOYED 7 REVIVALS ADMITTED 716 MEMBERS BAPTIZED 1,117 AND BURIED 1,126 OF HIS FLOCK

EPITAPH ON THE GRAVE OF BEZALEEL PINNEO, PASTOR OF THE CONGREGATIONAL CHURCH OF MILFORD, CONN.

VITEX AGNUS CASTUS THE BRANCHES OF WHICH ARE USED TO MAKE BASKETS, PRODUCES A FLOWER THAT WAS EATEN IN ANCIENT GREECE BY YOUNG GIRLS IN THE BELIEF IT *WOULD ENHANCE THEIR VIRTUES*

THE FAMED MUSICIAN WHO WAS COACHED BY A GHOST
VLADIMIR de PACHMANN (1848-1933) CELEBRATED RUSSIAN PIANIST, WAS CONVINCED THAT THE GHOST OF CHOPIN WAS ALWAYS BESIDE HIM AND HE *CONSULTED WITH THE GHOST WHILE PLAYING CONCERTS!* HE ALSO ASKED THE GHOST'S ADVICE BEFORE SIGNING ANY CONTRACT

A HUMAN FOOTPRINT IN THE CAVE OF FAUZAN, FRANCE, AMAZINGLY MODERN IN SIZE AND SHAPE, WAS IMPRINTED IN THE CAVE'S WET CLAY *20,000 YEARS AGO*

A **STATUE** of PRESIDENT ANDREW JACKSON FIGUREHEAD OF THE "S.S. CONSTITUTION" WAS DECAPITATED BY SAMUEL DEWEY, A CAPE COD SKIPPER, BUT ALTHOUGH THE COMMANDANT OF THE BOSTON NAVY YARD OFFERED A $1,000 REWARD FOR CAPTURE OF THE CULPRIT, PRESIDENT JACKSON, WHO NEVER LIKED THE STATUE, *REWARDED DEWEY WITH A POSTMASTERSHIP* July 3, 1834

THE SPIDER MONKEY HAS NO THUMBS BUT IT CAN CARRY FOOD TO ITS MOUTH *WITH THE FLEXIBLE END OF ITS TAIL*

THE WAVE THAT SAVED THREE LIVES!
The "Sally Ann" AN 80-TON SCHOONER SAILING FROM HALIFAX, NOVA SCOTIA, TO BERMUDA WITH 9 MEN AND BOYS ABOARD, WAS TOSSED SO VIOLENTLY DURING A STORM THAT THE MATE AND 2 SAILORS WERE WASHED OVERBOARD *BUT A MOMENT LATER ANOTHER WAVE SWEPT ALL 3 MEN BACK ABOARD THE SHIP UNHARMED* (November, 1827)

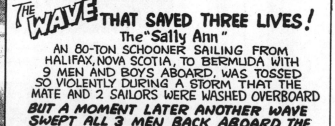

CUCUMBER 58 INCHES LONG Grown by Oscar Merrill in 1898, Landaff, N. Hampshire

Ripley's — ® Believe It or Not!

THE "VIKING" EXACT REPLICA OF A YACHT BUILT FOR KING OLAF OF NORWAY IN THE 10th CENTURY, WAS SAILED FROM NORWAY TO THE UNITED STATES IN 1893 AS AN EXHIBIT AT THE CHICAGO FAIR -- LOGGING UP TO 11 NAUTICAL MILES PER HOUR --
ON THE VOYAGE IT WAS DECIDED THAT THE SECRET OF ITS NAVIGABILITY WAS ITS SUPPLE CONSTRUCTION-- *BECAUSE THE SHIP WHIPPED AND TWISTED LIKE A SNAKE*

SHEPHERD DOGS in Hungary GUIDE SHEEP AND COWS BY *LEAPING ONTO THEIR BACKS*

MUSICAL MUGS USED IN GERMANY IN THE 16th, 17th AND 18th CENTURIES *PLAYED A TUNE WHEN THE DRINK WAS QUAFFED*

BENJAMIN BUTLER
(1818 -1893)
A STAUNCH SUPPORTER OF JEFFERSON DAVIS IN THE DEMOCRATIC NATIONAL CONVENTION IN 1860, WAS OFFERED THE VICE-PRESIDENCY BY ABRAHAM LINCOLN IN 1864 -- BUT DECLINED --
IF HE HAD ACCEPTED, HE WOULD HAVE BECOME PRESIDENT ONLY A FEW MONTHS LATER BECAUSE OF LINCOLN'S ASSASSINATION

THE VIOLET-SCENTED BUTTERCUP (Ranunculus pallasii) WHICH GROWS IN THE ARCTIC *IS THE ONLY BUTTERCUP THAT HAS A SCENT*

THE RING THAT WAS RETURNED BY A FISH !
MADAME EDUIGUE REREIT, of Paris, France, LOST HER RING WHILE WORKING IN HER KITCHEN AND RECOVERED IT A FEW DAYS LATER FROM *A FISH SHE HAD BOUGHT IN THE PUBLIC MARKET*

THE RING HAD SLID DOWN THE KITCHEN DRAIN, BEEN WASHED INTO THE RIVER -- AND WAS SWALLOWED BY A FISH THAT WAS PURCHASED BY MADAME REREIT HERSELF IN THE MOST AMAZING EXAMPLE OF COINCIDENCE IN MODERN TIMES (1903)

THE **FIRST "NO ADMITTANCE" SIGN IN HISTORY**
PICTURE WRITING FOUND IN THE PASIEGA CAVE, IN SPAIN, AND BARRING ADMITTANCE TO THE CAVERN, DATES BACK *TO THE CAVE MAN ERA*

Ripley's — ® Believe It or Not!

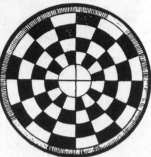

THE PURPLE SEA SNAIL
FLOATS ON THE SURFACE OF THE WATER—SUPPORTED BY A RAFT OF AIR BUBBLES *WHICH THE SNAIL CREATES BY RIPPLING THE SEA WITH ITS FOOT*

CIRCULAR CHESS-BOARD
Cottonian Library of the British Museum, London

THE MOST ILL-FATED GARMENT IN ALL HISTORY !
A CREMATION CEREMONY WAS STAGED BY A JAPANESE PRIEST IN TOKYO IN FEBRUARY, 1657, TO DESTROY THE BAD LUCK IN A KIMONO SUCCESSIVELY OWNED BY 3 TEEN-AGE GIRLS —*EACH OF WHOM HAD DIED BEFORE SHE COULD WEAR IT*
A VIOLENT WIND SPREAD THE FLAMES AND THE FIRE DESTROYED THREE-QUARTERS OF TOKYO — *LEVELING 300 TEMPLES, 500 PALACES, 9,000 STORES AND 61 BRIDGES AND KILLING 100,000 PEOPLE !*

THE NATIVE CHERRY
of Tasmania, Australia, GROWS ITS PIT *OUTSIDE THE FRUIT*

THE FARNESE PALACE,
ONE OF THE MOST IMPRESSIVE PALACES IN ROME, ITALY, WAS LEASED TO THE FRENCH FOR USE AS AN EMBASSY FOR 99 YEARS AT AN ANNUAL RENTAL OF *ONE LIRA—1/6th OF A CENT*　(1936)

A ROCKET-OPERATED TORPEDO AND A MINE WITH 3 FUSES
ILLUSTRATED IN AN ANCIENT WAR MANUAL, WERE INVENTED BY HASSAN AR-RAMMAH, AN ARAB SCIENTIST, *IN 1275*

DUTTON HALL
WAS DISMANTLED IN 1933 built in Cheshire, England, in 1542, AND WITH EVERY STONE AND TIMBER MARKED *WAS MOVED 250 MILES TO EAST GRINSTEAD, SUSSEX- WHERE IT WAS REASSEMBLED -* IT NOW SERVES AS A BOYS' SCHOOL

TREES
GROWING ALONG THE COLUMBIA RIVER GORGE, IN OREGON, ARE BUFFETED BY SUCH STRONG WINDS -*INVARIABLY FROM ONE DIRECTION-* THAT ALL THEIR BRANCHES EXTEND LEEWARD

THE RASPBERRY JAM TREE
of Australia IS SO CALLED BECAUSE ITS WOOD SMELLS JUST LIKE RASPBERRY JAM

THE COAT THAT HAD A TRAGIC PATTERN OF DEATH
JABEZ SPICER of Leyden, Mass. KILLED BY 2 BULLETS ON JAN. 25, 1787, IN SHAYS' REBELLION AT SPRINGFIELD ARSENAL, WAS WEARING THE COAT IN WHICH HIS BROTHER DANIEL HAD BEEN SLAIN BY 2 BULLETS ON MARCH 5, 1784

THE BULLETS THAT KILLED JABEZ PASSED THROUGH THE SAME 2 HOLES IN THE CLOAK THAT HAD BEEN MADE WHEN DANIEL WAS SLAIN 3 YEARS EARLIER

THE MAN WHO MADE HIS HOME HIS PRISON!
JAMES MACANDREW, CHIEF EXECUTIVE OF THE PROVINCE OF OTAGO, N.Z., ORDERED COMMITTED TO DEBTORS' PRISON IN 1871

ISSUED A DECREE DECLARING HIS OFFICIAL RESIDENCE WAS HENCEFORTH A JAILHOUSE

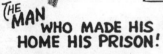

THE STRUCTURE DESIGNED BY A DREAM
THE CARTHAGINIAN RUIN in the park of Schoenbrunn, Vienna, Austria, *ACTUALLY A FAKE CONSTRUCTED IN 1778,* WAS ORDERED BUILT BY GERMAN EMPEROR JOSEPH II *AFTER HE HAD SEEN* **THE EDIFICE IN A DREAM**

THE MOST RADICAL TREATMENT FOR THE COMMON COLD
KINGS of the Shilluk Tribe in Africa *FOR CENTURIES WERE EXECUTED IF THEY CAUGHT A SLIGHT COLD* THE TRIBESMEN BELIEVED THEIR FORTUNES DEPENDED ON THE MONARCH'S STATE OF HEALTH—SO THEY STRANGLED ANY RULER WHO WAS NOT IN PERFECT HEALTH

THE DUKE of SUSSEX
(1773-1843)
SON OF KING GEORGE III of England, AS A BOY WAS WHIPPED SEVERELY BY HIS FATHER *FOR SUFFERING AN ATTACK OF ASTHMA*

THE ILLNESS WAS UNKNOWN AT THE TIME AND THE MONARCH THOUGHT THE CHILD WAS BEING MISCHIEVOUS

THE STRANGE MYSTERY OF THE GHOST SHIP THAT LOST ITS PASSENGERS AND CREW!

THE "JOYITA" A 70-TON MOTOR VESSEL THAT SAILED FROM APIA, SAMOA, ON MAR. 3, 1955, WAS FOUND ABANDONED 37 DAYS LATER *-ALTHOUGH IT WAS LINED WITH CORK AND COULD NOT HAVE BEEN IN DANGER OF SINKING*

NO TRACE HAS EVER BEEN FOUND OF ITS 16 CREWMEN AND 9 PASSENGERS!

THE MOST REMARKABLE SKI RACE IN HISTORY!

E. HEDLUND and S. UTTERSTRÖM COMPETING IN THE VASA SKI RACE IN SWEDEN IN 1954 OVER A 52-MILE RUN FROM SALEN TO MORA *BOTH FINISHED IN EXACTLY 5 HOURS, 23 MINUTES, 23 SECONDS-* THE GOLD AND SILVER MEDALS WERE CUT AND FUSED -SO EACH COMPETITOR RECEIVED A MEDAL THAT WAS HALF GOLD AND HALF SILVER

THE "DEAD LEAF" BUTTERFLY
ITS WINGS, EXPANDED, ARE BRILLIANTLY COLORED -*BUT WHEN FOLDED THEY LOOK EXACTLY LIKE A DEAD LEAF*

THE VISION THAT BECAME REALITY

NATHAN HUNT, A QUAKER AND ONE OF THE FOUNDERS OF GUILFORD COLLEGE, IN NO. CAROLINA, WAS PROMISED A $1,000 CONTRIBUTION FOR THE SCHOOL BY GEORGE HOWARD AS *SOON* AS THE LATTER'S WHALING SHIP DOCKED WITH A LOAD OF OIL-

IN JANUARY, 1837, HUNT REVEALED THAT IN A VISION HE HAD SEEN THE VESSEL DOCKING AT NEW BEDFORD, MASS., 800 MILES AWAY *-AND WEEKS LATER IT WAS CONFIRMED THAT THE SHIP ACTUALLY DOCKED ON THE VERY DAY AND HOUR OF HUNT'S VISION*

Ripley's Believe It or Not!

MUSICIANS of the Banda Tribe of Africa ARE FORBIDDEN TO PLAY THEIR INSTRUMENTS *UNLESS THEY ARE WEARING A FALSE BEARD OF MONKEY HAIR*

THE SPRING THAT RUNS HOT AND COLD near Ormea, Italy
IT IS STEAMING HOT IN WINTER AND ICE COLD EACH SUMMER

PUG DOGS ARE CONSIDERED CANINE ARISTOCRATS BY THE CHINESE WHEN THEY HAVE FOREHEAD WRINKLES THAT FORM THE *CHINESE CHARACTER FOR "PRINCE"*

GRANARIES BUILT BY AFRICAN NATIVES IN NIGERIA *IN THE BELIEF THEY WOULD BETTER PRESERVE THEIR GRAIN, WERE CONSTRUCTED IN THE SHAPE OF THERMOS JUGS*

THE FIRST LADY WHO WAS KIDNAPED BY AN ORANGUTAN!

MADAME RAYMOND POINCARÉ, wife of the President of France, WHILE SITTING IN THE GARDEN OF THE ELYSÉE PALACE, IN PARIS, IN 1914, *WAS SEIZED BY AN ORANGUTAN THAT HAD ESCAPED FROM A NEARBY CAGE, CARRIED TO THE TOP OF A TALL TREE AND HELD CAPTIVE IN ITS BRANCHES FOR SEVERAL HOURS* SHE WAS RESCUED UNHARMED BY THE ORANGUTAN'S JAVANESE ATTENDANT -BUT THE INCIDENT WAS KEPT SECRET FOR MORE THAN 40 YEARS

THE PATRIARCH

JOHN GILLEY (1718-1842) of Augusta, Maine, MARRIED A GIRL OF 18 WHEN HE WAS 80 AND BECAME THE FATHER OF 10 CHILDREN -THE LAST WHEN HE WAS *100 YEARS OF AGE*

HIS HAIR TURNED BLACK JUST BEFORE HE DIED AT THE AGE OF 124

Ripley's — Believe It or Not!

THE **STRANGEST**
BOOK COLLECTOR
IN ALL HISTORY

JUAN VICENTE
a librarian of Barcelona, Spain,
MURDERED 9 PEOPLE
BETWEEN 1830 AND 1835
—*EACH TIME TO GAIN*
POSSESSION OF A
SINGLE BOOK

THE
CROWNED
SWIFT
BUILDS THE
SMALLEST BIRD
NEST IN NATURE
—ONLY 1½ INCHES WIDE

IT HOLDS ONLY A SINGLE
EGG, AND THE SWIFT INCUBATES
THE EGG WHILE SITTING ON THE BRANCH
TO WHICH THE NEST IS ATTACHED

THE
CANDELABRA
PALM
AN *ARECA*
PALM
on the island
of Bourbon,
in the Indian
Ocean

EARL
COOLEY
of Denver, Col.,
DURING A
ONE-DAY TERM
AS GOVERNOR
OF COLORADO,
PARDONED A
CONVICT FOR
WHOM HE HAD
SERVED AS
DEFENSE
ATTORNEY
—*EXPLAINING*
THAT THE MAN
HAD BEEN
REPRESENTED
INADEQUATELY BY
COUNSEL AT THE TIME
OF HIS CONVICTION

THE
CROUCHING
HOUND
Baku, Russia
NATURAL ROCK
FORMATION

A **SWORD** THRUST INTO A ROCK
CREVICE BY SAN GALGANO
WHEN THE ITALIAN KNIGHT BECAME A
HOLY HERMIT, WAS DRIVEN HOME
WITH SUCH FORCE THAT IT IS STILL
THERE AS A POINT OF PILGRIMAGE
800 YEARS LATER (Siena, Italy)

A PALACE ON RUNNERS
USED BY EMPRESS CATHERINE II, of Russia, (1729-1796)
CONTAINED A DRAWING ROOM, A STUDY, A LIBRARY AND
A BEDROOM —AND OFTEN COVERED 100 MILES IN A
SINGLE DAY *PULLED BY 30 HORSES*

A *SPANIEL* OWNED BY JEAN DRUISY, of Chateaulin, France, REMAINED IN THE RIVER AULNE FOR 6 DAYS AND NIGHTS UNTIL ITS BARKING LED NEIGHBORS TO THE BODY OF ITS MASTER — WHO HAD BEEN MURDERED AND *THROWN INTO THE RIVER*

CALF BORN WITH THE OUTLINE OF A HEART ON *VALENTINE'S DAY*
Submitted by Richard E. Meriwether, Mobile, Ala.

A *RAILROAD PASS* of the SILVERTON RAILROAD, of Colorado, MADE OF BUCKSKIN (1888)

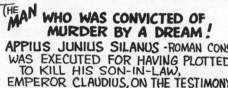

TRIPLE BANANA
Submitted by Joan Falk, Long Island City, N.Y.

THE *MAN* WHO WAS CONVICTED OF MURDER BY A DREAM!
APPIUS JUNIUS SILANUS - ROMAN CONSUL WAS EXECUTED FOR HAVING PLOTTED TO KILL HIS SON-IN-LAW, EMPEROR CLAUDIUS, ON THE TESTIMONY OF A SLAVE NAMED NARCISSUS *WHO HAD DREAMED HE SAW THE DEFENDANT ATTEMPT TO MURDER THE EMPEROR!*

CARIBOU HAVE HOLLOW HOOVES *WHICH SERVE AS SUCTION CUPS ON SMOOTH ICE*

BUTTERFLIES WITH A RANGE OF VISION THAT EXTENDS TO 9 FEET *ARE THE MOST FARSIGHTED OF INSECTS*

THE *BARKING FROG* WHEN DISTURBED INFLATES ITSELF TO MANY TIMES ITS NORMAL SIZE *AND WAILS LIKE A HUMAN INFANT*

THE TEMPLE OF NINGPO - China WAS CREATED EXCLUSIVELY AS A PLACE OF PRAYER FOR WOMEN WHO HOPE IN REINCARNATION *TO BE REBORN AS MEN*

THE *DUCK ORCHID* of Australia, SWAYING ON ITS SLENDER STEM, *ACTUALLY LOOKS LIKE A DUCK IN FLIGHT*

4 RAINBOWS - ONE INSIDE ANOTHER - SEEN BY ANTONIO de ULLOA, A SPANISH MARINER, AND 7 COMPANIONS AT SUNRISE *ON THE PEAK OF MT. PICHINCHA, ECUADOR, 1740*

THE **HUMAN CANNONBALL WHO COULD NOT BE KILLED!** ARUNA, AN INDIAN HOLY MAN, WHO INCENSED THE SULTAN OF MYSORE BY REFUSING TO BLESS A NEW GIANT MORTAR, WAS TWICE STUFFED INTO THE BIG GUN'S BARREL AND FIRED INTO THE AIR, AND *BOTH TIMES ESCAPED UNHARMED!*

THE FIRST TIME HE WAS BLOWN 800 FEET AND LANDED ON THE SOFT CANOPY ATOP AN ELEPHANT, AND THE SECOND TIME HE FELL WITHOUT A SCRATCH ON THE THATCHED ROOF OF A HUT (1782)

PRIZED VIOLINS IN THE 17th and 18th CENTURIES *MADE OF GLAZED AND ENAMELED POTTERY*

THE FIRST CHESS CHAMPION

THE TOMB OF QUEEN NEFERTARI, CONSORT OF KING RAMSES II, OF EGYPT, DISPLAYS A DESIGN COMMEMORATING THE FACT THAT SHE WAS *CHESS CHAMPION OF EGYPT* 3,250 YEARS AGO

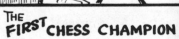

THE **STEIN OF THE 3 BROTHERS** ERFURT, GERMANY- 3 STEINS LINKED FIRMLY TOGETHER *FROM WHICH 3 BROTHERS ALWAYS DRANK SIMULTANEOUSLY*

THE CHATEAU OF OLD CHAMBORD France A BIRTHDAY PRESENT TO JEAN CHAMPROPIN FROM A FRIEND IS STILL OWNED BY HIS DESCENDANTS *694 YEARS LATER*

A **CACTUS** IN CACTUS FOREST, IN THE TUCSON MOUNTAINS, ARIZONA, *IN THE SHAPE OF AN ORNATE CROSS*

Ripley's — "Believe It or Not!"

IOACCHINO ROSSINI
(1792-1868) THE ITALIAN COMPOSER
ALWAYS KEPT HIS HEAD WARM
IN WINTER BY WEARING
3 WIGS

THE **TOMB** of ROMAN GENERAL LUCULLUS
-CONSTRUCTED IN 56 B.C.- WHICH MEASURES
88 FEET IN DIAMETER AND STANDS 28 FEET HIGH
IS NOW A MODERN TAVERN
Grotta Ferrata, Italy

**CAPTAIN
PERCIVAL DRAYTON**
(1812 - 1865)

COMMANDING THE U.S.
NAVY FRIGATE "POCAHONTAS"
IN THE CIVIL WAR,
ATTACKED AND CAPTURED
THE ISLAND OF
HILTON HEAD, N.C.,
OVERCOMING A
VALIANT DEFENSE BY
CONFEDERATE GENERAL
THOMAS F. DRAYTON
--HIS OWN BROTHER

**NEPTUNE'S
STAFF**
NATURAL
SHELL
FORMATION

THE GREAT CROSS
at Villargaudin, France,
DISPLAYS THE TOOLS
OF A CARPENTER

**FRIEDRICH
von SCHILLER**
(1759 - 1805)
THE FAMED
GERMAN POET
COULD ONLY
COMPOSE POETRY
WHILE SITTING
WITH HIS
**BARE FEET
IMMERSED
IN ICE-COLD
WATER**

Ripley's ® Believe It or Not!

THE CORONET
A BARNACLE WHICH ATTACHES ITSELF TO THE SKIN OF WHALES

LOOKS EXACTLY LIKE A DUCAL CROWN

CHRIST ON THE CROSS
A 6-FOOT FIGURE ON MT. SOURA SASS, in Tyrol, Austria, WAS CREATED BY NATURE

THE FIGURE WAS PART OF A DEAD PINE TREE FOUND GROWING OVER A PRECIPICE BY 2 TYROLEANS-WHO HUNG IT ON THE CROSS

THE MOST ASTOUNDING NAVAL VICTORY IN HISTORY
2 SMALL SHIPS
COMMANDED BY MAXIMILIEN AND GABRIEL ABOS, BROTHERS, FLYING THE FLAG OF THE KNIGHTS OF MALTA, WERE ATTACKED OFF THE ISLAND OF NIOS, GREECE, BY 50 TURKISH GALLEONS MANNED BY 15,000 SAILORS

AFTER A BATTLE THAT LASTED AN ENTIRE DAY EVERY SHIP IN THE TURKISH FLEET WAS SUNK, DAMAGED OR FORCED TO FLEE, AND, ALTHOUGH ONE OF THE BROTHERS WAS FATALLY WOUNDED, BOTH THEIR VESSELS WERE ABLE TO CONTINUE THEIR JOURNEY

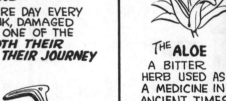

THE ALOE
A BITTER HERB USED AS A MEDICINE IN ANCIENT TIMES

HAS BEEN FOUND BY MODERN MEDICAL SCIENCE TO BE THE ONLY REMEDY FOR X-RAY BURNS

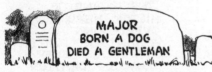

MAJOR BORN A DOG DIED A GENTLEMAN
EPITAPH in the Aspen-Hill cemetery for pets, Rockville, Md.

BOOMERANGS
MANY SHAPED TO RETURN TO THE THROWER, WERE FOUND IN TUTANKHAMEN'S TOMB- THE WEAPON ASSOCIATED WITH AUSTRALIAN BUSHMEN WAS USED AGES EARLIER BY KING TUT TO HUNT FOWL

THE "APPLE" of the Garden of Eden ACTUALLY WAS A LEMON
THE EDIBLE APPLE WAS UNKNOWN IN BIBLICAL TIMES

THE DUKE of MONTMORENCY-LAVAL
(1747-1817)
AFTER HEARING A MILITARY MARCH PLAYED WHEN HE WAS ONLY 10, BECAME A COMPULSIVE HUMMER OF THAT TUNE EVERY HOUR OF THE DAY FOR 60 YEARS

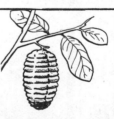

A LEOPON
OFFSPRING OF A LIONESS AND A LEOPARD
Hanshin Park Zoo, Tokyo, Japan

THE **MARBLED SEA PERCH**
the chameleon
of the sea
CAN CHANGE ITS
COLORING TO MATCH ITS
SURROUNDINGS ANYWHERE
IN THE OCEAN DEPTHS

CHARLES BAUDELAIRE
(1821-1867) famous French poet
DYED HIS HAIR GREEN

THE **GREATEST GEYSER IN THE WORLD**
A GEYSER in the Poás Volcano, Costa Rica,
COVERS AN AREA OF **37 ACRES**, IS **1,000 FEET DEEP** AND
SENDS UP A COLUMN OF WATER **350 FEET HIGH**

SUNFLOWER
12 FEET HIGH
**WITH 46
SEPARATE BLOOMS**
Submitted by Edward
Arsenault, Freeport, Me.

THE **INSIGNIA**
WORN BY PRIESTS IN
pre-Columbian Michoacan, Mexico,
*WAS A GOURD STUDDED
WITH TURQUOISES*

MOST ORNATE WEDDING INVITATION
THE WEDDING ANNOUNCEMENT PREPARED IN 1812
FOR JOHANN BUCHEGGER AND VIKTORIA SCHADLER
OF OHMINGEN, GERMANY, CONSISTED OF LETTERS
IN THE LIKENESS OF EACH INVITED GUEST

TOMATO CHICK
Submitted by
Eddie Danks,
Tulsa, Okla.

**NGEST MARRIAGE
PROPOSAL**

FRANCESCO COLONNA
(1449-1527)
the Italian author
O TIMID TO PROPOSE IN
ERSON TO A GIRL NAMED
OLIA, WROTE A BOOK
TITLED, "A DREAM OF LOVE"
*CONTAINING
165,000 WORDS*

THE INITIAL LETTERS OF
TS 37 CHAPTERS SPELL
OUT IN LATIN:
RANCESCO COLONNA
LOVES POLIA"

MRS.
CLARA CARTER
of West Ellworth, Me.
SIX DAYS EACH
WEEK FOR YEARS
COOKED AT 5 A.M. FOR
A FAMILY OF FIVE—
DROVE A MAIL COACH
OVER A 14-MILE ROUTE—
PICKED 10 QUARTS OF
BLUEBERRIES DAILY
(IN SEASON)—SERVED
HER BROOD DINNER
—AND THEN DID THE
FAMILY WASH

A **WATERFALL** in Assam, India, CREATED BY AN EARTHQUAKE IN 1897 - AND STILL RUNNING **70 YEARS LATER**

THE **SKELETON** THAT RULED THE ROMAN EMPIRE!

EMPEROR NUMERIANUS, WHO SUCCEEDED TO THE THRONE OF ROME WHEN HIS FATHER WAS KILLED IN 283 DURING A CAMPAIGN AGAINST PERSIA, LED HIS ARMY ON A RETREAT OF 1,500 MILES - BUT WAS NEVER SEEN BY HIS TROOPS DURING THE ENTIRE 8 MONTHS OF THE JOURNEY.
AIDES ANNOUNCED HE WAS SUFFERING FROM AN EYE DEFECT - BUT WHEN SUSPICIOUS ARMY OFFICERS FORCED THEIR WAY INTO THE EMPEROR'S TENT THEY FOUND HE HAD *DIED MONTHS EARLIER AND HAD BEEN REDUCED BY THE DESERT HEAT TO A SKELETON*

AN **AREA OF 49,000 SQUARE MILES** IN THE NORTHWEST SECTION OF THE PROVINCE OF ONTARIO, CANADA, **IS SERVED BY A SINGLE TELEPHONE DIRECTORY OF 60 PAGES**
Submitted by H.P. Ratchford, Terrace Bay, Ont.

THE **UPSIDE-DOWN CATFISH** of South America SWIM NORMALLY FOR A TIME WHEN THEY ARE YOUNG - *THEN TURN OVER ON THEIR BACKS FOR THE REMAINDER OF THEIR LIFETIMES*

THE UNPROPHETIC GIFT
A **BED OF ROSES** WAS PRESENTED BY THE CITY OF NANCY TO MARIE ANTOINETTE WHEN SHE ARRIVED IN FRANCE FROM HER NATIVE AUSTRIA -*TO SYMBOLIZE HER FUTURE AS QUEEN OF FRANCE* 23 YEARS LATER SHE DIED ON THE GUILLOTINE

GRAVES of members of the Sara Tribe, of Africa, AS A SHELTER FOR THE SOUL OF THE DEPARTED, ARE COVERED *WITH INVERTED RAINBOW-HUED WATER POTS*

THE **PARROT FISH** of Australia HAS 2 SETS OF TEETH -*ONE IN ITS BEAK AND THE OTHER IN ITS THROAT*

PRINCE VON KAUNITZ (1711-1794) Chancellor of Austria WAS SO FEARFUL OF CATCHING COLD THAT IN SUMMER AS WELL AS WINTER *HE ALWAYS WORE 6 SUITS OF CLOTHES*

Ripley's— Believe It or Not!

WOMEN of the Kirdi Tribe of Africa BEAUTIFY THEMSELVES BY FORCING A PLUG THROUGH THEIR LIP AND GREET EVERY ACQUAINTANCE WITH A CURTSY

THE FLOWERS of the Australian FIRE-WHEEL TREE ARE A BRILLIANT RED AND GROW IN THE SHAPE OF A PINWHEEL

ROBERT G. ARMSTRONG (1865-1956) English jockey and horse trainer ATTENDED EACH ANNUAL NORTHUMBERLAND PLATE RACE FOR 72 YEARS

The MAN who CROSSED THE SNOW-COVERED ALPS ON BARE FEET! HENRI DUKE de JOYEUSE (1567-1608) TO REPENT FOR HIS HAVING ABANDONED THE CAPUCINE ORDER ATTEMPTED TO WALK BAREFOOTED FROM PARIS, FRANCE, TO ROME THROUGH THE SNOWS OF A SEVERE WINTER HE CROSSED FRANCE, TRAVERSED THE ICY ALPS, AND REACHED RIVOLI, IN ITALY —WHERE HE DIED OF EXHAUSTION AT THE AGE OF 41

THE GALLOPING GALLOWS Rome CRIMINALS DURING THE MIDDLE AGES WERE HANGED BY DANGLING THEM FROM A ROPE FASTENED TO THE EARS OF THE BRONZE HORSE IN THE STATUE OF EMPEROR MARCUS AURELIUS

A FLOCK OF DUCKS LIVES IN A "PENTHOUSE" ATOP THE Sheraton-Peabody Hotel, in Memphis, Tenn., AND EACH DAY TAKES AN OUTING AND SWIM BY USING AN ELEVATOR AND PARADING THROUGH THE MAIN LOBBY

Ripley's ® Believe It or Not!

THE SPIROBIS WORM CONSTRUCTS A TUBULAR HOME OF MUD THAT RESEMBLES A SPIRAL SHELL

A MILITARY DRUM MADE FROM THE SKIN OF JAN ZISKA, CZECH LEADER - AT HIS OWN REQUEST SO HE COULD CONTINUE TO PARTICIPATE IN HIS COUNTRY'S WAR AGAINST THE GERMANS EVEN AFTER HIS DEATH

THE KNIGHT WHO RISKED DEATH 727 TIMES FOR A WOMAN HE NO LONGER LOVED!

SUERO de QUINONES, a Castilian knight, HAVING HAD A METAL RING FORGED AROUND HIS NECK AS A TOKEN OF LOVE, COULD NOT FREE HIMSELF OF THIS REMINDER OF A FORMER SWEETHEART WITHOUT VIOLATING HIS CODE OF CHIVALRY
- UNLESS IT WAS LOST IN BATTLE
A LANCE FINALLY FREED HIM OF HIS YOKE AFTER HE HAD FOUGHT 68 KNIGHTS A TOTAL OF 727 JOUSTS (1434)

THE STAR OF THE SOUTH

A 125-CARAT DIAMOND *IS THE ONLY LARGE DIAMOND EVER FOUND BY A WOMAN*
A BRAZILIAN SLAVE DISCOVERED IT IN 1853 AND AS A REWARD WAS GIVEN HER FREEDOM

THE FLESH OF THE CUTTLEFISH

LONG WAS USED BY SCHOOLCHILDREN in the French Pyrenees AS A *PENCIL ERASER*

THE MOST AMAZING PAINTER IN HISTORY

FRANCISCO HERRERA THE ELDER (1576-1656) WHO HAS BEEN CALLED SPAIN'S MICHELANGELO
CREATED HIS MASTERPIECES BY WIELDING A BRUSH ON GLOBS OF PAINT SPLASHED ON THE CANVAS BY A SERVANT WHO USED *A BROOM DIPPED IN BUCKETS OF PAINT*

THE ENEMY THAT WAS OUTSHOT WITH ITS OWN AMMUNITION!

GUNNERS of the U.S. Cutter "Eagle" DROVE OFF THE MORE POWERFUL BRITISH BRIG, "DISPATCH" OFF LONG ISLAND IN 1813 BY SALVAGING THE ENEMY'S SHOT AND FIRING IT BACK AT THE BRIG IN CARTRIDGES MADE OF BITS OF CLOTH AND PAGES TORN FROM THE CUTTER'S LOG! THE AMERICANS HAD DRAGGED THEIR GUNS TO A HILL OVERLOOKING THE FOE AND WHEN THEY RAN OUT OF AMMUNITION, SALVAGED SHOT THAT HAD RIDDLED THE HULL OF THEIR BEACHED CUTTER

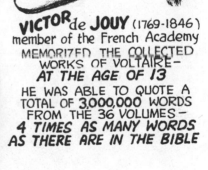

VICTOR de JOUY (1769-1846) member of the French Academy MEMORIZED THE COLLECTED WORKS OF VOLTAIRE— *AT THE AGE OF 13*

HE WAS ABLE TO QUOTE A TOTAL OF 3,000,000 WORDS FROM THE 36 VOLUMES— *4 TIMES AS MANY WORDS AS THERE ARE IN THE BIBLE*

THE **CROWN** of Our Lady of Covadonga, Spain, COMPLETED IN 1918 BY DONATIONS FROM RESIDENTS OF ASTURIAS PROVINCE CONTAINS 3,155 DIAMONDS, 32 PEARLS, 983 RUBIES, 2,572 SAPPHIRES, 18 OUNCES OF GOLD AND HALF A POUND OF PLATINUM

ELEPHANT KILLED in Angola, Africa, by Joseph Fenykovi, *WAS 13'2" TALL AND WEIGHED 12 TONS* NOV. 13, 1955

THE LARGEST BRIBE OF ANCIENT TIMES

GABINIUS, Roman proconsul of Syria, FOR USING ROMAN TROOPS TO RESTORE KING PTOLEMY OF EGYPT TO HIS THRONE, *WAS PAID A BRIBE OF $12,000,000*

THE **BABY** IN THE CRADLE ORCHID

ACTUALLY APPEARS TO HAVE A BABY ROCKING IN A YELLOW CRADLE

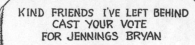

BABOONS ON A TUN
(Baboon Tun)
ARE PORTRAYED ON THE
COAT OF ARMS OF THE
BABINGTON FAMILY
OF ENGLAND

THE MAN WHO KILLED A LION WITH A SHEATH KNIFE!
HARRY WOLHUTER, a game ranger in Kenya National Park, in Africa,
DRAGGED FROM HIS HORSE BY A FULL-GROWN LION
KILLED THE BEAST BY PLUNGING HIS KNIFE
INTO ITS HEART (August, 1903)

THE SACRED CANNON OF BASRA
Iraq
AN ANCIENT GUN- SPARED BECAUSE IT WAS CONSIDERED
TOO EXPENSIVE TO REMOVE WHEN THE CITY WALL WAS
DEMOLISHED IN 1869 - NOW IS WORSHIPED BY LOCAL
RESIDENTS AS THE REVERED GUARDIAN OF LOCAL
WEATHER AND CROPS

A HUGE STATUE OF BUDDHA
WHICH LAY IGNORED IN THE FIELDS NEAR
BANGKOK, SIAM, FOR 300 YEARS
WAS FOUND TO HAVE UNDER ITS
TOP COATING OF PLASTER
400 POUNDS OF GOLD

THE PERFECT SON
LOUIS LA CAZE
(1799 - 1869)
BEGAN THE STUDY OF MEDICINE
AT THE AGE OF 66
- JUST TO TAKE CARE OF HIS
AILING MOTHER
HE BECAME A DOCTOR
- BUT HE DIED A FEW MONTHS LATER
Paris, France

Ripley's Believe It or Not!

THE MUSK OX IS NOT AN OX
IT IS A SHEEP -AND ALTHOUGH IT LOOKS AWKWARD ACTUALLY IT IS VERY FLEET

AN ORANGE 19½ INCHES IN CIRCUMFERENCE
Submitted by Fred C. Van Duyne, Brooklyn, N.Y.

THE CITY WALL of Porrentruy, Switzerland, HAS BEEN CONVERTED INTO A CONTINUOUS ROW OF INHABITED HOUSES -MANY CONSTRUCTED BY ACTUALLY DIGGING ROOMS OUT OF THE MASONRY

THE IRON MAN
SULTAN BEYBARS of Egypt TO SET AN EXAMPLE OF HARDIHOOD FOR HIS SOLDIERS SWAM ACROSS THE RIVER NILE AND BACK EVERY DAY FOR 17 YEARS -CLAD IN FULL ARMOR AND DRAGGING A 38-LB. WEIGHT!
(1260-1277)

"OUR LADY OF THE FIRE"
A PICTURE IN THE HOME OF LOMBARDINO di RIOPETROSO, of Forli, Italy, WAS THE ONLY OBJECT NOT DESTROYED WHEN THE HOUSE BURNED TO THE GROUND -YET THE PICTURE HAD BEEN PAINTED ON WOOD

A BULLFIGHT THAT DECIDED A WAR!
A BATTLE BETWEEN THE ARMIES OF JAVA AND MALAYA, FOR POSSESSION OF SUMATRA, WAS AVERTED IN THE 4th CENTURY WHEN EACH GENERAL DESIGNATED A BUFFALO TO FIGHT FOR HIS ARMY!
THE MALAY BUFFALO WON - AND A LARGE SECTION OF SUMATRA STILL IS CALLED MINANGKABAU -WHICH MEANS "THE BUFFALO'S VICTORY"

Ripley's — Believe It or Not!

THE MOST DARING ACT OF GALLANTRY IN ALL HISTORY!

RODRIGO PONCE de LEON (1443-1492) famed Spanish army officer, TO RETRIEVE A GLOVE DROPPED BY ANA de MENDOZA AT A RECEPTION ATTENDED BY KING FERDINAND AND QUEEN ISABELLA, **LEAPED INTO A PIT FILLED WITH FEROCIOUS LIONS!** *HE RECOVERED THE GLOVE AND ESCAPED UNHARMED* (1483, Seville, Spain)

SHIPWRECK CASTLE

A HOUSEBOAT IN THE SHAPE OF A CASTLE LOCATED on Lake Pepin, Minn., WAS BUILT ENTIRELY FROM THE WRECKAGE OF SHIPS *DEMOLISHED BY THE LAKE'S VIOLENT STORMS*

A POSTAGE STAMP

ISSUED BY EAST GERMAN COMMUNIST OFFICIALS IN 1956, TO OBSERVE THE 100th ANNIVERSARY OF COMPOSER ROBERT SCHUMANN, WAS DESIGNED TO FEATURE SCHUMANN'S HEAD AND *ONE OF HIS FAMOUS COMPOSITIONS.* THE STAMP WAS HURRIEDLY RECALLED WHEN IT WAS DISCOVERED THAT THE COMPOSITION *ACTUALLY WAS THE WORK OF FRANZ SCHUBERT*

THE GRAND VIZIER WHO PAID $8,800,000 FOR HIS POST

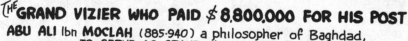

ABU ALI Ibn MOCLAH (885-940) a philosopher of Baghdad, TO SERVE AS GRAND VIZIER FOR 3 YEARS, PAID THE CALIPH $2,200,000 AT THE TIME OF HIS APPOINTMENT **AND PROMISED TO PAY ANOTHER $2,200,000 EACH TIME HE WAS UNABLE TO SOLVE A PUZZLE PROPOUNDED BY THE RULER** ONCE EACH YEAR THE GRAND VIZIER DELIBERATELY GAVE THE WRONG SOLUTION SO HE COULD KEEP IN THE CALIPH'S GOOD GRACES

THE MAGIC MUSHROOM of Mexico IS TOPPED BY A TYPICAL MEXICAN SOMBRERO

BENJAMIN FRANKLIN'S LIBRARY CHAIR BY RAISING ITS SEAT *BECAME A LADDER*

THE POLKA DOT SHELL (Voluta junonia) *RAREST OF ALL AMERICAN SHELLS*

THE STAR-OF-DAVID ORCHID

THE MADAGASCAR ORCHID CONSISTS OF 2 TRIANGLES INVERTED ONE ATOP THE OTHER - *RESEMBLING THE STAR OF DAVID*

GRAPEFRUIT
WITH HALF ITS SECTIONS WHITE AND *THE OTHERS RED*
Submitted by Garfield Williamson, Mt. Vernon, N.Y.

THE **BIRCH WEEVIL** TO HOLD HER EGGS *ROLLS A PERFECT FUNNEL* OF BIRCH LEAVES

A **MUSEUM** in Millau, France, IS LOCATED OVER THE TARN RIVER ATOP THE ARCH OF A BRIDGE -ALL THE REST OF WHICH WAS CARRIED AWAY BY A FLOOD 400 YEARS AGO

A **CANDYROASTER**
a species of pumpkin MEASURING 68 INCHES IN DIAMETER AND WEIGHING 150 POUNDS
Grown by
MRS. JARVIS CHAMBERS
Iron Duff, N.C.

BEAR KISSING A LION
NATURAL ROCK FORMATION
near Casteljau, France

DRUSILLA
SISTER OF ROMAN EMPEROR CALIGULA, WAS HONORED FOLLOWING HER DEATH IN 40 A.D. BY A MONTH OF MOURNING, DURING WHICH IT WAS *A CRIME TO TAKE A BATH!*

THE **PILGRIM** WHO TRAVELED 1,400 MILES ON HIS KNEES!
ABUL KASIM JONEID, the Persian philosopher, MADE 30 PILGRIMAGES TO MECCA, TRAVELING 82,600 MILES ON FOOT
-BUT HIS FIRST JOURNEY OF 1,400 MILES WAS MADE ENTIRELY ON HIS KNEES!

THE GROUNDED GOOSE
THE SEBASTOPOL GOOSE of the Danube River area, Germany, **CANNOT FLY**
THE FEATHERS ON ITS WINGS ARE FRIZZLED AND SO THIN THEY BLOW IN THE SLIGHTEST BREEZE

THE CELL KEYS
CARRIED BY EARLY ENGLISH JAILERS *WERE ALSO PISTOLS*

THE AMAZING "KING OF THE CUT-UPS"

JEAN HUBER (1721-1786) of Geneva, Switzerland, CREATED OUTSTANDING PORTRAITS AND LANDSCAPES OUT OF PAPER

-ALWAYS WIELDING HIS SCISSORS BEHIND HIS BACK

THE FRIENDLY VULTURE

THE HOUSE BUILT BY A FISHERMAN NEAR PUNTA LANZINOSA, ON SARDINIA, IS SHELTERED BY A HUGE ROCK SHAPED LIKE A HOVERING VULTURE

BARBED WIRE IS MADE IN 600 DIFFERENT FORMS

Submitted by Jesse S. James of Maywood, Calif., WHO HAS COLLECTED 250 DIFFERENT KINDS OF BARBED WIRE

BELLE LEONARD

AN INSTRUCTOR AT THE ILLINOIS FEMALE COLLEGE, Jacksonville, Ill., WAS SO DEVOUT THAT SHE WOULD NOT MAIL A LETTER UNLESS SHE WAS FIRST ASSURED THAT IT WOULD NOT STILL BE IN TRANSIT ON SUNDAY

THE SEA ANGEL

IS A SNAIL WITH WINGS

BERNICE THOMAS

a New York City housewife HAS WON 300 LARGE DOLLS FOR NEEDY YOUNGSTERS LIVING AT THE CHILDREN'S SHELTER OF THE QUEENSBORO SOCIETY FOR THE PREVENTION OF CRUELTY TO CHILDREN

BY HER SKILL AT THROWING A BASEBALL AT AMUSEMENT PARKS

WILD CABBAGES

ARE THE ONLY PLANTS THAT GROW ON THE PRINCE EDWARD ISLANDS South Africa

Ripley's — Believe It or Not!

GOLD COINS EACH VALUED AT $228 WERE MINTED BY HUNGARIAN MAGNATE MICHAEL APAFI IN 1661 *JUST FOR USE IN TIPPING*

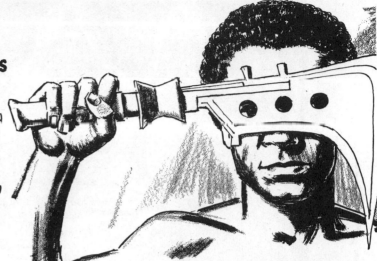

THE **MEN** WHO **LOOK DAGGERS** NATIVES of the Feradje Tribe of the Congo ARE FORBIDDEN TO GAZE UPON THEIR CHIEF *EXCEPT THROUGH SPECIAL EYEHOLES IN THE BLADES OF THEIR KNIVES*

A **SAPLING** 18 INCHES HIGH FOUND GROWING INSIDE THE TRUNK OF AN ELM TREE WHEN THE OLD TREE WAS CUT DOWN Submitted by Edward Capobianco, Sea Cliff, N.Y.

THE **CHOCOLATE ORCHID** (Nigritella rubra) WHICH GROWS IN EUROPE *HAS BOTH THE COLOR AND SCENT OF CHOCOLATE*

A **HOUSE** on 2 acres of land WAS BEQUEATHED BY ROSALIE DECROLY, A WEALTHY WIDOW OF BERCHIES, BELGIUM, *THE INCOME TO PROVIDE THE KITTY FOR AN ANNUAL CARD GAME IN THE TOWN SQUARE*

THE **BIRD THAT LIVES IN A "GLASS HOUSE"** THE EAST INDIAN SWALLOW BUILDS A NEST OF GELATINOUS THREADS *THAT IS TRANSPARENT AND LOOKS LIKE AMBER GLASS*

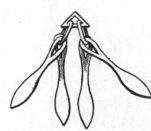

4 POT STIRRERS ATTACHED BY CHAIN LINKS— ALL CARVED BY THE SARAMACCANER TRIBE OF DUTCH GUIANA *FROM A SINGLE PIECE OF WOOD*

THE RULER WHO WAS AFRAID TO CLOSE HIS EYES!

SULTAN JANNARY WHO RULED THE CARMATHIANS FROM 900 TO 913 TRAINED HIMSELF TO SLEEP FULLY DRESSED AND ARMED *- WITH HIS EYES WIDE OPEN!* HE WAS FINALLY SLAIN BY 2 CONSPIRATORS WHO REALIZED THE SULTAN WAS VULNERABLE AFTER THEY TOO HAD *LEARNED TO SLEEP WITHOUT CLOSING THEIR EYES*

Ripley's — Believe It or Not!

THE BANQUETS OF THE "DEAD!"

THE PRINCE de CONDÉ (1643-1709)
ONE OF THE RICHEST MEN IN ALL FRANCE,

SUDDENLY REFUSED TO EAT AT THE AGE OF 56
— *INSISTING THAT HE HAD DIED*

FOR THE NEXT 10 YEARS HIS DOCTORS STAGED
ELABORATE BANQUETS AT WHICH ALL THE GUESTS
ARRIVED IN COFFINS AND WEARING SHROUDS
— *TO CONVINCE THE MENTALLY ILL PRINCE
THAT "EVEN CORPSES MUST EAT"*

THE OLDEST GREEK WRITING EVER FOUND

IS ON A WINE PITCHER PRESENTED
IN ATHENS 2,800 YEARS AGO
AS A PRIZE IN A DANCE CONTEST.
IT BEARS IN GREEK THE INSCRIPTION:
"The dancer who will give the best
performance here will get me"

A PROPOSAL SCENE

CARVED IN 1835 BY A
WHALER FROM NEW BEDFORD, MASS.,
FROM THE TEETH OF A WHALE
— *AND THEN SENT TO HIS
SWEETHEART BECAUSE HE
WAS TOO BASHFUL TO
PROPOSE IN PERSON*

"BARON"

A POODLE GIVEN BY
FRENCH AUTHOR VICTOR HUGO
TO THE MARQUIS DE FALETANS
AND TAKEN TO MOSCOW,
FOUND ITS WAY BACK TO HUGO'S
APARTMENT IN PARIS, FRANCE,
*TRAVELING 1,500 MILES
IN 3 MONTHS*

PARIS →

VANILLA BEANS in Genale, Somaliland, GROWING FROM THE TRUNK OF A COCONUT PALM

PHOENICIAN BOTTLE

COLORED VIOLET,
BROWN AND PURPLE—
MADE 2,400 YEARS
AGO BY WINDING A
*CONTINUOUS STRIP
OF OPAQUE GLASS*

THE 4 R's — READING, 'RITING, 'RITHMETIC AND RAFTING

CHILDREN in New Caledonia WHO LIVE ACROSS THE PONERIHOUEN RIVER FROM THE SCHOOL MAKE THE CROSSING EACH MORNING AND EVENING ON *INDIVIDUAL RAFTS*

THE TOMBSTONE

ON THE GRAVE OF A MERCHANT
in Neumaten, Germany,

COMMEMORATES HIS BIGGEST SALE
— DELIVERY OF A SHIPLOAD OF
MOSELLE WINE TO ROMAN
LEGIONS STATIONED ON
THE RHINE RIVER

THE SHIP WAS EQUIPPED WITH
AN EYE — TO HELP KEEP IT ON
A STRAIGHT COURSE

THE **POWDER PUFF COCKATOO**

THE GREAT PALM COCKATOO HAS A GLAND ON ITS BACK THAT EMITS A POWDER WHICH WATERPROOFS ITS FEATHERS - IT USES ONE OF ITS FLUFFY FEATHERS AS *A POWDER PUFF*

THE **BELLS THAT HAVE RUNG IN 654 NEW YEARS**

THE BELLS in the belfry of the temple at Seikenji, Japan, EACH NEW YEAR'S EVE SINCE 1314 HAVE BEEN PEALED 108 TIMES AS A REMINDER TO ABSTAIN FROM SIN *BECAUSE THE JAPANESE BELIEVE THERE ARE 108 HUMAN SINS*

HOHUA AHOWHENUA
(1765-1889) of Matamata Plains, New Zealand,

IN ACCORDANCE WITH TRIBAL CUSTOM *AFTER HAVING TILLED HIS FIELDS UNTIL THE AGE OF 122 WAS ABANDONED IN A DESERTED VILLAGE TO STARVE -* HE LIVED TO THE AGE OF 124 BY CAPTURING AND EATING PEACOCKS

RASP COINS USED IN ANCIENT CHINA *LOOKED LIKE A METAL CURRY COMB*

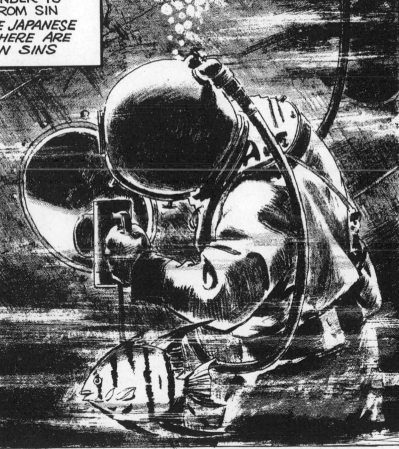

THE **GREEN TREE ANT** of Australia

MORE INDUSTRIOUS THAN ITS MANY KIN *FORCES EVEN ITS UNDEVELOPED YOUNG TO WORK* ITS NEST IS MADE BY SEWING TOGETHER LEAVES WITH THREAD PRODUCED BY ITS LARVA

A **PAIR OF PARAKEETS** REGULARLY SOLD IN JAPAN IN 1927 FOR **$500**

THE JAPANESE GOVERNMENT HAD TO FORBID IMPORTATION OF THE BIRDS TO HALT THE CUSTOM OF GIVING THEM TO SWEETHEARTS AS A TOKEN OF LOVE

THE MOST EERIE DISCOVERY IN ALL HISTORY !

GIULIO BARDI -an Italian deep-sea diver - WHOSE BROTHER AND SISTER-IN-LAW HAD VANISHED MYSTERIOUSLY- STUMBLED ON THEIR BODIES BY CHANCE WHILE SEARCHING FOR GOLD 5 YEARS LATER *IN A SHIP LYING AT THE BOTTOM OF THE SEA OFF THE CANARY ISLANDS*

MOREOVER, THE WOMAN HAD A DAGGER IMBEDDED IN HER CHEST - AND NO EXPLANATION OF THE CRIME WAS EVER DISCOVERED

THE **FRONT** OF THE DUCAL PALACE, in Sassuolo, Italy,

APPEARS TO BE A SERIES OF GALLERIES, COLUMNS, DOORWAYS AND RECESSES, YET ACTUALLY *IT IS A GIGANTIC OPTICAL ILLUSION* THERE IS A REAL DOOR - BUT EVERYTHING ELSE IS A PART OF A FALSE FAÇADE

Emperor COMMODUS
(161-192) of Rome
WAS SO CONCEITED THAT DURING HIS REIGN ALL 12 MONTHS OF THE CALENDAR WERE RENAMED IN HIS HONOR. THE ROMAN NATION WAS CALLED COMMODIANA, THE CITY OF ROME WAS NAMED COLONIA COMMODIANA, THE ARMY WAS CALLED COMMODIANI, THE ROMAN SENATE BECAME THE COMMODIANUS, AND THE PERIOD BECAME *"THE GOLDEN CENTURY OF COMMODUS"*

THE **MOST BEREAVED FATHER OF WORLD WAR II**
ALCIDE CERVI of Reggio Emilia, Italy, WAS THE FATHER OF 7 SONS
-ALL OF WHOM WERE EXECUTED BY A FASCIST FIRING SQUAD ON THE SAME DAY (Dec.28,1943)

SODA DAM across Jemez Creek, New Mexico, 400 FEET LONG, 50 FEET HIGH AND 50 FEET THICK— *A NATURAL SODA DAM BUILT BY THERMAL SPRINGS*

ORANGE 14" IN CIRCUMFERENCE
Submitted by F. L. LOVE, Miami, Fla.

THE **TOWN SEAL** of Gelnhausen, Germany, DISPLAYS THE HEADS OF EMPEROR FRIEDRICH BARBAROSSA AND HIS WIFE - *BECAUSE ITS DESIGNERS, WHO WERE STANDING BEFORE THE EMPEROR, TOOK LITERALLY HIS ORDER THAT THEY "FEATURE WHAT YOU SEE"*

TIMOTHY RYAN DIED 1814
A 1,000 WAYS CUT SHORT OUR DAYS NONE ARE EXEMPT FROM DEATH A HONEY BEE BY STINGING ME DID STOP MY MORTAL BREATH

EPITAPH in Greenwood Cemetery Manchester, N.Y.

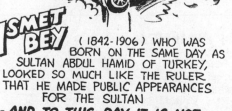

ISMET BEY (1842-1906) WHO WAS BORN ON THE SAME DAY AS SULTAN ABDUL HAMID OF TURKEY, LOOKED SO MUCH LIKE THE RULER THAT HE MADE PUBLIC APPEARANCES FOR THE SULTAN
-*AND TO THIS DAY IT IS NOT CERTAIN WHICH OF THEM OUTLIVED THE OTHER!*

Ripley's Believe It or Not!

BAKER ANTS IN MASS CHEWING SESSIONS, PRODUCE A SALIVA WHICH CONVERTS GRAIN SEEDS *INTO BREAD*

THE **TWENTYEIGHT PARAKEET** of Australia WAS GIVEN THAT NAME BECAUSE IN ITS WILD STATE *IT CONSTANTLY REPEATS "28...28"*

T^HE **PILGRIMS** near Cavus, Turkey NATURAL STONE FORMATION

A **CHINESE JUNK** WAS MAROONED ON A ROCK IN THE HARBOR OF AMOY WHEN THE TIDE *SUDDENLY FELL 20 FEET* (1933)

THE STUDENT WHOSE LIFE WAS SAVED BY HIS TEXTBOOK!

ANTONIO CORDEYRO (1641-1722) TRAVELING AT THE AGE OF 15 FROM HIS HOME IN THE AZORES TO THE UNIVERSITY OF COIMBRA, IN PORTUGAL, ON A BRITISH SHIP, WAS SEIZED BY THE CAPTAIN OF A SPANISH WARSHIP, WHO ORDERED **THE BOY HANGED FROM THE YARDARM IN THE BELIEF HE HAD TRAITOROUSLY SERVED AS AN ENGLISH SEAMAN** *ANTONIO SAVED HIS LIFE BY SHOWING THE CAPTAIN A VOLUME OF VIRGIL AND RECITING HALF THE ENTIRE BOOK FROM MEMORY- INCLUDING ONE PAGE HE HAD MEMORIZED BACKWARDS (1656)*

A PALACE

BUILT IN ESSEN, GERMANY, IN 1870 BY STEEL MAGNATE ALFRED KRUPP WAS CONSTRUCTED WITHOUT A SINGLE PIECE OF WOOD AND WITH WINDOWS WHICH COULD NOT BE OPENED *-BECAUSE HE WAS FANATICALLY FEARFUL OF COLDS AND FIRE*

THE RAILWAY BEETLE
The female of Phengodes Hieronymi IS SO NAMED BECAUSE ON EITHER SIDE OF HER BODY SHE DISPLAYS A ROW OF RED AND GREEN LIGHTS

CAN YOU DRAW THIS DESIGN WITH A CONTINUOUS LINE, WITHOUT RETRACING A LINE ANYWHERE AND WITHOUT CROSSING ANY LINE?

SOLUTION:
Submitted by
DAVID W. TESKE
New York City

THE PROPHECY THAT KILLED A KING!

KING ALEXANDER III
(1241 - 1286)
of Scotland
WARNED BY A SOOTHSAYER THAT HIS HORSE WOULD BE THE CAUSE OF HIS DEATH
KILLED THE CHARGER WITH HIS DAGGER!

MONTHS LATER ALEXANDER'S NEW MOUNT SHIED AT THE SIGHT OF THE BLEACHED SKELETON—AND BOTH HORSE AND RIDER PLUNGED OVER A PRECIPICE TO THEIR DEATHS!

THE PEOPLE WHO USE THEIR SKINS AS WRITING PAPER!

SCHOOLBOYS
in Gujarat, India,
DO THEIR HOMEWORK
BY WRITING ON THEIR TANNED THIGHS WITH WOODEN SLIVERS!

THE WORDS AND NUMERALS REMAIN LEGIBLE FOR MORE THAN 12 HOURS

THE TOWER of the Cathedral of Antwerp, Belgium, 400 FEET ABOVE THE GROUND, PROVIDES A VIEW OF OTHER BELL TOWERS IN 124 DIFFERENT LOCALITIES

THE HAT OF W.J. CAVERLY, WHO WAS KILLED IN A RAILROAD ACCIDENT IN Silver Plume, Colo., WAS HUNG ON A NAIL IN AN UNDERTAKER'S ESTABLISHMENT IN 1906 AND IS STILL THERE 58 YEARS LATER

THE GAMBLER WHO VALUED HIS HONOR ABOVE HIS LIFE!

ROBERT REMINE of Silver City, N. Mexico, SENTENCED TO DEATH FOR MURDER, WAS PERMITTED TO LEAVE HIS PRISON CELL TO VISIT GAMBLING HALLS EVERY NIGHT FOR MONTHS —YET HE ALWAYS RETURNED BY 10 P.M.!

WHEN HIS SENTENCE WAS AFFIRMED BY THE HIGHER COURTS REMINE WENT TO THE GALLOWS WITHOUT A WORD OF COMPLAINT

THE BODY OF A MAIL TRUCK used in Copenhagen, Denmark, FROM 1815 UNTIL 1865, WAS SHAPED LIKE A BALLOON

THE PALACE OF KNOLE in Kent, England, HAS 12 COURTYARDS FOR THE MONTHS IN EACH YEAR, 52 STAIRWAYS TO CORRESPOND WITH THE NUMBER OF WEEKS, AND A WINDOW FOR EACH OF THE 365 DAYS IN A YEAR

A HUGE WILLOW TREE IN FRONT OF THE NOYES HOUSE IN Litchfield, Conn., GREW FROM A RIDING STICK IT WAS STUCK IN THE GROUND BY COLONEL BENJAMIN TALMADGE OF WASHINGTON'S STAFF DURING THE REVOLUTION

MONEY ISSUED BY GOV. JOHN ROSS FROM 1910 TO 1913 FOR USE IN THE COCOS KEELING ISLANDS in the Pacific, WAS MADE OF SHEEPSKIN

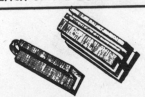

CHINESE COINS SHAPED TO REPRESENT FOLDED LENGTHS OF SILK WERE USED IN THE 12th CENTURY AND THEY COULD PURCHASE AS MANY FOLDS OF SILK AS THERE WERE SIMULATED FOLDS IN THE COIN

THE AGAVE PLANT of Brazil HAS ITS ONLY LEAVES ON THE GROUND, BUT ITS STEM GROWS TO A HEIGHT OF **30 FEET.** IT DIES AS SOON AS IT REACHES ITS FULL HEIGHT

THE HUMAN STEAMROLLERS

CAPT. ORME DENNY

RESPONSIBLE FOR EVACUATING 90 BRITISH CITIZENS FROM MOUNT HAGEN, NEW GUINEA, TO ESCAPE JAPANESE INVADERS, HAD ONLY 2 PLANES, SUFFICIENT FUEL FOR ONLY 2 TRIPS – BUT THE GROUND WAS SO RAIN-SOAKED, THE PILOTS REFUSED TO TAKE OFF WITH MORE THAN 7 PASSENGERS !

CAPT. DENNY MADE THE RUNWAYS USABLE FOR EVACUATION OF THE ENTIRE PERSONNEL BY STAGING A MAMMOTH DANCE BY 2,000 NATIVES – WHO STAMPED ON THE SPONGY GROUND CONTINUOUSLY FOR 24 HOURS !
(April, 1942)

THE FORBIDDEN FOUNTAIN of PERNES-les-Fontaines, France

THE FOUNTAIN IS NEVER USED BECAUSE OF A LEGEND THAT ANYONE WHO DRINKS FROM ITS WATERS *WILL GO MAD*

THE PIRARUCU A SWEET-WATER FISH OF BRAZIL WHICH GROWS TO A LENGTH OF **10 FEET** AND **1,100 POUNDS** IN WEIGHT, HAS A TONGUE SO ROUGH THAT IT IS USED BY THE INDIANS *AS A GRATER*

THE HEDGEHOG CACTUS of Mexico IS PLEATED LIKE AN ACCORDION SO IT CAN EXPAND WITH WATER IN *PREPARATION FOR PERIODS OF DROUGHT*

SALLY EAGER 1810-1905 of Harlan County, Ky., AFTER LOSING HER EYEGLASSES AT THE AGE OF 90, *COULD THREAD A NEEDLE WITHOUT GLASSES* FOR THE REMAINING 5 YEARS OF HER LIFE

KING AGO LI AGBO of Abomey, Africa, WHO WAS DEPORTED BY THE FRENCH IN 1900 FOR MUTINY, WAS PERMITTED TO RETURN TO HIS COUNTRY IN 1905. *BUT FOR THE NEXT 37 YEARS HE ALWAYS WORE A MASK OVER HIS NOSTRILS* –INSISTING THAT THE AIR OF HIS KINGDOM HAD BEEN CONTAMINATED

THE INQUISITIVE SEX — **FEMALE KOEL BIRDS** of India HAVE A SHRIEK THAT SOUNDS EXACTLY LIKE *"WHO ARE YOU?"*

Ripley's Believe It or Not!

LILACS SENT TO ONE'S BETROTHED BROKE THE ENGAGEMENT IN MEDIEVAL ENGLAND

FROM 14 MATCHES ARRANGED AS ABOVE, REMOVE 2 AND REARRANGE 3 TO FORM A WORD EXPRESSING WHAT MAKES A GOOD MATCH

Answer:

LOVE

PAUL MULBERRY a pitcher for the Eldred (III.) Stars WAS THE FIRST PLAYER TO USE RESIN JULY 30, 1916

THE DIAMOND THAT AVERTED A WAR THE SHAH DIAMOND, WEIGHING 88.70 CARATS, SENT BY THE SHAH OF PERSIA TO CZAR NICHOLAS I OF RUSSIA AFTER THE RUSSIAN AMBASSADOR TO PERSIA HAD BEEN MURDERED BY A PERSIAN MOB - *ACTUALLY PREVENTED A WAR!* (1829)

THE **STALK-EYED FLY** (Diopsida) of the Tropics HAS ITS EYES AT THE TIP ENDS OF 2 LONG ANTENNAE

THE CHAPEL OF ST. ORAN on the island of Iona, in the Hebrides, HOLDS THE TOMBS OF 48 KINGS of SCOTLAND, 8 KINGS of NORWAY, 4 KINGS of IRELAND and 4 KINGS of FRANCE

THE BURGUNDY SNAIL (Helix pomatia) HAS AN EYE ON EACH OF ITS 2 LONG TENTACLES - *YET ITS VISION IS SO POOR IT MUST FIND ITS WAY BY FEELING OBJECTS WITH ITS 2 SHORTER TENTACLES*

THE AFRICAN LOCUST (Gongylus gongoloides) LOOKS SO MUCH LIKE A FLOWER *THAT THE INSECTS ON WHICH IT FEEDS SETTLE ON IT IN SEARCH OF NECTAR*

THE **SON** WHO FOLLOWED IN HIS FATHER'S FOOTSTEPS - *TO THE GRAVE!* BARON RODEMIRE de TARAZONE of France WAS SLAIN IN 1872 BY AN ASSASSIN NAMED CLAUDE VOLBONNE, AND 21 YEARS EARLIER HIS FATHER ALSO WAS MURDERED BY A CLAUDE VOLBONNE - *YET THE TWO ASSASSINS WERE NOT RELATED!*

A DRINKING GLASS DROPPED BY ANNA HARDING IN RENO, NEV., ON ST. VALENTINE'S DAY *BROKE TO FORM A PERFECT HEART*

Submitted by TIBBY and 'FIRPO' GAZZIGLI Las Vegas, Nev.

THE STRANGEST INITIATION RITE IN THE WORLD
YOUTHS in New Guinea, TO PREPARE FOR THE EVILS OF MANHOOD, MUST STAND IN A GROUP BENEATH A MASK REPRESENTING THE FEATURES OF A MONSTER *ALL DAY LONG FOR 30 CONSECUTIVE DAYS!*

BOTTLE DECORATED BY ITS ROMAN MANUFACTURER WITH GLASS THREADS WAS FOUND IN Cologne, Germany, WHERE IT HAD BEEN BURIED FOR *1,800 YEARS*

THE STRANGEST LIBRARY IN THE WORLD
A GIANT STATUE OF BUDDHA IN THE LAMASERY OF YUNG-NING, CHINA, DOUBLES AS AN OBJECT OF VENERATION AND A LIBRARY ITS INTERIOR HOLDING 317 VOLUMES OF TIBETAN CLASSICS

THE COAT of ARMS of ADAM RIES (1492-1559) THE CELEBRATED GERMAN MATHEMATICIAN EMBRACES THE FORMULAS $2 \times 2 = 4$ AND $4 \div 2 = 2$ —WHICH HE CONSIDERED THE GREATEST REPRESENTATIONS OF TRUTH

THE S.S. BEDFORDSHIRE
ORDERED BROKEN UP FOR SCRAP, BROKE AWAY FROM A TUG IN ST. GEORGE'S CHANNEL ON HER LAST JOURNEY AND *POUNDED TO PIECES ON THE ROCKS OF CARDIGAN ISLAND* 1934

JACQUES DELMOTTE
of Tournai, Belgium, DECORATED BY A PRACTICAL JOKER WITH THE ORDER OF THE PADLOCK, WHICH LINKED THE 2 LAPELS OF HIS COAT, *WORE THE GARMENT DAY AND NIGHT FOR THE REMAINING 19 YEARS OF HIS LIFE*

TREE LIGHTNING
ARBORESCENT LIGHTNING WHICH OCCURS ONLY DURING TROPICAL STORMS IN SOUTH AMERICA TRACES IN THE SKY THE OUTLINE OF A LEAFLESS TREE AND, UNLIKE NORMAL LIGHTNING, *ITS FLASHES ALWAYS ASCEND*

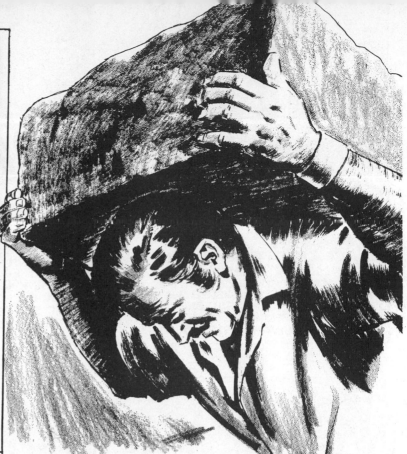

THE LUMBERJACK WHO SINGLEHANDEDLY CHANGED THE BOUNDARY OF SWITZERLAND
JEAN COSTAUD, A POWERFUL LUMBERJACK OF LIECHTENSTEIN, SETTLED A FRONTIER DISPUTE BETWEEN HIS COUNTRY AND SWITZERLAND BY THE SUPERHUMAN FEAT OF CARRYING A STONE WEIGHING 1,040 POUNDS *A DISTANCE OF 1 MILE, 4,500 FEET!*

WHERE HE FINALLY FELL EXHAUSTED THE STONE WAS ERECTED AS THE OFFICIAL BOUNDARY MARKER-- *AND HAS SO SERVED FOR 235 YEARS*

THE MISERONI VASE
OWNED BY THE PRINCE OF LIECHTENSTEIN IS CARVED FROM A SINGLE PIECE OF TOPAZ AND WEIGHS 3 POUNDS, 5 OUNCES

THE ELEPHANT SNOUT
AN AFRICAN FISH COMMUNICATES WITH OTHER FISH BY EMITTING AN ELECTRICAL SIGNAL --A PISCATORIAL VERSION OF THE MORSE CODE

GIRLS
of the Murundi Tribe, of the Congo, WIND THEIR LEGS IN HUNDREDS OF YARDS OF CORD *BECAUSE THICK LEGS ARE CONSIDERED A MARK OF BEAUTY*

THEIR LEGS SEEM TO BE 5 TIMES NORMAL SIZE

THE WEB
OF GATERACANTHA PALLIDA, A SOUTH AMERICAN SPIDER, IS ANCHORED BY STRAPS TO WHICH ITS OCCUPANT AFFIXES SECTIONS OF SILKY FLUFF - TO DIVERT THE ATTENTION OF PREDATORS FROM *THE SPIDER ITSELF*

DOROTHEA SCHAU
(1795-1878) of ODENSE, DENMARK, WAS THE MOTHER OF 7 OFFICERS IN THE DANISH ARMY -- *EVERY ONE OF WHOM DIED IN THE SERVICE*

THE LIGHT THAT FAILED
SARAH COOPER (1782-1850) WHO LIVED AT 28th STREET AND 4th AVENUE, IN NEW YORK, AFTER HER SAILOR FIANCÉ VANISHED WITH HIS SHIP AT SEA, KEPT A LIGHT BURNING IN HER WINDOW IN EXPECTATION OF HIS RETURN *EVERY NIGHT FOR 45 YEARS*

THE COUGH THAT WAS A DEATH SENTENCE FOR 1,200 MEN!
NAPOLEON BONAPARTE, AS A FRENCH GENERAL FIGHTING IN THE MIDDLE EAST IN 1799, WAS ABOUT TO RELEASE 1,200 TURKS CAPTURED AT JAFFA, WHEN HE WAS SEIZED WITH A FIT OF COUGHING--*"MA SACRÉ TOUX,"* ("MY CONFOUNDED COUGH") HE EXCLAIMED -- HIS NEXT IN COMMAND THOUGHT NAPOLEON HAD SAID, *"MASSACREZ TOUS"* ("MASSACRE EVERYONE") --AND ALL 1,200 PRISONERS WERE EXECUTED!

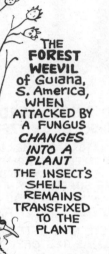

THE **FOREST WEEVIL** of Guiana, S. America, WHEN ATTACKED BY A FUNGUS *CHANGES INTO A PLANT* THE INSECT'S SHELL REMAINS TRANSFIXED TO THE PLANT

A **TAVERN SIGN** in Hamburg, Germany, MADE FROM THE SHOULDER BLADE OF A WHALE, GAVE THE STREET ON WHICH IT HANGS ITS NAME *"THE STREET OF THE WHALE'S SHOULDER BLADE"*

THE **NEST** OF THE JAVANESE ZETHUS BEE COMPRISES CHIPS OF MILKWEED LEAVES WHICH IT GLUES TOGETHER AND WHICH IT PROTECTS FROM RAIN BY *A SEPARATE ROOF OF CHIPS*

THE JEST THAT PROVED PROPHETIC!
PIERRE-ROGER de BEAUFORT, A YOUNG PRIEST INJURED AND ROBBED BY THUGS IN 1321 AND NURSED BACK TO HEALTH BY THE PRIOR OF THE MONASTERY OF THURET, REMARKED: "WHEN WILL I EVER BE ABLE TO REPAY YOU?" **"WHEN YOU ARE POPE,"** THE PRIOR REPLIED -- *21 YEARS LATER THE YOUNG PRIEST WAS CROWNED POPE CLEMENT VI - AND APPOINTED THE PRIOR ARCHBISHOP OF TOULOUSE AND PAPAL CHAMBERLAIN*

THE **TURPENTINE INSECT** WHICH BUILDS ITS NEST IN THE TEREBINTH TREE, CONSTRUCTS ITS SHELTER BY TWISTING LEAVES INTO *THE SHAPE OF A HORSESHOE*

THE **LARVA** of the **LATERNARIA INSECT** FRIGHTENS OFF PREDATORY MONKEYS BY CAMOUFLAGE THAT MAKES IT LOOK LIKE *A BABY ALLIGATOR* - PAINTED ALONGSIDE ITS SNOUT ARE ROWS OF FEROCIOUS-LOOKING TEETH

Ripley's Believe It or Not!

THE BATTLE FORMATION of the armies of the ancient Siamese RESEMBLED THE HEAD OF A BUFFALO

THE NATIONAL EMBLEM of the Empire of the Incas of Peru WAS THE RAINBOW

BELÉM DO PARÁ, a city in Brazil, IS RAINED ON BETWEEN 2 AND 4 P.M. EVERY DAY OF THE YEAR

AN OVAL TOMB FOUND IN THE MARI DESERT, Lebanon, WAS USED 5,000 YEARS AGO SO THE DECEASED COULD LEAVE THE WORLD FOLDED IN THE SAME POSITION AS HE ENTERED IT

MOUNT HIKURANGI in New Zealand, A PEAK 5,735 FEET HIGH, IS THE FIRST SPOT ON WHICH THE RISING SUN SHINES IN THE ENTIRE AREA THAT ONCE COMPRISED THE BRITISH EMPIRE

THE COAT OF ARMS of the PELHAM FAMILY FEATURES THE BELT BUCKLE OF KING JOHN THE GOOD, OF FRANCE, WHICH WAS SNATCHED BY AN ENGLISH ANCESTOR OF THE PELHAMS IN THE BATTLE OF POITIERS IN 1356

THE SLAVE WHO BECAME A QUEEN

BATHILDE A BRITISH GIRL WHOM PIRATES SOLD INTO SLAVERY TO KING CLOVIS II, OF NEUSTRIA, FRANCE, WON THE MONARCH'S LOVE, BECAME HIS QUEEN AND RULED AS REGENT AFTER HIS DEATH — SHE BECAME THE MOTHER OF 3 KINGS AND AS REGENT OUTLAWED SLAVERY IN HER COUNTRY FOREVER

THE FIJIAN WEDDING RING IS THE TOOTH OF A SPERM WHALE-SUSPENDED FROM A ROPE OF BRAIDED COCONUT HUSK FIBER THE PROSPECTIVE GROOM SENDS IT TO HIS SWEET-HEARTS FATHER, AND IF HE ACCEPTS THE PROPOSAL, THE TOOTH IS HUNG FROM A RAFTER IN THE COUPLE'S HUT AS A CERTIFICATE OF THEIR MARRIAGE

SAMUEL L. SOUTHARD (1787-1842) SERVED AS SECRETARY OF THE ARMY SECRETARY OF THE NAVY AND SECRETARY OF THE TREASURY SIMULTANEOUSLY

Ripley's Believe It or Not!

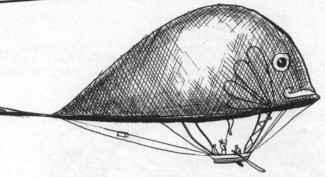

A **BALLOON** DEMONSTRATED IN ENGLAND IN 1816, WAS SHAPED LIKE A GIANT DOLPHIN

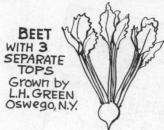

BEET WITH **3** SEPARATE TOPS Grown by L.H. GREEN Oswego, N.Y.

JOSEF MITTELSTADT (1681-1793) SERVED IN THE PRUSSIAN ARMY FOR 67 YEARS, FOUGHT IN 17 WARS, MARRIED HIS THIRD WIFE AT THE AGE OF 109, AND LIVED TO BE 112

THE **BRAMAH LOCK** SO IMPREGNABLE THAT ITS ENGLISH MAKER OFFERED A $1,000 REWARD FOR 64 YEARS TO ANYONE WHO COULD PICK IT, WAS FINALLY OPENED WITHOUT A KEY BY AN AMERICAN NAMED A.C. HUBBS *WHO LABORED ON THE LOCK FOR 51 HOURS*

THE **NYIMI** CHIEF OF THE BAKUBA TRIBES OF THE CONGO WEARS CEREMONIAL ROBES THAT WEIGH **230** POUNDS - *3 TIMES AS MUCH AS THE ARMOR OF A MEDIEVAL KNIGHT*

Peru LAND OF THE LLAMA HAS AN OUTLINE SHAPED LIKE THE *HEAD AND NECK OF A LLAMA*

THE **SEAL** OF SIR FRANCIS GALTON (1822-1911) FATHER OF THE MODERN SCIENCE OF FINGERPRINTING *FEATURED HIS OWN FINGERPRINT*

KITES ARE USED IN Indonesia and Malaya *FOR FISHING* A LINE WITH A BAITED HOOK IS FASTENED TO THE KITE - FREEING THE FISHERMEN FOR OTHER TASKS

THE **WILLIAM TELL SHELTER** IN THE BOTANICAL GARDENS OF Melbourne, Australia, *IS AN EXACT REPLICA OF SWITZERLAND WILLIAM TELL CHAPEL*

THE UNIVERSITY OF KIEV, in the Ukraine, WHEN ITS STUDENTS RIOTED IN 1901 TO PROTEST THE DRAFTING OF FELLOW STUDENTS INTO THE ARMY AS PUNISHMENT FOR POLITICAL ACTIVITY, WAS PAINTED RED TO IMPLY THAT THE INSTITUTION WAS BLUSHING WITH SHAME

MOST AMAZING ARCHER IN ALL HISTORY

WASA DAIHARACHIRO, a Japanese samurai, SHOT HIS BOW CONTINUOUSLY FOR 24 HOURS IN KYOTO, JAPAN, FIRING 13,053 ARROWS AT A TARGET 396 FEET AWAY - AND SCORED 8,133 BULL'S-EYES! (April 27, 1686)

THE CARD GAME OF THE CORPSES!

A GATEHOUSE OF THE FORTRESS OF MALINES, Belgium, BLOWN UP WHEN LIGHTNING STRUCK 2,000 BAGS OF GUNPOWDER, WAS DUG INTO 3 WEEKS LATER BY WORKMEN WHO FOUND IN A VAULTED CHAMBER 4 SOLDIERS "PLAYING CARDS"-AND A 5th STILL STANDING BEHIND IN THE ROLE OF A KIBITZER!

THE 5 SOLDIERS WERE INSTANTLY KILLED BY THE EXPLOSION, BUT THE BLAST HAD CREATED A VACUUM THAT PRESERVED THE BODIES INTACT
THE GROUP WAS BURIED IN A SINGLE GRAVE - -WITH THE PLAYERS STILL CLUTCHING THEIR CARDS

GLASS COINS

A DIFFERENT COLOR FOR EACH DENOMINATION WERE USED IN EGYPT FROM 908 TO 1171 -AND WERE EXCHANGEABLE FOR GOLD ON DEMAND

A PUDDING BAKED FOR A FESTIVAL in Vienna, Austria, CONTAINED 4,500 EGGS, 660 POUNDS OF RAISINS, 275 POUNDS OF SUGAR, 220 POUNDS OF ALMONDS, 110 POUNDS OF LEMON EXTRACT, 220 POUNDS OF FAT, 23 POUNDS OF SPICES, 10 BOTTLES OF RUM -AND WEIGHED OVER 1,500 POUNDS IT REQUIRED 10 DAYS AND NIGHTS TO PREPARE THE PUDDING - BUT IT WAS EATEN IN JUST 75 MINUTES (1864)

Tomato SHAPED LIKE A 4-LEAF CLOVER Grown by Nino Carrara, Redwood City, Calif.

RODERIQUE a French sailor WHOSE SWEETHEART DIED IN TAHITI, HAD HER TOMB TATTOOED OVER HIS HEART

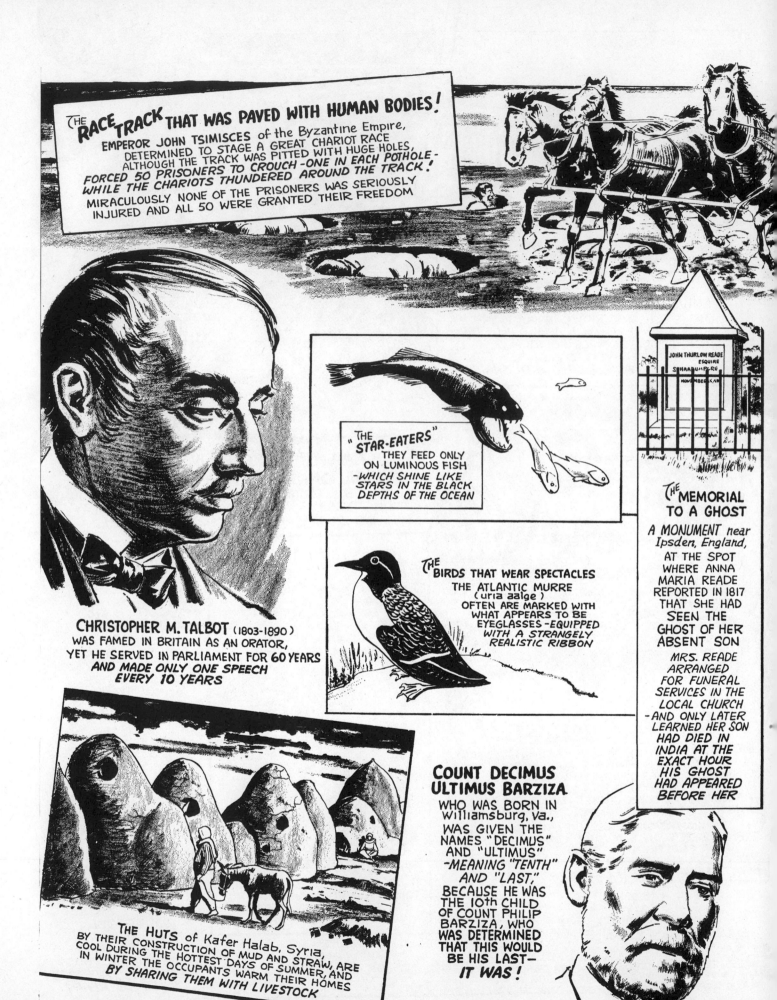

THE RACE TRACK THAT WAS PAVED WITH HUMAN BODIES!
EMPEROR JOHN TSIMISCES of the Byzantine Empire, DETERMINED TO STAGE A GREAT CHARIOT RACE ALTHOUGH THE TRACK WAS PITTED WITH HUGE HOLES, FORCED 50 PRISONERS TO CROUCH -ONE IN EACH POTHOLE- WHILE THE CHARIOTS THUNDERED AROUND THE TRACK! MIRACULOUSLY NONE OF THE PRISONERS WAS SERIOUSLY INJURED AND ALL 50 WERE GRANTED THEIR FREEDOM

"THE STAR-EATERS" THEY FEED ONLY ON LUMINOUS FISH -WHICH SHINE LIKE STARS IN THE BLACK DEPTHS OF THE OCEAN

CHRISTOPHER M. TALBOT (1803-1890) WAS FAMED IN BRITAIN AS AN ORATOR, YET HE SERVED IN PARLIAMENT FOR 60 YEARS AND MADE ONLY ONE SPEECH EVERY 10 YEARS

THE BIRDS THAT WEAR SPECTACLES THE ATLANTIC MURRE (uria aalge) OFTEN ARE MARKED WITH WHAT APPEARS TO BE EYEGLASSES -EQUIPPED WITH A STRANGELY REALISTIC RIBBON

THE MEMORIAL TO A GHOST A MONUMENT near Ipsden, England, AT THE SPOT WHERE ANNA MARIA READE REPORTED IN 1817 THAT SHE HAD SEEN THE GHOST OF HER ABSENT SON

MRS. READE ARRANGED FOR FUNERAL SERVICES IN THE LOCAL CHURCH -AND ONLY LATER LEARNED HER SON HAD DIED IN INDIA AT THE EXACT HOUR HIS GHOST HAD APPEARED BEFORE HER

COUNT DECIMUS ULTIMUS BARZIZA WHO WAS BORN IN Williamsburg, Va., WAS GIVEN THE NAMES "DECIMUS" AND "ULTIMUS" -MEANING "TENTH" AND "LAST," BECAUSE HE WAS THE 10th CHILD OF COUNT PHILIP BARZIZA, WHO WAS DETERMINED THAT THIS WOULD BE HIS LAST— IT WAS!

THE HUTS of Kafer Halab, Syria, BY THEIR CONSTRUCTION OF MUD AND STRAW, ARE COOL DURING THE HOTTEST DAYS OF SUMMER, AND IN WINTER THE OCCUPANTS WARM THEIR HOMES BY SHARING THEM WITH LIVESTOCK

Ripley's — ® Believe It or Not!

THE MOST GENEROUS TIP IN ALL HISTORY

THE CHAULAKHI - A GROUP OF BUILDINGS THAT COST $194,000 TO BUILD WAS GIVEN BY KING WAJID ALI SHAH OF OUDH, INDIA *TO HIS BARBER* Lucknow, India - 1847

THE OASIS OF TODRHA in Morocco HAS SOIL SO RICH THAT IT BEARS *3 DIFFERENT CROPS EACH YEAR*

BAUDOUIN I
Duke of Flanders
ATTACKED BY A POWERFUL BEAR
STRANGLED THE BEAST WITH HIS BARE HANDS!

THE FIRST SPORTS TROPHY A COPPER CUP DEPICTING 2 WRESTLERS- FOUND IN IRAQ IN 1938 *IS MORE THAN 4,700 YEARS OLD*

THE HALLOWED COFFIN IN WHICH CALIPH MOKTAFI WAS BURIED IN 1160 WAS MADE FROM THE ORIGINAL DOORS OF THE KAABAH, in Mecca *-THE MOST VENERATED SHRINE OF THE MOHAMMEDANS*

Ripley's ® Believe It or Not!

THE BABIRUSA
(PIG-DEER)
HAS 4 TUSKS--EACH
MORE THAN A FOOT
LONG--YET ALL OF
THEM ARE USELESS

MRS. OZIAS H. MCFADDEN
A TEACHER OF
Embden, Maine,
TAUGHT FOR **30** TERMS
- *EACH TERM IN A
DIFFERENT SCHOOL*

THE LONDON HOSPITAL
TODAY ONE OF THE GREATEST MEDICAL CENTERS IN
THE WORLD, WAS OPENED IN 1740 WITH A CAPITAL
OF ONE SHILLING (24 CENTS)

THE **CRICKET** IS A
VENTRILOQUIST

A **CHURCH** on Ocracoke Island, N.C.,
HOUSING THE CONGREGATIONS OF 2 OTHER CHURCHES
*WHICH WERE DEMOLISHED AT THE TIME OF THEIR MERGER,
SO A NEW CHURCH COULD BE BUILT FROM
THEIR SALVAGED MATERIALS*

ADAM MOLTKE (1710-1792)
A FRIEND OF KING FREDERICK V
of Denmark
WAS THE FATHER OF 22 SONS
-OF WHOM 5 BECAME CABINET MINISTERS
4 WERE AMBASSADORS
2 BECAME GENERALS
AND THE OTHER 11 WERE MAYORS,
PROVINCIAL GOVERNORS, OR
PRIVY COUNCILORS OF STATE

A **CALENDULA BLOOM**
FROM WHICH
9 OTHER
CALENDULAS
GREW,
EACH ON ITS
OWN STEM
Grown by
MRS. MARTHA FREDERICI
ARBORG, MANITOBA

THE **MOST
LAVISH
EXECUTION
IN HISTORY!**

JORG HONAVER,
EXECUTED FOR
FRAUDULENTLY
CLAIMING HE
COULD
CHANGE IRON
INTO GOLD

*WAS COATED
WITH A
COVERING
OF GOLD
AND
HANGED ON
A GOLDEN
GALLOWS*
April 2, 1597

from an old print

KINGSGATE CASTLE in England ACTUALLY WAS CONSTRUCTED BY THE FIRST LORD HOLLAND (1705-1774) AS A STABLE FOR HIS HORSES

THE NILE CROCODILE IS THE ONLY ANIMAL IN NATURE THAT MAKES AUDIBLE SOUNDS WHILE IT IS STILL IN ITS EGG THE EGG IS BURIED IN THE GROUND, AND THE YOUNG CROCODILE'S "HONK" IS A SIGNAL TO ITS PARENT THAT IT IS TIME TO DIG UP THE EGG

HONK

?

MUSTAFA A DERVISH of Scutari, Turkey, TO ATONE FOR HAVING ONCE FALLEN ASLEEP DURING A SERMON, SAT UPRIGHT WITH HIS HAIR ATTACHED TO THE CEILING BY A STRING EVERY NIGHT FOR THE NEXT 21 YEARS OF HIS LIFE! (1891-1912)

THE ROLLER COASTER TREE ACHTERMANN PEAK, GERMANY

THE MAN WHOSE LIFE WAS SAVED BY AN EARTHQUAKE! LOUIS GALDY of Port Royal, Jamaica, WAS BURIED ALIVE BY AN EARTHQUAKE ON JUNE 7, 1692, BUT ANOTHER QUAKE REOPENED THE GROUND AND CATAPULTED HIM TO SAFETY! GALDY SURVIVED FOR ANOTHER 47 YEARS

3 IRON BOATS TRAVEL LASHED TOGETHER on Lake Chad, Africa, THE CENTER ONE HAVING THE MOTIVE POWER AND THE OTHERS PROVIDING LIVING QUARTERS FOR PASSENGERS AND CREW

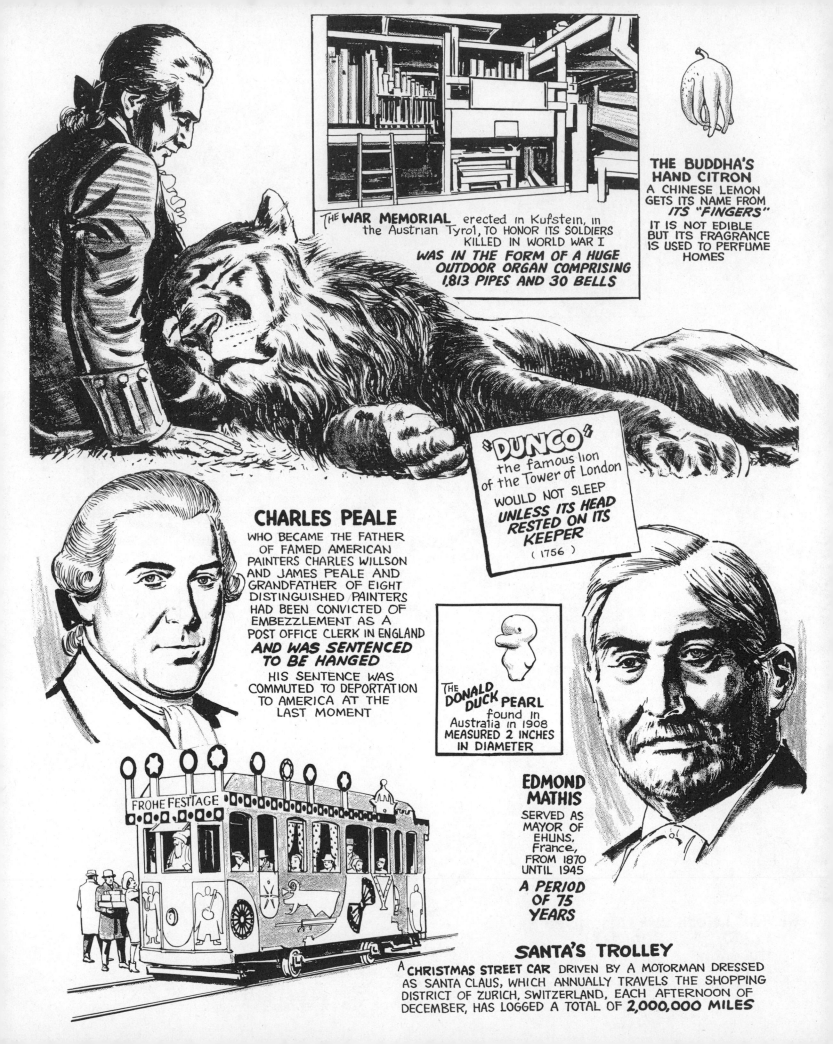

THE **WAR MEMORIAL** erected in Kufstein, in the Austrian Tyrol, TO HONOR ITS SOLDIERS KILLED IN WORLD WAR I **WAS IN THE FORM OF A HUGE OUTDOOR ORGAN COMPRISING 1,813 PIPES AND 30 BELLS**

THE BUDDHA'S HAND CITRON
A CHINESE LEMON GETS ITS NAME FROM *ITS "FINGERS"* IT IS NOT EDIBLE BUT ITS FRAGRANCE IS USED TO PERFUME HOMES

"DUNCO" the famous lion of the Tower of London WOULD NOT SLEEP **UNLESS ITS HEAD RESTED ON ITS KEEPER** (1756)

CHARLES PEALE
WHO BECAME THE FATHER OF FAMED AMERICAN PAINTERS CHARLES WILLSON AND JAMES PEALE AND GRANDFATHER OF EIGHT DISTINGUISHED PAINTERS HAD BEEN CONVICTED OF EMBEZZLEMENT AS A POST OFFICE CLERK IN ENGLAND **AND WAS SENTENCED TO BE HANGED** HIS SENTENCE WAS COMMUTED TO DEPORTATION TO AMERICA AT THE LAST MOMENT

THE **DONALD DUCK PEARL** found in Australia in 1908 MEASURED 2 INCHES IN DIAMETER

EDMOND MATHIS SERVED AS MAYOR OF EHUNS, France, FROM 1870 UNTIL 1945 **A PERIOD OF 75 YEARS**

FROHE FESTTAGE

SANTA'S TROLLEY
A **CHRISTMAS STREET CAR** DRIVEN BY A MOTORMAN DRESSED AS SANTA CLAUS, WHICH ANNUALLY TRAVELS THE SHOPPING DISTRICT OF ZURICH, SWITZERLAND, EACH AFTERNOON OF DECEMBER, HAS LOGGED A TOTAL OF **2,000,000 MILES**

THE MOST PROFITABLE SWINDLE IN ALL HISTORY!

BELESIS AN ASSYRIAN REBEL, AFTER KING ASSUR-BANI-PAL OF ASSYRIA HAD BURNED HIMSELF ALIVE, PERSUADED THE NEW RULER, ARBACES, TO GRANT HIM PERMISSION TO *GIVE THE LATE MONARCH'S ASHES PROPER BURIAL*

UNKNOWN TO ARBACES, THE PYRE HAD CONTAINED 2,500,000 GOLD BRICKS -AND BELESIS SALVAGED THE MOLTEN GOLD AND *NETTED $2,000,000,000 BY HIS RUSE!* (885 B.C.)

THE **ALTAR** in the Chapel of the Castle of Issogne, Italy *CONSISTS OF SOLID GOLD* IT WAS MADE BY MELTING DOWN GOLD COINS

MATCHES
USED IN THE U.S. IN 1840 *COULD BE IGNITED FROM EITHER END*

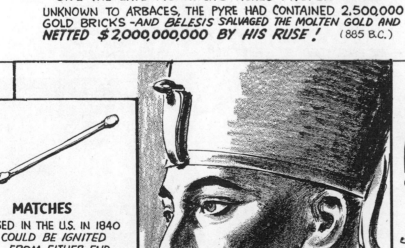

THE **FATHER** OF **TIME!**
IMHOTEP WHO WAS CHIEF JUSTICE OF EGYPT AND COURT PHYSICIAN TO PHARAOH ZOSER *INVENTED THE FIRST CALENDAR IN 2,780 B.C.*

WOMEN
of Latour-d'Auvergne, France, WEAR A BAND ON THEIR HEADDRESS TO HONOR WOMEN OF THE VILLAGE WHO KILLED A TROOP OF SARACENS WITH STONES AND THEN PROUDLY ATTACHED THE INVADERS' CHIN STRAPS TO THEIR HEADDRESSES *1,200 YEARS AGO*

Ripley's Believe It or Not!

HORSES
BEFORE THE
INVENTION OF THE
STIRRUP IN 420
WERE TRAINED TO
RECEIVE THEIR
RIDERS BY
DROPPING TO
THEIR KNEES
LIKE CAMELS

THE **BIG CATCH**
A MUSKELLUNGE, 5 FEET LONG, HOOKED BY
ALICE PRATT OFF GRENELL'S ISLAND, N.Y.
HAD JUST SWALLOWED A 19-INCH PICKEREL
INSIDE OF WHICH WAS FOUND A PERCH

THE **GREATEST GRAFTER OF ALL TIME**

HO SHEN, PRIME MINISTER AND TAX COLLECTOR UNDER CHINESE
EMPEROR CHIEN LUNG, CONFESSED, AFTER THE EMPEROR'S
DEATH IN 1796, THAT HE HAD ACCUMULATED GOLD AND
SILVER BARS, JEWELS AND FURS WORTH $612,000,000
THE EQUIVALENT TODAY OF APPROXIMATELY $12,000,000,000
EMPEROR CHIA CHING REWARDED HO SHEN FOR HIS
CO-OPERATION IN REVEALING THE HIDING PLACE OF HIS LOOT
BY PERMITTING HIM TO HANG HIMSELF IN HIS CELL

BRITISH DOLLARS
THE BANK OF
ENGLAND
FROM 1804
TO 1806
*MINTED
SILVER
DOLLARS*

RICORD'S **FROG** of the Bahamas
IS THE ONLY FROG THAT
HATCHES ITS YOUNG AS FROGS
-SKIPPING THE TADPOLE STAGE

AN **ARTIFICIAL PLANT**
CREATED BY FAMED FRENCH
GOLDSMITH FABERGE ENTIRELY
OF GOLD AND DIAMONDS
*IS SO DELICATELY
WROUGHT THAT IT IS
IN PERPETUAL MOTION*

THE **RAILROAD BRIDGE** OVER THE CLAVEY RIVER, IN TUOLUMNE COUNTY, CALIF.,
325 FEET LONG AND 65 FEET HIGH
*ORIGINALLY WAS BUILT IN THE TUOLUMNE RAILROAD YARDS - THEN
WAS TAKEN APART AND TRANSPORTED TO ITS PERMANENT SITE*

A **GOLDEN STAND** STUDDED WITH PEARLS, EMERALDS AND RUBIES CREATED BY THE DUKE OF FERRARA IN 1501 TO HOLD HIS ENGAGEMENT PRESENT FROM HIS FUTURE BRIDE, LUCREZIA BORGIA -*A LOCK OF HER GOLDEN HAIR*

THE DANCE OF THE DEAD!
THE BASQUES of France PERFORM A DANCE IN WHICH A TRUSSED-UP MAN IS PASSED OVERHEAD AS A RE-ENACTMENT OF AN ANCIENT FUNERAL CUSTOM, IN WHICH *THE BASQUES ALWAYS DANCED WITH THE BODY OF A DEAD CHIEF!*

HOT DOG! THE MEXICAN HAIRLESS HAS A CONSTANT BODY TEMPERATURE OF 104 DEGREES
Submitted by DR. F.C. COULTER, Orange, Conn.

"HAWAIIAN MUSIC" IS THE CREATION OF A GERMAN BANDMASTER
CAPTAIN HENRY BERGER (1844-1929) a German military bandmaster INVITED TO HAWAII BY KING KAMEHAMEHA V IN 1872, COMPOSED THE FIRST HAWAIIAN SONGS WHICH *HE ADAPTED FROM GERMAN FOLK TUNES* HE COMPOSED 72 FAMOUS HAWAIIAN SONGS, INCLUDING "ALOHA OE" AND THE HAWAIIAN NATIONAL SONG

THE **QUEEN** OF **THE NIGHT** A CACTUS THAT BLOOMS AT MIDNIGHT, HAS A PERFUME SO POWERFUL THAT IT CAN BE DETECTED *HALF A MILE AWAY*

THE MAN WHO CLIMBED A MOUNTAIN BAREFOOTED!
FRITZ SIEGEL CLIMBED 9,728 FEET TO THE SNOW-COVERED PEAK OF GERMANY'S ZUGSPITZE *WITHOUT SHOES* (July 15, 1932)

THE **FIDDLE** IS WORSHIPED BY THE PARDHANS of India *AS A PORTABLE TEMPLE SHELTERING THEIR GOD* PLAYING THE FIDDLE IS CONSIDERED PRAYER, AND HENS AND GOATS ARE SACRIFICED TO IT

THE **HAMMERHEAD FLY** (DIOPSIS) IS NATURE'S ONLY REPLICA OF THE *HAMMERHEAD SHARK*

THE *BIGGEST* BIG-GAME HUNTER OF THEM ALL
ARCHDUKE FRANZ FERDINAND WHOSE ASSASSINATION BROUGHT ON WORLD WAR I, KEPT A CAREFUL RECORD OF HIS HUNTING BAGS, AND *HIS KILLS TOTALLED 276,000*

THE **DRUGSTORE**
of Lemgo, Germany, HAS BEEN LOCATED FOR *400* YEARS IN THE *GREAT BAY WINDOW OF THE TOWN HALL*

TAIL BRISTLES of the African porcupine ARE USED BY THE MAEJE TRIBE AS ARROWHEADS

THE LAKE THAT WAS PUT IN HOCK
LAKE ATTER, largest Alpine lake in Austria, WITH AN AREA OF 18 SQUARE MILES *WAS PAWNED BY THE AUSTRIAN GOVERNMENT IN 1592 FOR A LOAN OF $50* HANS KHEVEHULLER, WHO PUT UP THE MONEY, RECEIVED TEMPORARY OWNERSHIP OF THE LAKE, ITS FISH, AND ALL THE FISHERMEN DWELLING ON ITS SHORES

THE SPIDER CRAB
CAMOUFLAGES ITSELF BY HANGING *LAYERS OF SEAWEED* ON HOOKS ON ITS BACK

THE MARTIAN WRITTEN LANGUAGE
AS COPIED DOWN BY CATHERINE MULLER, OF Geneva, Switzerland, WHO INSISTED SHE LEARNED IT *FROM A DEPARTED ASSOCIATE DURING A SEANCE*

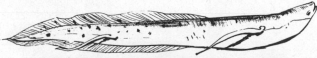

THE FIRST CREATURE WITH LUNGS
THE PROTOPTERUS, A FISH WITHOUT FINS OR GILLS, BREATHES BY COMING TO THE SURFACE OF THE WATER *—AS IT HAS FOR 400,000,000 YEARS*

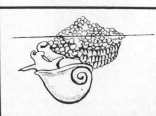

THE VIOLET SHELL
a snail, SAILS ABOUT ON A RAFT OF AIR BUBBLES *BUILT FROM MUCUS STORED IN ITS FOOT*

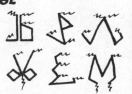

Ripley's Believe It or Not!

A LEMON THAT GREW IN THE SHAPE OF A **TEAPOT**
Submitted by James Hilliard San Francisco, Calif.

AIMÉE RAPIN famed Swiss artist WAS BORN WITHOUT ARMS, YET SHE KNITTED AT THE AGE OF 5, DEVELOPED A BEAUTIFUL 'HANDWRITING' AND BECAME A LEADING PAINTER —*USING HER FEET!*

THE **ROUND FISHBOWL** WAS INVENTED BY *COUNTESS DUBARRY, MISTRESS OF KING LOUIS XV OF FRANCE*

THE **MUSICAL MONARCH** *KING FREDERICK II of Prussia* WHO LOVED TO PLAY THE FLUTE *GAVE 50,000 PUBLIC CONCERTS—* AT LEAST 3 CONCERTS EVERY DAY FOR A PERIOD OF 40 YEARS

THE MEN WHO FIREPROOF THEIR BODIES

MEDICINE MEN of the Kondoa Tribe, in Tanganyika, Africa, HAND DOWN FROM GENERATION TO GENERATION THE SECRET OF MIXING A VEGETABLE JUICE THAT *MAKES THEIR NAKED SKIN IMPERVIOUS TO A BLAZING TORCH*

PAUL DESCHANEL (1856-1922) WAS THE ONLY FRENCH PRESIDENT *WHO WAS NOT BORN IN FRANCE* HE WAS BORN IN BELGIUM AND SERVED AS PRESIDENT OF FRANCE IN 1920

Ripley's Believe It or Not!

THE TOP of CORINTHIAN COLUMNS CONSIDERED THE MOST BEAUTIFUL COLUMN DESIGN, WAS INSPIRED BY THE PRICKLY LEAVES OF THE MEDITERRANEAN ACANTHUS PLANT

GEN. THOMAS JEFFERSON CHAMBERS (1802-1865) AFTER WHOM CHAMBERS COUNTY, TEXAS, WAS NAMED, WAS GIVEN 66,420 ACRES OF LAND FOR SERVING AS A JUDGE OF THE SUPERIOR COURT OF TEXAS -- *YET HE NEVER ONCE CONVENED COURT*

THE LAND DEEDED TO HIM INCLUDED THE PRESENT SITE OF AUSTIN

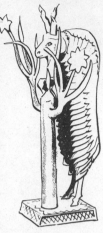

A PUBLIC STATUE OF A RAM CAUGHT IN A BUSH, WHICH STOOD IN THE STREETS OF UR of the Chaldees, Babylonia, WAS MADE OF SOLID GOLD

THE RIVER WITH FISH THAT CATCH THEMSELVES! Ornans, France FISH ARE NEVER HOOKED IN THIS SECTION OF THE RIVER LOUE -- *THEY SWIM INTO THE HOMES OF THE FISHERMEN!*

A RAKE MADE BY AMERICAN INDIANS *FROM THE ANTLERS OF A DEER*

THE MAN WHO WAS MADE A MONARCH BY A PARROT! GENERAL ABD-el MOUMEN (1101-1163) WAS ELECTED CALIPH OF AN EMPIRE INCLUDING ALL OF NORTH AFRICA AND SOUTHERN SPAIN BECAUSE THE ASSEMBLY, DEADLOCKED IN ITS ATTEMPT TO DECIDE ON A NEW LEADER, WAS STARTLED BY A PARROT THAT FLEW INTO THE TENT AND SCREECHED: "GLORY TO CALIPH ABD-el MOUMEN!" THE ASSEMBLY TOOK UP THE CRY AND THE GENERAL RULED THE EMPIRE FOR 11 YEARS -TO BE FOLLOWED ON THE THRONE BY 12 OF HIS DESCENDANTS (1152)

DOGMAR a village in Tibet, CONSISTS OF HOUSES CLINGING TO A TALL CLAY CLIFF —UP WHICH NATIVES *MUST SCRAMBLE TO REACH THEIR HOMES*

KING ROBERT III (1340-1406) of Scotland, UPON LEARNING THAT HIS SON JAMES HAD BEEN IMPRISONED BY THE ENGLISH, BECAME SO GRIEF-STRICKEN THAT HE *STARVED HIMSELF TO DEATH*

AT HIS OWN DIRECTION HE WAS BURIED IN AN ANTHILL BENEATH AN EPITAPH THAT READ : "*HERE LIES THE WORST KING AND THE MOST MISERABLE MAN IN THE KINGDOM*"

PETER L. JAYCOCKS of Key West, Fla., WALKED 80 FEET *WITH 2 MEN BALANCED ON THE PALMS OF HIS HANDS*

GOLD WEDDING RINGS DECLARED TO BE IN THE SHAPE OF THE TEMPLE OF JERUSALEM, MADE A VENETIAN JEWELER WEALTHY IN THE 16th CENTURY -*UNTIL IT WAS DISCOVERED THEY IN NO WAY RESEMBLED THE TEMPLE*

WITCH HAZEL WAS SO NAMED BECAUSE EARLY AMERICANS BELIEVED THE PLANT HAD THE POWER TO LOCATE UNDERGROUND SPRINGS AND MINERALS WHEN *USED AS A DIVINING ROD*

DRAGONS SHAPED FROM BLOCKS OF ICE BUILT ON THE NEVA RIVER AT ST. PETERSBURG, RUSSIA. EACH WINTER TERRIFIED *THE POPULACE BY SPOUTING FLAMES WITHOUT MELTING* THE PUBLIC NEVER LEARNED THEY WERE LINED WITH ASBESTOS

THE **MOON SNAIL** *HAS NO EYES*— IT HAS AN ENORMOUS FOOT OUT OF WHICH THE SNAIL MUST SQUEEZE WATER TO BE ABLE TO FIT INTO ITS SHELL

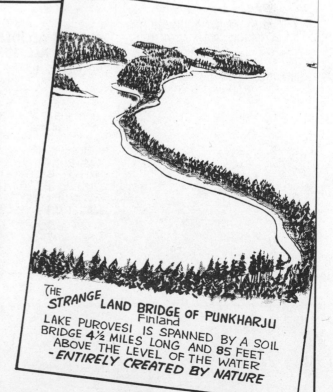

THE **STRANGE LAND BRIDGE OF PUNKHARJU** Finland LAKE PUROVESI IS SPANNED BY A SOIL BRIDGE 4½ MILES LONG AND 85 FEET ABOVE THE LEVEL OF THE WATER -*ENTIRELY CREATED BY NATURE*

A BRITISH OBSERVATION PLANE on the Western front in World War I FLEW IN WIDE CIRCLES FOR SEVERAL HOURS AND THEN LANDED WITHOUT MISHAP -ALTHOUGH ITS PILOT AND OBSERVER WERE BOTH DEAD! June 18, 1918

A **NATIVE** of New Guinea HONORS HIS DEAD FATHER BY WEARING A NECKLACE **WOVEN FROM HIS FATHER'S HAIR**

IT'S EMBARRASSING!

"Barney" A YOUNG DUCK OWNED BY CYRIL SKINNER **CANNOT SWIM** Sevenoaks, England

THE MOST COLOSSAL BANQUET OF MODERN TIMES

THE GOVERNMENT OF FRANCE TO EXPRESS ITS GRATITUDE FOR ITS ELECTION VICTORY OF 1900, ENTERTAINED AT AN ENORMOUS BANQUET IN THE GARDEN OF THE TUILERIES EVERY MAYOR IN ALL FRANCE – *SIMULTANEOUSLY* **SERVING 22,295 MAYORS**

THE BANQUET REQUIRED 3,600 WAITERS, 300 DISHWASHERS, 250,000 DISHES –AND **50,000** BOTTLES OF WINE

A **POPPY** THAT GREW THROUGH A BRICK WALL *BLOOMED BEFORE 2 SIMILAR PLANTS IN AN ADJACENT FLOWER BOX* Submitted by MRS. JOSEPH BERGLAR, Creve Coeur, Missouri

THE MOST ACCIDENT PRONE MAN IN ALL HISTORY

THE REV. JOHANNES OSIANDER (1657-1724) of Tubingen, Germany, WAS KNOCKED DOWN BY A WILD BOAR, HAD HIS HORSE FALL ON HIM DURING A FLOOD, WAS SHOT AT BY BANDITS AND BURIED UNDER AN AVALANCHE, WAS BLOWN INTO THE RHINE RIVER BY A BLIZZARD, CRUSHED BY A FALLEN TREE, WAS SHIPWRECKED – AND EVEN **WAS RUN OVER BY A SHIP** *HE ESCAPED UNHARMED EVERY TIME*

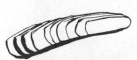

THE **RAZOR CLAM** CAN BURY ITSELF IN THE SAND IN **8 SECONDS** IT DIGS A HOLE WITH ITS FOOT –*WHICH THEN SWELLS AND ENLARGES THE OPENING TO FIT THE ENTIRE CLAM*

PINOCCHIO TOMATO Submitted by WILLIAM CUSHING Yarmouth, Nova Scotia

THE **BLUE** DANUBE IS NOT BLUE NEAR PASSAU, AUSTRIA, THE BROWN ILZ RIVER, THE GREEN DANUBE AND THE YELLOW INN RIVER FLOW SIDE BY SIDE **TO CREATE A STRIPED DANUBE**

Ripley's Believe It or Not!

A **DAGGER** found in the tomb of King Tut HAD A BLADE OF IRON THAT WAS STILL BRIGHT AND SHINY ALTHOUGH IT HAD BEEN BURIED FOR NEARLY 3,300 YEARS

MYKONOS a Greek island HAS A POPULATION OF ONLY 5,000 —YET IT HAS **360** CHURCHES

THE **MONUMENT TO A POEM** Schaffhausen, Switzerland IT WAS ERECTED TO COMMEMORATE FREDERICK von SCHILLER'S FAMOUS POEM "THE BELL"

THE **JOEPYEWEED** IS A MEMORIAL TO AN INDIAN MEDICINE MAN, JOE PYE, WHO USED IT TO CURE 12 DIFFERENT AILMENTS

FRANCESCO MOROSINI (1618 - 1694) WARRIOR RULER OF VENICE, ALWAYS PRAYED BEFORE HE LEFT HIS HOME AND ALWAYS CARRIED A PRAYER BOOK —BUT THE BOOK WAS HOLLOWED OUT TO CONCEAL A PISTOL AS A PRECAUTION AGAINST ASSASSINS!

THE **PLAY THAT WAS WRITTEN WITH A NEEDLE!** LAURENT de la BAUMELLE (1728-1773) French poet and playwright WHILE A PRISONER IN THE BASTILLE IN 1752 WROTE A TRAGEDY OF 700 STANZAS —SCRATCHING THE WORDS ON 2 TIN PLATES WITH A NEEDLE! THE PLATES WERE TAKEN FROM HIM BUT HE HAD MEMORIZED THE PLAY —AND IT WAS PRODUCED MANY TIMES IN FRENCH THEATRES

THE BLUE CRAB FOUND IN THE RED SEA OFF the Sinai Peninsula DIES WITHIN 2 MINUTES AFTER BEING TAKEN FROM THE WATER

Acanthurus Xanthurus A FISH FOUND IN THE INDIAN AND PACIFIC OCEANS IS A BRIGHT BLUE COLOR DURING THE DAYTIME AND A VIVID WHITE AT NIGHT

"MAGIC" NEEDLES EUROPEAN SCIENTISTS FROM THE 16th TO 18th CENTURIES BELIEVED THAT 2 NEEDLES CUT FROM THE SAME BAR OF STEEL AND RUBBED BY THE SAME MAGNET WOULD ALWAYS POINT THE SAME WAY —EVEN WHEN FAR APART THE NEEDLES WERE MOUNTED ON ALPHABET DIALS IN THE BELIEF THAT MOVING ONE TO SUCCESSIVE LETTERS WOULD SPELL OUT MESSAGES ON THE DISTANT DIAL

Ripley's — Believe It or Not!

TIBETAN MEDALS
ARE CONSTRUCTED BY MIXING RED CLAY WITH *CRUSHED BONES FROM THE CORPSES OF TIBETAN HOLY MEN*

The **TOMB** OF THE CAMEL
Tibba, India
IT WAS ERECTED OVER THE GRAVE OF A CAMEL NAMED "MELU" WHICH DAILY CARRIED A BEGGING BOWL FROM DOOR TO DOOR *COLLECTING GRAIN FOR CHARITY*

The **RAIN** THAT FELL FOR **100** YEARS !
ALL THE OCEANS FOR MILLIONS OF YEARS *WERE SUSPENDED ABOVE THE EARTH IN AN UNBROKEN BLACK CLOUD* WHEN THE MOLTEN ROCK OF THE EARTH COOLED, THE CLOUD RELEASED A TORRENT OF RAIN THAT LASTED FOR 100 YEARS AND FORMED OUR OCEANS

The **MAN WHO KILLED HIS OPPONENT IN A PISTOL DUEL WITHOUT FIRING A SHOT!**
FREDERIC THUYETTE
CHALLENGED BY ARCHAMBAULT NIVLICH, HIS BEST FRIEND, OVER A MISUNDERSTANDING, AGREED TO A DUEL IN THE BOIS de Boulogne, near Paris, France, BUT INSISTED HE WOULD NOT SHOOT HIS PISTOL. TO MAKE CERTAIN THAT THUYETTE WOULD NOT SHOOT, NIVLICH TAMPERED WITH THE FORMER'S PISTOL, BUT HIS OWN *BULLET RICOCHETED BACK FROM THUYETTE'S WEAPON - KILLING NIVLICH INSTANTLY!* (1823)

DR. MARIANO GALVEZ
(1794 - 1838)
WHO BECAME PRESIDENT OF GUATEMALA IN 1831
BEGAN LIFE AS A FOUNDLING ABANDONED ON A DOORSTEP

A STALACTITE CURTAIN
10 FEET WIDE
in a cave near Syrau, Germany,
IS 1,000,000 YEARS OLD

A FAMILY MAN
KING PHILIP II
(1527-1598) of Spain
WHO HAD 4 WIVES,
MARRIED 2 OF HIS COUSINS,
AN AUNT AND A NIECE

THE FISH THAT CARRIES A TORCH
ANOMALOPS KATOPTRON
of India
LIGHTS ITS WAY THROUGH THE DARK DEPTHS OF THE SEA
BY CARRYING IMMEDIATELY BELOW ITS EYES A COLONY OF LUMINOUS BACTERIA

"POMPEY" A LION
LIVED IN THE TOWER OF LONDON, IN ENGLAND,
from 1690 to 1760
- A SPAN OF 70 YEARS

2 TREES
GROWING FROM A CONCRETE ROOF
Submitted by Mrs. Ophelia Elston, Chicago, Ill.

THE PIGGYBACK DANCE OF THE DEAD!
THE CORPSE OF A MEMBER OF THE KAPSIKI TRIBE of the Cameroons, Africa,
IS ALWAYS ATTIRED IN FINERY, INCLUDING A CROWN, AND PARTICIPATES IN A DANCE THAT LASTS FOR HOURS
ASTRIDE THE SHOULDERS OF THE TRIBE'S BLACKSMITH!

DR.
BENJAMIN
KITTREDGE
(1740-
1826)
of Tewksbury,
Mass.,

WAS THE
FATHER OF
8 SONS
-ALL OF
WHOM
BECAME
PHYSICIANS

DEVIL
WORSHIPERS
a sect in
Syria and Iraq
ARE FORBIDDEN ONLY
2 TYPES OF FOOD
-LETTUCE AND
CAULIFLOWER

THE
MIMECITON
a beetle
MIMICS THE ACTIONS
OF ANTS SO
PERFECTLY IT IS
PERMITTED TO ENTER
AN ANTHILL AND
GET A WORKING
ANT'S SHARE OF THE
STORED HONEY

THE
BLUE PEOPLE of MOROCCO
BERBERS of the Draa Valley
USE A BLUE INDIGO DYE ON THEIR
CLOTHING WHICH GRADUALLY
TURNS THEIR ENTIRE BODIES
AN INDELIBLE BLUE !

THE
STRANGEST CASTLE
IN THE WORLD!
THE CASTLE OF MUSSO
in Italy
CONSISTING OF MANY FORTS
AND TOWERS AND A LONG WALL
REPEATEDLY GIRDLES A
TALL MOUNTAIN FROM ITS
BASE TO ITS PEAK

ROCK-A-BYE
BIRDIE

A
HUMMING
BIRD
BUILT ITS NEST
near Santa Fe, Argentina,
IN A LOOP OF WIRE THAT
SWUNG BACK AND FORTH
FROM A FENCE

THE
FIRST ALUMINUM POT
A STEW PAN WAS MADE OF
ALUMINUM BY HENRY W. AVERY
of Cleveland, Ohio, in 1890
-AND WAS USED BY HIS
WIFE FOR 43 YEARS

GENERAL
ATHA MOSSANA
WHO RULED TRANSOXIANA,
IN ASIA, FROM 759 TO 779
CONCEALED THE FACT THAT HE
HAD LOST AN EYE IN BATTLE
BY WEARING DAY AND NIGHT
A MASK OF SOLID GOLD

THE
OLDEST HARP IN THE WORLD
IT WAS FOUND IN THE GRAVE OF QUEEN
SHUB-AD IN THE CITY OF UR OF THE CHALDEES,
HOME OF THE BIBLICAL PATRIARCH, ABRAHAM
- AND WAS CONSTRUCTED 5,000 YEARS AGO

Ripley's Believe It or Not!

"DELPHINUS" THE STAR CONSTELLATION, BEARS THE GREEK NAME FOR THE DOLPHIN—TO HONOR THE LEGENDARY DOLPHIN THAT CARRIED ARION ON ITS BACK TO SAFETY IN 626 B.C. *BECAUSE IT ADMIRED THE WAY HE PLAYED THE LYRE*

WALLAGIE A MALAYAN WOODCUTTER OF CAPE TOWN, SO. AFRICA, ALONE CONSUMED A BANQUET CONSISTING OF SOUP, CHICKENS AND RICE, RICE CAKES, PASTRIES, CURRIES AND SWEET POTATOES IN BATTER —*THAT HAD BEEN PREPARED FOR 16 PEOPLE!* Feb.,1931

The **TOMB** of the 13th **DALAI LAMA** of Tibet ON THE ROOF OF THE POTALA PALACE IN LHASA IS **70** FEET HIGH AND COVERED WITH A SHEET OF SOLID GOLD THAT WEIGHS A TON *AND IS VALUED AT MORE THAN* **$1,000,000**

The **Steeple** of the **CALVARY CHURCH,** in Arlington, Mass., WAS BUILT ORIGINALLY FOR A BOSTON MARKET, AND FOR YEARS BEFORE IT BECAME A CHURCH STEEPLE *IT ADORNED A CHARLESTOWN BREWERY*

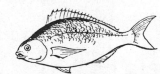

A **SEA BREAM** *MUST BE SERVED WHOLE TO EACH GUEST AT EVERY JAPANESE WEDDING* THE FISH'S NAME IN JAPANESE MEANS "HAPPINESS" – AND IT WOULD BE UNTHINKABLE TO REDUCE A GUEST'S PORTION

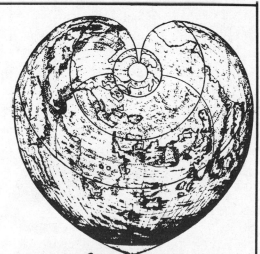

COLUMBUS DID NOT BELIEVE THE EARTH WAS ROUND! THE EARTH, CHRISTOPHER COLUMBUS SAID, *IS SHAPED LIKE A PEAR*

A **TOMB** in Serachs, Afghanistan, BELIEVED TO BE THAT OF CAIN, *HISTORY'S FIRST MURDERER*

Ripley's — Believe It or Not!

HE FORTUNE THAT LAY UNDETECTED IN A TAVERN FOR 62 YEARS

RICHARD FRYER WHO PURCHASED WOLVERHAMPTON INN, IN WOLVERHAMPTON, ENGLAND, IN 1807, OPENED A HEAVY OAK CHEST THAT STOOD WITH A NAILED-DOWN LID BEHIND THE BAR-- AND FOUND 25,000 GOLD SOVEREIGNS -- *WORTH $121,682*
THE MONEY HAD BEEN LEFT AT THE INN BY BONNIE PRINCE CHARLIE--WHO HAD FORGOTTEN TO CLAIM IT WHEN HE LEFT FOR FRANCE

EDWARD WORTLEY *MONTAGU*
(1713 - 1776)
AN ECCENTRIC ENGLISHMAN
WORE A WIG MADE
OF SOLID IRON

A WEDDING RING
LOST BY MRS. STELLA CIEPIELA IN 1955
WHILE GARDENING
IN Chelsea, mass.,
*WAS FOUND BY
ITS OWNER IN
AN AREA SHE
HAD TILLED FOR
11 YEARS*

THE BUILDING THAT WAS CONDEMNED FOR MURDER

THE PARIS OPERA HOUSE, in the French capital, WAS ORDERED DEMOLISHED BY THE AUTHORITIES *BECAUSE THE DUKE OF BERRY WAS SLAIN BY AN ASSASSIN AS HE WAS LEAVING THE OPERA*
THE STRUCTURE WAS PUNISHED AS A CO-CONSPIRATOR (Feb. 13, 1820)

"Loopy"
A CAT OWNED BY
W. MARTIN ROSS,
VANISHED FROM
ROSS' CAR IN
MEDFORD, ORE., ON
ITS FIRST VISIT TO THAT CITY AND RETURNED TO ROSS
3 DAYS LATER AT A HOUSE ITS OWNER HAD RENTED AS A
TEMPORARY RESIDENCE -*AFTER THE CAT VANISHED*

A **SINGLE** **PAIR OF GUPPIES**, IF ALL ITS PROGENY SURVIVED, WOULD PRODUCE 3,000,000 DESCENDANTS A YEAR— YET OF ALL THESE NO 2 MALES WOULD LOOK EXACTLY ALIKE

THE CYNHYENA of Africa HAS A COAT OF BROWN, GRAY AND BLACK THAT LOOKS LIKE A MODERNISTIC PAINTING —*AND NO TWO ARE EVER MARKED ALIKE*

THE CLIFF CASTLE OF TARN-ET-GARONNE THE CHATEAU de la CAZE (France) WAS CONSTRUCTED ENTIRELY FROM THE DEBRIS OBTAINED WHEN ITS MOAT AND CELLAR WERE DUG *OUT OF A MOUNTAIN OF SOLID ROCK*

THE STRONGEST STRONGARM MAN IN ALL HISTORY! GUSTAVE REHARD, CHIEF OF A BAND OF THUGS IN LONS, FRANCE, TO BREAK UP A FIGHT BETWEEN 2 MEMBERS OF HIS GANG WHO WERE DUELING WITH KNIVES ON A BILLIARD TABLE, *LIFTED THE SLATE-BED TABLE ON HIS SHOULDERS AND* **CARRIED THE TABLE AND STRUGGLING HIGHWAYMEN A DISTANCE OF 20 FEET!** (1793)

OLIVE TREE near Palma, Mallorca, MORE THAN 1,000 YEARS OLD, GROWING IN THE SHAPE OF ITS OWN INITIAL, THE LETTER "O"

THE TAHR an Asian mountain goat, WHEN CAPTURED IN A NET, ALWAYS FAINTS

THE FIRST BLOND WIG THE CROWN of the Kings of Ur (now in Iraq) WORN ON CEREMONIAL OCCASIONS 5,000 YEARS AGO WAS A WIG *MADE OF SOLID GOLD*

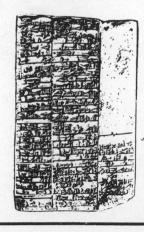

THE OLDEST PRESCRIPTION IN THE WORLD A CUNEIFORM TABLET FOUND IN THE RUINS OF Nippur, Babylonia, CARRIES THIS 4000-YEAR-OLD PRESCRIPTION: "Pulverize the root of the moon plant and let the patient drink it dissolved in beer."

THE STRANGEST DISCIPLINARIAN IN ALL HISTORY! SHAMYL (1797-1871) LEADER OF THE CAUCASIAN TRIBES IN A STRUGGLE AGAINST RUSSIA *SENTENCED HIS OWN MOTHER TO 100 LASHES FOR ADVISING HIM TO SURRENDER!* THEN, CITING A KORAN INJUNCTION THAT CHILDREN SHOULD ASSUME PUNISHMENT ORDERED FOR THEIR PARENTS, SHAMYL INSISTED THAT *HE RECEIVE THE WHIPPING*

THE FAIRY-TALE THEATRE
AN OPEN-AIR THEATRE NEAR HOMBURG-SAAR, GERMANY, BUILT FOR THE PERFORMANCE OF PLAYS BASED ON FAIRY TALES *IN A FAIRY-TALE SETTING IN RABENHORST FOREST*

KING JAMES I (1566-1625) of England
IN THE 22 YEARS HE OCCUPIED THE THRONE, *NEVER WASHED HIS RIGHT HAND -*
HE MERELY DAUBED HIS FINGERTIPS WITH A DAMP CLOTH EACH MORNING - FEARING *THAT WASHING WOULD MAKE THE SKIN FEEL COARSE WHEN HE SHOOK HANDS*

THE DEATH THAT FULFILLED A VICTIM'S CRY FOR VENGEANCE!
PIETER GIJSBERT NORDT
DUTCH GOVERNOR OF THE CAPE COLONY, BRUTALLY SENTENCED 9 SOLDIERS TO BE HANGED, MERELY **BECAUSE HE SUSPECTED THEY PLANNED TO DESERT** - AS THE 9th SOLDIER WAS LED TO THE GALLOWS HE EXCLAIMED: *"Governor Nordt, I summon thee at this very moment before the Judgment Seat of God to answer for our souls!"*
A FEW MOMENTS LATER THE GOVERNOR WAS FOUND SITTING IN HIS OFFICE - **STONE DEAD!**
1729

AN ENGRAVING FOUND ON A TEMPLE WALL IN SAKKARA REVEALED THAT PRIESTS IN ANCIENT EGYPT *HAD TO DOUBLE AS COWBOYS AND LASSO BULL DESTINED FOR SACRIFIC*

THE WELL HOUSE
IN THE MOSQUE OF IBN TULUN AT CAIRO, EGYPT, WAS CONSTRUCTED BY SULTAN AHMED IBN TULUN *AS A TOMB FOR HIS TUTOR*
THE BUILDING IS STILL CONSIDERED A TOMB - USED "TEMPORARILY" AS A WELL HOUSE - ALTHOUGH THE TUTOR WAS BURIED ELSEWHERE *1,080 YEARS AGO*

THE COFFIN THAT UNITED 2 BITTER ENEMIES
KING ADOLPH of Germany AND HIS SUCCESSOR, KING ALBRECHT I, MORTAL ENEMIES IN LIFE, WERE BURIED IN ADJOINING BIERS IN THE CATHEDRAL OF SPEYER *BUT FIRE DESTROYED THE CATHEDRAL IN 1689, AND THE REMAINS OF THE TWO FOES - REDUCED TO UNIDENTIFIABLE ASHES - WERE PUT IN A SINGLE COFFIN*

THE CLEAR OUTLINE OF A CINNAMON LEAF FOUND IN A ROCK near Fritzlar, Germany, *5,000 MILES FROM THE NEAREST CINNAMON TREE -* DATES BACK TO WHEN SUCH TREES ACTUALLY GREW IN THE AREA *200,000,000 YEARS AGO*

Ripley's Believe It or Not!

"MANDOR" A POODLE OWNED BY AN AUSTRIAN CUSTOMS OFFICIAL, NIGHTLY CHECKED EVERY SENTRY ALONG THE AUSTRO-GERMAN FRONTIER AND BARKED TO AWAKEN ANY GUARD HE FOUND ASLEEP- POLICING AN 18-MILE STRETCH OF BORDER ON HIS OWN !

THE FIRST PANTOMIMIST ANDRONICUS LIVIUS A ROMAN ACTOR OF THE 3d CENTURY B.C., ORIGINATED THE ART OF PANTOMIME BECAUSE AT THE VERY HEIGHT OF HIS CAREER, *HE LOST THE USE OF HIS VOICE*

THE BUG CORYTHUCHA CILIATA WEARS A COAT OF LACE

THE GREATEST CHARIOTEER IN ALL HISTORY !
ANNICERIS FAMED GREEK CHARIOT DRIVER COULD MAKE 1,000 TURNS IN AN ARENA AT FULL SPEED *WITHOUT DEVIATING FROM HIS ORIGINAL TRACK*

THE CAVE CHARACIN
FISH FOUND ONLY IN A MEXICAN CAVE, HAVE EYES AS YOUNG FRY, BUT *THE ADULT FISH ARE ALWAYS BLIND*

THE LARGEST CAMERA EVER MADE
A CAMERA MADE IN 1899 TO PHOTOGRAPH AN ENTIRE TRAIN IN DETAIL, WEIGHED 1,400 POUNDS, WAS 20 FEET LONG, AND USED A NEGATIVE THAT MEASURED **10** FEET BY **8** FEET

Ripley's Believe It or Not!

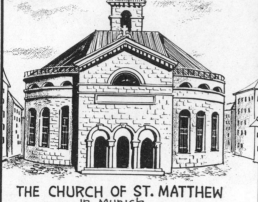

THE CHURCH OF ST. MATTHEW
in Munich
WAS DEMOLISHED IN 1938 BECAUSE AN
AIDE MISUNDERSTOOD AN ORDER BY
ADOLF HITLER --WHO SAW A PILE OF
PAVING STONES ON THE SONNENSTRASSE
AND MURMURED -- "THAT PILE OF
STONES WILL HAVE TO BE REMOVED"

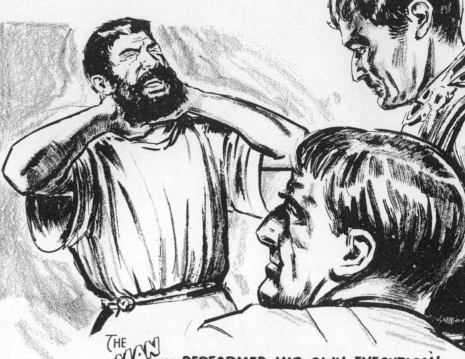

THE MAN WHO PERFORMED HIS OWN EXECUTION!
EX-EMPEROR MAXIMIANUS I, WHO RESIGNED
AFTER RULING THE ROMAN EMPIRE FROM 286 TO 305,
WAS CONVICTED OF PLOTTING THE MURDER OF
EMPEROR CONSTANTINE, HIS SON-IN-LAW
-BUT WAS PERMITTED TO SPECIFY THE
MANNER OF HIS EXECUTION
*HE CHOSE TO STRANGLE HIMSELF
WITH HIS OWN HANDS!* (310)

TRIPLE ROSE
Submitted by J.P. FURNER, Belmont, Calif.

A **SEAL** SIGHTED IN 1954
near the Scilly
Isles, England,
WORE AS A "COLLAR"
AROUND ITS NECK, AN
AUTOMOBILE TIRE

**THE MOST ILL-STARRED FASHION
DESIGN IN ALL HISTORY**
MELIK el AZIZ
ruler of Yemen from 1196 to 1202,
DESIGNED AN IMPERIAL CLOAK
WITH A TRAIN 60 FEET LONG
*HIS SARTORIAL EXTRAVAGANCE
SO ENRAGED HIS SUBJECTS
THEY ROSE IN REBELLION
AND KILLED HIM*

CAN YOU FIND IN
THIS FLOWER DESIGN
OF A SUMMER PRINT
DRESS WORN BY
ENGLISH WOMEN IN
THE 19th CENTURY
*PROFILES OF BOTH
QUEEN VICTORIA
AND PRINCE ALBERT?*

CYPRESS ROOT
SHAPED LIKE
*THE HEAD OF
A HORSE*
Submitted by
EDWARD A. ILLSCHE
Fort Myers, Fla.

EMPEROR ASOKA
of India
COLLECTED THE ASHES OF BUDDHA AND BUILT A SEPARATE TEMPLE FOR EACH PARTICLE OF ASH
A TOTAL OF 84,000 TEMPLES

THE APRON THAT IS A SHIELD AGAINST MISFORTUNE
EVERY BRIDE IN THE Admiralty Islands BRINGS TO HER HUSBAND AS A DOWRY AN APRON WOVEN FROM SHELL MONEY
-WHICH SERVES AS THE FAMILY'S CASH RESERVE AND IS USED ONLY IN AN EMERGENCY

LEECHEE NUTS ARE NOT NUTS THEY ARE DRIED FRUIT

THE LARGE-MOUTH BLACK BASS IS KNOWN BY *44 DIFFERENT NAMES*

THE **EAGLE** in the Coat of Arms of Indonesia
HAS 17 FEATHERS IN EACH WING AND 8 IN ITS TAIL – SYMBOLIZING THE 17th DAY OF THE 8th MONTH –THE DATE ON WHICH THE COUNTRY WON INDEPENDENCE

SIOUX INDIAN PLAYING CARDS
MADE FROM THE SKIN OF DRIED FISH

BEEHIVES in Appelwerder, Poland, ARE CARVED IN THE FORM OF *HUMAN FIGURES*

BHINNEKA TUNGGAL IKA

THE FIRST CHRISTMAS SEAL
A CHRISTMAS SEAL TO RAISE FUNDS TO FIGHT TUBERCULOSIS *WAS CREATED BY EINAR HOLBOLL, A DANISH POSTMASTER, IN 1904*

THE **LARGEST COIN** EVER MINTED
A SILVER COIN MINTED BY THE DUKE OF BRAUNSCHWEIG-CELLE, IN GERMANY, IN 1639 WAS VALUED AT $16, MEASURED 5" IN DIAMETER *AND WEIGHED 1 1/8 POUNDS*

THE FIRST KEY RINGS
KEYS, used by the ancient Romans, COULD BE WORN AS RINGS *AND ALSO SERVED AS A PERSONAL SEAL*

THE **WALL** OF THE CHURCH in St. Gilles-du-Gard, France, IN WHICH ST. GILES WAS BURIED HAS CRUMBLED AWAY TO FORM *AN AMAZING PROFILE OF THE SAINT*

THE TRAGIC TRIP OF THE TRUNK THAT DELIVERED A BRIDE'S TROUSSEAU

THE SCHOONER "SUSAN AND ELIZA" WAS WRECKED IN A STORM OFF CAPE ANN, MASS., AS IT WAS CARRYING SUSAN HICHBORN- ONE OF ITS OWNER'S DAUGHTERS- TO HER WEDDING IN BOSTON
ALL 33 PERSONS ON BOARD PERISHED, AND NO TRACE OF THE SHIP WAS EVER FOUND -EXCEPT FOR A TRUNK BEARING SUSAN'S INITIALS AND CONTAINING HER TROUSSEAU WHICH WAS CAST ASHORE AT THE FEET OF HER WAITING FIANCÉ!

LEROI HENRI
A MUSICIAN OF
Paris, France,
WHOSE NAME IN
FRENCH MEANS
"KING HENRY"
NAMED HIS 5 SONS
LEROI HENRI I
LEROI HENRI II
LEROI HENRI III
LEROI HENRI IV
AND
LEROI HENRI V

THE **TOWER**
OF THE
CHURCH OF OSTHEIM
Alsace, France
-SURMOUNTED BY
A STORK'S NEST-
WAS UNHARMED
BY A WORLD
WAR II
BOMBING
RAID
ALTHOUGH
ALL THE
REST
OF THE
STRUCTURE
WAS
LEVELED

THE TOWER AND ITS NEST STILL STAND AS A MEMORIAL TO THE STORKS OF ALSACE

PIGEONS
in China
OFTEN HAVE
BAMBOO FLUTES
WIRED TO THEIR
TAILS IN THE
BELIEF THAT THE
*MUSIC WILL SCARE
AWAY HAWKS*

THE **OLDEST DRINKING GLASS** IN THE **WORLD**
A GOBLET FOUND IN THE RUINS OF KING SARGON'S PALACE AT Khorsabad BEARS THE NAME OF THE BIBLICAL RULER OF ASSYRIA WHO USED IT 2,682 YEARS AGO
- Iraq -

THE CUCKOO RAY
IS THE ONLY CREATURE IN NATURE THAT HAS EYELIDS
INSIDE ITS EYES

4 TOMATOES
GROWING TOGETHER
Submitted by
MRS. LILLIAN PERES,
Rochester, N.Y.

THIS TALISMAN
in the 18th century
WAS BELIEVED SO
POTENT IN ITS
ABILITY TO FREE
A PRISONER THAT
GIVING IT TO ONE
*WAS PUNISHABLE
BY DEATH*

A **ROMAN GOBLET**
CARVED FROM A SINGLE
BLOCK OF GLASS, WAS
BLOWN FROM AN ANCIENT
TOMB IN TRIER, GERMANY,
BY AN ALLIED BOMBER
IN WORLD WAR II
-STILL USABLE AFTER
1,600 YEARS DESPITE
THE EXPLOSION!

THE **CHURCH BUILT BY ONE MAN!**
THE CHURCH OF WIRVIGNES, Picardy, France,
WAS ERECTED BY ABBÉ PAUL LECOUTRE
WHO LABORED ALONE FOR 43 YEARS

A **LARGE TURTLE**, FOUND ON MAY 26,1900,
in Washburn, No. Dakota, HAD INSCRIBED
ON ITS SHELL *THE YEAR 1807*

Ripley's® Believe It or Not!

MONEY THAT "RAN OUT" — ON ITS OWN TWO FEET A BRONZE COIN, CIRCULATED 1,900 YEARS AGO IN NIMES, in ancient Gaul, WAS SHAPED LIKE THE HINDQUARTERS OF A PIG EVEN TO ITS 2 LEGS—AND WAS WORTH EXACTLY THE COST OF A HAM

A **COUNTERFEIT** ENGLISH SOVEREIGN PRODUCED BY A SPANIARD IN 1880 CONSISTED OF A THIN COATING OF GOLD ON A GRAY METAL HE CONSIDERED WORTHLESS— THE GRAY METAL WAS LATER IDENTIFIED AS PLATINUM—WORTH **3 TIMES AS MUCH AS GOLD**

SKANDERBEG
(1403-1468)
FAMED HERO OF ALBANIA, WORE ON HIS BROW THE HEAD OF A MOUNTAIN GOAT —SO HIS MOUNTAINOUS HOMELAND WOULD ALWAYS BE ON HIS MIND

THE **HOME** of the Bishop of Jebeil, in Syria, CONSISTS OF A SERIES OF SPACIOUS CAVES IN RUGGED Mt. LAKLOUK — AND ITS EXTERIOR DESIGN IS FORMED BY THE NATURAL FANTASTIC SHAPES OF ROCKY CRAGS

3 NUMBERS 19 33 AND 42 ARE CONSIDERED UNLUCKY IN JAPAN
19 IS CALLED JUKU—MEANING SORROWS
33 IS SAN ZAN — MEANING DISASTERS
42 IS SHI NI —WHICH MEANS DEATH

THE **WORM THAT CARRIES A FEATHER DUSTER** THE SEA PEACOCK BREATHES THROUGH GILLS THAT RESEMBLE A BEAUTIFULLY COLORED **FEATHER DUSTER**

THE MAGIC MEDICINE RING
A RING BESTOWED ON A SUFFERING SUBJECT BY EARLY BRITISH MONARCHS WAS CONSIDERED CAPABLE OF CURING THE WEARER OF CRAMPS

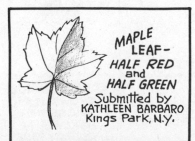

MAPLE LEAF— HALF RED and HALF GREEN Submitted by KATHLEEN BARBARO Kings Park, N.Y.

THE **ORCHESTRA** THAT CAME "BAKED" IN A PIE ! Paris, France, A HUGE PIE SERVED AT THE WEDDING OF PRINCE HENRY OF FRANCE AND CATHERINE de MEDICI CONTAINED, IN ADDITION TO ITS EDIBLE INGREDIENTS, A 4-PIECE ORCHESTRA —1533—

Ripley's Believe It or Not!

THE CONTRADICTORY CAT
KITTEN WITH "OK" ON ONE SIDE AND "NO" ON THE OTHER
—BOTH NATURAL MARKINGS
Submitted by Mrs. Stephen E. Randall, Gouverneur, N.Y.

A GIANT TORTOISE
LIVED IN THE LONDON, ENGLAND, ZOO
FOR 200 YEARS
(1699-1899)

A STATUE OF 2 SAINTS
CARRIED ANNUALLY IN A PROCESSION in San Cosmo, Italy, IS THE TARGET OF THOUSANDS OF BANKNOTES IN THE BELIEF THAT *HITTING THE STATUE WITH MONEY WILL ASSURE PROSPERITY FOR THE THROWER*

THE SAGUARO CACTUS
ATTAINS A WEIGHT OF 12 TONS AND CAN STORE UP *A TON OF WATER*— IT ANNUALLY PRODUCES 275,000 SEEDS —ONLY ONE OF WHICH EVER BECOMES A NEW PLANT

POTATOES
GROWING INSIDE ANOTHER POTATO
Submitted by WAYNE HARBOUR, Bedford, Iowa

The MOST DARING ESCAPE IN HISTORY!
Nürnberg, Germany
—
EPPELEIN von GAILINGEN
—GRANTED PERMISSION TO MOUNT HIS FAVORITE CHARGER AS HIS LAST REQUEST BEFORE BEING HANGED— SPURRED THROUGH AN ENTIRE REGIMENT OF CAVALRY, RODE UP A RAMP TO THE TOP OF THE CITY WALL, THEN LEAPED HIS HORSE TO A MOAT 100 FEET BELOW —*AND ESCAPED WITHOUT INJURY EITHER TO HIMSELF OR HIS HORSE!*

Amharic
THE LANGUAGE OF ETHIOPIA *HAS AN ALPHABET OF 267 LETTERS* THE VOWELS ALONE ARE REPRESENTED BY 49 DIFFERENT CHARACTERS.

THE POLYPTERUS
A FISH OF TROPICAL AFRICA, BREATHES EQUALLY WELL UNDERWATER *AND FROM THE AIR*

CORNEL SHRUB
GROWS ITS BLOSSOMS *BEFORE IT SPROUTS LEAVES*

THE KING MAKER
RICIMER
A GERMAN MILITARY LEADER OF ANCIENT ROME,
3 TIMES REFUSED INVITATIONS TO RULE ROME
*BUT PERSONALLY GAVE THE CROWN TO 5 EMPERORS
-AND THEN DEPOSED EACH OF THEM*

THE VOLCANO THAT SAVED 29 MEN FROM THE SEA!
THE RT. REV. WILLIAM McCRAIT, Bishop of the Church of England,
ADRIFT WITH 28 OTHER PASSENGERS AND CREWMEN FROM THE SCHOONER
HARRIET COWPER, 1,000 MILES FROM THE NEAREST LAND, HAD GIVEN UP HOPE
*WHEN A COLUMN OF FIRE SUDDENLY SHOT UP FROM THE OCEAN
AND A NEW ISLAND ROSE 50 FEET ABOVE THE WATER*

THE MEN NAMED IT "TIMELY ISLAND"- AND 3 DAYS LATER THEY
WERE RESCUED FROM IT BY THE ENGLISH SLOOP *SPRY'S* CREW, WHO
SAW THE UNDERWATER VOLCANO EXPLODE IN THE DISTANCE

KHUSRO KHAN
THE GOVERNOR OF TATTA, IN WHAT IS
NOW PAKISTAN, BUILT **300** MOSQUES
TO ATONE FOR ONCE HAVING
*ACCIDENTALLY GLIMPSED A
NEIGHBOR'S WIFE IN HER BATH* (1612)

MARY OWENS of Danville, Pa.,
DONNED THE UNIFORM OF A UNION SOLDIER AND
FOUGHT BESIDE HER HUSBAND IN THE CIVIL WAR
FOR 18 MONTHS
SHE WAS IN 3 BATTLES, WAS WOUNDED TWICE
-AND SAW HER HUSBAND SLAIN AT HER SIDE

HOUSE
in Almas do Freire, Portugal,
WHICH HAS AS ITS FOUNDATION
AN ANCIENT OVEN

THE **WOUND** THAT SAVED A MAN'S LIFE
JACKIE MARMON
SHIPWRECKED OFF NEW ZEALAND AFTER HAVING ESCAPED FROM
A CONVICT SETTLEMENT, REACHED SHORE WITH 2 OTHER SURVIVORS
- *BUT SAVAGE MAORIS KILLED BOTH OF HIS COMPANIONS*
HIS LIFE WAS SPARED BECAUSE HE HAD SUFFERED A HEAD
WOUND ON THE SHIP AND THE RAG HE HAD TIED AROUND HIS
HEAD AS A BANDAGE RESEMBLED THE EMBLEM OF A MAORI CHIEF
MAKING HIM UNTOUCHABLE   (1800)

HARALD
(850-933)
THE FIRST
KING OF
NORWAY

RULED THAT
COUNTRY FOR
70 YEARS
*AND WAS
THE FATHER
OF 20
KINGS*

THE **NORTHERNMOST TREE**
IN THE WORLD
A LONE TREE GROWING OUTSIDE
HAMMERFEST, NORWAY,
*WHICH IS THE MOST NORTHERN
TOWN IN THE WORLD*

A *GOLD* **WATCH**
CONSTRUCTED IN 1800 IN
THE SHAPE OF A TULIP,
*IS STUDDED WITH
HUNDREDS OF PEARLS*
Neufchatel, Switzerland

WOMEN of the Akha Tribe
of Northern Thailand
DON A TALL HEADDRESS WHEN THEY MARRY
AND, EXCEPT FOR A FEW MINUTES A
MONTH WHEN THEY DRESS THEIR HAIR,
NEVER REMOVE IT DAY OR NIGHT
WHEN THEY DIE THEY ARE
BURIED STILL WEARING IT

Ripley's—® Believe It or Not!

THE **TRUNK** OF THE THUYA TREE, OF THE FRENCH RIVIERA, IS *COMPLETELY COVERED BY GREEN LEAVES*

A **PIKE** in the Stour River, near Keynston, England, SEIZED A FULL-GROWN DUCK, HELD IT UNDER WATER UNTIL IT DROWNED — *AND THEN DINED ON IT* September, 1948

THE **AMAZING MATRIARCH** OF MAUERKIRCHEN
BARBARA VIERTALER IN 1712 ATTENDED THE CELEBRATION OF THE 700th ANNIVERSARY OF THE CHURCH IN MAUERKIRCHEN, AUSTRIA, AND IN 1812 WALKED 12 MILES FROM ASPACH TO MAUERKIRCHEN TO OBSERVE THE CHURCH'S 800th ANNIVERSARY- *WHEN SHE WAS 119 YEARS OF AGE!*

SLEEPING GIRL
NATURAL FORMATION EL VALLE, PANAMA Submitted by Marta Narimatser, Curundee, Canal Zone

THE **LATTICE MUSHROOM** IS COVERED BY A *PEEKABOO HOOD*

THE SEAL of a Babylonian physician FEATURES HIS LIKENESS AND THE TOOLS USED IN HIS PROFESSION- *5,000 YEARS AGO*

RICHARD C. MOYER of Harleysville, Pa., WORKED STEADILY AS A PRINTER *FOR 70 YEARS*

"MACHS NA" INSCRIBED ON THE BALUSTRADE OF THE CATHEDRAL OF BERNE, Switzerland, IS A CHALLENGE TO OTHER ARCHITECTS THAT MEANS " *TRY AND COPY IT* "

THE **CEPHALOTUS** A CARNIVOROUS PLANT, HAS A LID WHICH *PREVENTS RAIN FROM DILUTING ITS POISON*

THE MUSSEL'S BEARD WHICH GROWS ON THE SHELLS OF LIVING MUSSELS, ACTUALLY COMPRISES COLONIES OF TINY HYDROID ANIMALS ON EACH "HAIR" -*COUNTLESS MILLIONS OF THEM ON EACH MUSSEL*

Ripley's Believe It or Not

"JAMES CROW" a raven exhibited in the Tower of London **FOR 44 YEARS**

"Pal" PART WOLFHOUND AND PART COLLIE, ON TREKS THROUGH MOUNTAINOUS TERRAIN WITH REVENUE AGENT S. GLENN YOUNG IN SEARCH OF MOONSHINERS -*CARRIED SADDLEBAGS CONTAINING RATIONS FOR 10 DAYS FOR BOTH HIMSELF AND HIS MASTER* THE DOG COULD GIVE HIMSELF A BATH IN A REGULAR BATHTUB - ADJUSTING THE HOT AND COLD FAUCETS WITHOUT ASSISTANCE

A **SILVER BED** made in London, England, FOR AN INDIAN MAHARAJAH IS EQUIPPED WITH MOTORIZED STATUES OF *4 GIRLS WHO WAVE FANS TO ASSURE THE MAHARAJAH COOL SLUMBER*

GLOBE SPONGE Tethya fissurata LOOKS LIKE A GOLF BALL

MARIE de BOURGOGNE (1457-1482) WIFE OF ARCHDUKE MAXIMILIAN OF AUSTRIA, THROWN BY HER HORSE DURING A HUNT, DIED OF GANGRENE AT THE AGE OF 25 *BECAUSE SHE WAS TOO MODEST TO PERMIT A PHYSICIAN TO TREAT HER INJURIES*

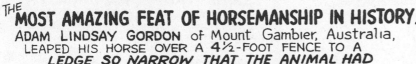
THE MOST AMAZING FEAT OF HORSEMANSHIP IN HISTORY!
ADAM LINDSAY GORDON of Mount Gambier, Australia, LEAPED HIS HORSE OVER A 4½-FOOT FENCE TO A *LEDGE SO NARROW THAT THE ANIMAL HAD TO LAND SIDEWAYS TO AVOID PLUNGING 300 FEET OVER A SHEER PRECIPICE* THE HORSE THEN STOOD QUIETLY ON THE LEDGE UNTIL SPECTATORS DISMANTLED THE FENCE (1860)

THE **BAR** in the Hochreither Inn, in Leonfelden, Austria, BUILT INTO AN ANCIENT STAGECOACH

THE RUINED CASTLE
on Peacock Island, Berlin, Germany,
WAS NEVER AN ACTUAL
CASTLE -HAVING BEEN
CONSTRUCTED AS A RUIN IN 1797

THE
YUCCA
PLANT
IS
POLLINATED
ONLY BY
*ONE SPECIES
OF MOTH*

SPADE MONEY
used in China
2,600 YEARS AGO
WAS SHAPED LIKE
A MINIATURE
SPADE – *EVEN
TO A ROUND,
HOLLOW
HANDLE*

THE
MAN WHO KILLED A BEAR WITH HIS BARE HAND!
DUKE GEORG II THE STRONG
RULER OF ANHALT, GERMANY,
KILLED A BEAR ON THE BANK OF THE ELBE RIVER IN 1509
WITH A BLOW OF HIS FIST !

THE **RIGOROUS RAIN DANCE OF BRAZIL**
THE KRAHO INDIANS, IN A CEREMONY
THEY BELIEVE WILL BREAK A DROUGHT,
RACE FOR DISTANCES AS LONG AS 7 MILES-
EACH MAN CARRYING A 7-FOOT HARDWOOD LOG
WEIGHING 220 POUNDS

THE **FLOWER MUSHROOM**
(Aseroe rubra)
*LOOKS AND SMELLS
LIKE A WATER LILY*

**SWEET
WILLIAM**
a flower

AND

**STINKING
WILLIE**
a weed

BOTH WERE NAMED
FOR THE SAME MAN
-WILLIAM, DUKE OF
CUMBERLAND, WHO
DEFEATED THE SCOTS IN
THE BATTLE OF CULLODEN
THE GRATEFUL ENGLISH
NAMED A FLOWER IN HIS
HONOR AND THE SCOTS GAVE
HIS NAME TO A WEED

A **TURTLE**
BEARING ON ITS HEAD
THE NUMERAL 30

Submitted by
Clarence L. Howle
Fisherman's Wharf,
San Francisco, Calif.

THE WILD BOAR NATURAL ROOT GROWTH found at Death Valley, Calif., by Mrs. Myron Bishop of Port Townsend, Wash.

THE SONG THRUSH HAVING CAPTURED A SNAIL, GETS AT ITS MEAT BY *SMASHING THE SHELL AGAINST A ROCK*

THE BIRD THAT PLANTS A FLOWER GARDEN
THE GARDENER BOWER BIRD (Amblyornis inornatus) BUILDS A GARDEN ENHANCED BY COLORFUL BLOSSOMS AND SHELLS AND A SPECIAL HUT *AS A ROMANTIC SETTING IN WHICH TO COURT ITS MATE* THEY THEN SHARE A NORMAL TREETOP NEST

NAHARIN FASSI (1741-1840) A POET OF Shiraz, Persia, AND EACH OF HIS 3 SONS *WERE BORN AT INTERVALS OF EXACTLY 25 YEARS*

2 IRON HOUSES SHIPPED TO Melbourne, Australia, from England DURING THE GOLD RUSH OF 1851 ARE STILL *INHABITED TODAY - 115 YEARS LATER*

THE RICHEST DESSERT IN ALL HISTORY
SHAH RUKH (1377-1447)
WHO RULED MONGOLIA, PERSIA, INDIA AND TURKESTAN, CELEBRATED 43 SUCCESSIVE BIRTHDAYS BY GREAT BANQUETS AT WHICH THE DESSERT SERVED TO EACH GUEST WAS A BASIN *FILLED WITH DIAMONDS, PEARLS, RUBIES AND EMERALDS!*

THE AFRICAN LUNGFISH HAS BOTH LUNGS AND GILLS - AND WALKS ON ITS FINS

The CHURCH of NOTRE DAME in St. Omer, France, WAS ORDERED DEMOLISHED DURING THE FRENCH REVOLUTION BUT WAS PRESERVED INTACT BY CONVERTING IT FOR USE AS A STOREHOUSE FOR FODDER

Ripley's ® Believe It or Not!

THE MOST VULNERABLE CREATURE IN ALL NATURE
IPNOPS, A BLIND DEEP-SEA FISH, IS HELPLESS TO DEFEND ITSELF OR ELUDE PURSUIT AND BEARS ON ITS HEAD A LUMINOUS PATCH *—WHICH ATTRACTS THE ATTENTION OF PREDATORS*

THE MAN WHO CROSSED THE ATLANTIC WITHOUT FOOD OR WATER!
DR. ALAIN BOMBARD, a Frenchman, SAILED A SMALL RAFT FROM THE CANARIES TO BARBADOS - A VOYAGE OF 65 DAYS - *EXISTING ON SEA WATER AND FISH HE CAUGHT ON THE TRIP!* 1953

DR. MELCHIOR SEBISCH
(1578 - 1674)
PROFESSOR OF MEDICINE AT THE University of Strasbourg, France, WAS GIVEN HIS MEDICAL DEGREE AT THE UNIVERSITY OF BASLE, Switzerland, IN 1610 ONLY AFTER HE HAD *STUDIED MEDICINE IN 27 SUCCESSIVE UNIVERSITIES*

THE WOODCOCK NEVER SEES ITS FOOD
ITS 3-INCH BEAK IS DRIVEN DEEP INTO THE MUD AND IT DEVOURS EARTHWORMS IT HAS LOCATED BY SENSE OF FEEL

THE SCALLOP
HAS 100 EYES, *EACH OF ITS SHINY GREEN EYES HAS A LENS, A RETINA AND AN OPTICAL NERVE*

COUNT ANTON SZTARAY
(1740 - 1809)
A GENERAL IN THE AUSTRIAN ARMY, TOOK PART IN 89 BATTLES IN A PERIOD OF 47 YEARS *AND WAS SERIOUSLY WOUNDED IN 84 OF THEM*

A U.S. $2 BILL
WITH ITS REVERSE SIDE PRINTED UPSIDE DOWN Submitted by JACOB BAUER, Biloxi, Miss.

THE FISH THAT DROWN EASILY
MACROPODUS OPERCULARIS CAN STAY ALIVE ONLY BY COMING TO THE SURFACE FOR A BREATH OF FRESH AIR

Ripley's Believe It or Not!

THE ONLY DISINFECTANT AVAILABLE WHEN AN EPIDEMIC OF SMALLPOX SWEPT THE TOWN OF Oglethorpe, Ga., in 1855 *WAS GARLANDS OF ONIONS*

A **WARNING** TO MOTORISTS TO BEWARE OF LIONS at Serengeti Wildlife Park, in Tanganyika, Africa, *FEATURES THE SKULL AND CROSSED BONES OF A LION*

STAY IN YOUR CAR

THE MOURNING PIGEON
DURING THE BURIAL SERVICE OF CAPTAIN JOSEPH G. BELAIN IN THE CHURCH OF GAY HEAD, MASS., *A CARRIER PIGEON FLEW IN FROM THE SEA, ALIGHTED ON THE BIER AND STAYED TILL THE SERVICE WAS CONCLUDED-* AS IF IN TRIBUTE TO THE MAN WHO HAD DEDICATED HIS LIFE TO SAVE THE CARRIER PIGEON FROM EXTERMINATION

THE **CURTAIN FIG TREE** of YUNGABURRA Australia A GIANT TREE WITH BRANCHES SO DENSE *THEY FORM A NATURAL CURTAIN*

THE FISH THAT WARNS OF EARTHQUAKES
THE MISGURN (Misgurnus fossilis) A EUROPEAN LOACH, NORMALLY LIES SLUGGISH IN THE MUDBED OF SLOW STREAMS *BUT IT DARTS RAPIDLY ABOUT WHEN AN EARTHQUAKE IS IMPENDING* THE MISGURN IS KEPT UNDER OBSERVATION BY SEISMOLOGICAL STATIONS IN INDIA

ADMIRAL JAMES H. WHITSHED (1762-1849) JOINED THE BRITISH NAVY AT THE AGE OF 11 AND BECAME ITS COMMANDER-IN-CHIEF **76 YEARS LATER**

PUTNAM CONN OCT 17 84 11 AM

THE CANCELLATION STAMP USED BY THE POSTMASTER of Putnam, Conn., in 1884 *WAS THE BIBLICAL NAME "JEHOVA" PRINTED IN HEBREW*